Jesus of Korea

Jesus of Korea

Savior of the People

Paul Hyoshin Kim

Fortress Press
Minneapolis

JESUS OF KOREA
Savior of the People

Copyright © 2016 Fortress Press. All rights reserved. Except for brief quotations in critical articles or reviews, no part of this book may be reproduced in any manner without prior written permission from the publisher.
Visit http://www.augsburgfortress.org/copyrights/ or write to Permissions, Augsburg Fortress, Box 1209, Minneapolis, MN 55440.

Cover image: Getty Image #113904334
Cover design: Ivy Palmer Skrade

Library of Congress Cataloging-in-Publication Data
Print ISBN: 978-1-5064-0681-7
eBook ISBN: 978-1-5064-0682-4

This book was produced using Pressbooks.com, and PDF rendering was done by PrinceXML.

Dedicated to my wife, Christie

Contents

Foreword — xi

Introduction — 1

PART I. CHRISTIAN AMERICA AND CONFUCIAN KOREA

1. Jones 1867–1887: Experiencing the American Christ — 9

   1.1 The Conversion of George Heber Jones — 9
   1.2 Jones's Early Life — 15
   1.3 Learning the Faith through The YMCA — 21
   1.4 The Triumphant Christ of Nineteenth-Century America — 24
   1.5 Jones and Nineteenth-Century American Revivalism — 27
   1.6 Student Volunteer Movement for Foreign Missions (SVMFM) and "Evangelization of the World in Our Generation" — 32
   1.7 Jones and the American Christ — 35

2. Choe, 1858–1887: Confronting the Confucian Challenge — 39

   2.1 Choe's Growing Reservations about the Status Quo — 39
   2.2 Korea's Great Confucian Experiment Nears its End — 42
   2.3 Choson's Need for Reform — 46
   2.4 The Persecution of Catholics in Korea (1784–1871) — 53
   2.5 Early Life of Choe Pyonghon — 58
   2.6 Choe's Life Goal — 60

PART II. ENCOUNTERING THE OTHER

3. Jones, 1887–1892: Going as an Apostle to Old Choson — 65

   3.1 The Macedonian Call to Choson — 65
   3.2 Early Years of Missionary Service in Korea — 71
   3.3 Three Discoveries about the Korean People — 84
   3.4 Hananim and the Christian God — 86
   3.5 Jesus and the Korean Demons — 88
   3.6 Called To Be an Apostle from Birth — 92

4. Choe, 1888–1892: Drawing Near to Jesus the Western Savior — 95

   4.1 The Initial Contact with the Missionaries — 95
   4.2 Choe's Conversion to Christianity — 102
   4.3 Jesus, the Self-Sacrificing Savior — 110
   4.4 Can a Western Savior Save the East? — 115

PART III. PART 3: JESUS THE SAVIOR OF THE KOREAN PEOPLE

5. Jones, 1892–1903: Witnessing God's Power to Save — 121

   5.1 Overview of the Missionary Work at Chemulpo — 121
   5.2 How Jesus, the Incarnate Mediator, Saves the Common People — 122
   5.3 Jesus of the Bible Seen in Chemulpo — 126
   5.4 Jesus and the Common People — 130
   5.5 "Ancestor Worship" = Old Korea — 132
   5.6 Jesus the Savior in Chemulpo — 141

6.	Choe, 1893–1903: Preaching the Great Way of Truth	143
	6.1 Overview of Choe's Work as an Evangelist	143
	6.2 Jesus and the Founders of Eastern Religions	149
	6.3 Jesus and the Human Problem in "The Doctrine of Sin"	152
	6.4 The Evangelist's Work I: Preaching the Great Way of Jesus (Chili Taedo)	158
	6.5 The Evangelist's Work II: Renewing the Nation through the Jesus Way (Tohak)	162
	6.6 "The Song of Independence"	164
	6.7 An Evangelist of God's Salvation in Korea	167

PART IV. PART 4: JESUS THE SAVIOR OF THE KOREAN NATION

7.	Jones, 1903–1910: Building God's Kingdom in Korea	171
	7.1 Jones's Last Years of Service in Choson	171
	7.2 Jesus as the "Ethical Standard" (Totokui pyojun)	173
	7.3 Jesus, the Purifying Lord of the Church	178
	7.4 1905 and Its Effect on Jones's Ethical Jesus	185
	7.5 Jesus and the 1907 Korean Pentecost	187
	7.6 What Would Jesus and Jones Do about Japan and Korea?	193
	7.7 A Recap of Jones's Life and Work in Choson	203
8.	Choe, 1903–1910: Birthing a New Korea	211
	8.1 Choe's Pastoral Goals at Chongdong Church	211
	8.2 Jesus, the Foundation of a New Nation	214
	8.3 Jesus in Reflections on the Holy Mountain	218
	8.4 Jesus Builds a New Nation: Spiritually	222
	8.5 Jesus Builds a New Nation: Politically	227
	8.6 Jesus Builds a New Nation: Heroically	232
	8.7 Pastor Choe, a Nation-Builder in the Jesus Way	237
	8.8 A Recap of Choe Pyonghon's Thought and Work	240
	Conclusion	247
	Primary Sources	253

Foreword

Paul Hyoshin Kim was a respected and beloved Korean American pastor and theologian whose untimely death in 2014 occurred before he was able to see this book through to publication. Born in South Korea in 1958, Paul immigrated to the United States with his family when he was ten years old. A PhD graduate from Princeton Theological Seminary, he served as pastor of churches both in New Jersey and California. In addition to his pastoral responsibilities, his life was devoted to peace and social justice work. He served as the first director of the National Campaign for Peace and Reunification of Korea, sponsored by the National Council of Churches. He was also involved in interfaith dialogues and advocacy for responsible care of the environment. It is largely due to the dedication of his wife, Christie Huh, that Paul's research is now available to a wider public.

In his provocative study, Paul Kim tells the story of two early Methodist missionaries in Korea, George Heber Jones (1867–1919) and Choe Pyonghon (1858–1927). The story is significant for more than historical reasons. Kim shows that Jones and Choe wrestled with issues that continue to face the church today—especially the question of how best to understand the interplay between the Christian gospel and the various cultures in which it is proclaimed and lived out and the question of the extent to which the universalism of the Christian gospel is compatible with the national aspirations of a people.

Jones was born in Mohawk, New York, of English-Scottish-Welsh ancestry. His faith journey began with a heartfelt conversion experience as a youth in a Methodist church. An exceptionally disciplined and self-educated person, he rose to a leadership role in the YMCA movement and learned much from his involvement in that movement. Although he lacked formal college and seminary education, he felt called to become a missionary and was eventually able to convince the missionary council of the Methodist Episcopal Church of his qualifications. He arrived in Korea in 1888, only twenty-one years old and one of the first missionaries from America to what was often called the "Hermit Kingdom," a land whose people and culture were entirely unknown in the West.

From the beginning of his time in Korea, Jones received stellar assistance from Choe Pyonghon, a young Korean who taught him the Korean language and introduced him to the history, religion, and culture of the Korean people. The strong and mutually formative friendship of Jones and Choe is one of the fascinating aspects of the story that Kim tells. In no small part, due to the help of Choe, Jones entered deeply into the life of his adopted land. With his genuine respect for and love of the Korean people, he became an effective preacher of the Christian gospel in their own language. Jones' desire to assist in the indigenization of the Christian message did not mean his withholding judgment on certain features of traditional Korean religion and culture. In particular, he sharply criticized the practice of ancestor worship as the de facto state religion undergirding the repressive government of that time and its moribund social order.

While Kim describes both the difficulties that Jones faced and the many accomplishments of his missionary endeavors, the intent of the book is in no way to provide the reader with a hagiography. On the contrary, the author clearly acknowledges that Jones brought an "American Christ" to Korea, a Savior who bore the marks of late-nineteenth- and early-twentieth-century American confidence in the supremacy of its culture and the inherent rightness of its expansionist destiny. "Jones was not able to disengage himself completely from his cultural worldview," Kim writes.

Perhaps the most striking evidence of this fact is the attitude of Jones to Japan's long domination, and then, complete control of Korea after the end of the Russo–Japanese war in 1905. Jones discouraged Korean Christians from actively resisting Japan's encroachment on the sovereignty and independence of the Korean people. He did so, Kim explains, for both ideological and pragmatic reasons. Ideologically, Jones believed that the Japanese domination would be a benefit to Koreans since the Japanese were fast becoming a powerful nation, far closer to the industrially advanced nations of Europe and the United States, and thus, able to contribute to the "civilizing" process that was part of the motto of Jones' missionary work: "Christianize and civilize." Pragmatically, Jones, no doubt, judged that public acts of resistance against the superior power of Japan would only result in disaster for the young Christian movement in Korea. Kim agrees that under the circumstances, armed resistance would have been neither politically realistic nor spiritually justifiable. Nevertheless, he contends that Jones missed the opportunity to support the growth of social and political responsibility as part of the living out of the Christian gospel that had begun to form in the hearts and minds of many Koreans in these crisis years of the early twentieth century. What Jones failed to see, in Kim's judgment, was that "Jesus was changing a despairing people into a people of the way of the cross, willing to sacrifice themselves in non-violent resistance against evil."

Choe, Jones' older assistant for several years, was a gentleman scholar of the ancient Confucian texts. His decision to confess to Christ as savior and become a member of the church came only after a deep personal struggle. At the heart of this struggle was the question of whether a Western Savior could save people of the East, including Koreans. Choe's eventual answer to this question would be that Jesus was not a foreigner, but the universal Savior and that his message and life of self-sacrificial love, far from requiring a betrayal of the Korean people and their cultural heritage, was the power of God for their salvation, both as individuals and as a nation.

Neither for Jones nor for Choe was the gospel restricted to the salvation of souls. They both believed that faith and practice are inseparable, that salvation has both a spiritual and a social dimension, that it encompasses both soul and body, both individual and society. But Choe was, in Kim's reading, more consistent in this emphasis. While Jones and Choe agreed that the decadence of Korean neo-Confucianism was incompatible with the spirit of Christianity, Choe sought to retrieve the ancient teachings of Confucianism, which he would come to understand as a kind of *praeparatio evangelica*. Christianity, in his view, was not the antithesis of Confucianism, but its fulfillment. He held that there was important continuity as well as real discontinuity between the texts of his fathers and the new texts of the Bible.

Choe became not only an impressive preacher of the gospel, but a well-respected author. His critics have inclined to label him as a cultural theologian, a comparative religious scholar, a poetical preacher, or a mere consciousness-raiser. According to Kim, however, seeing the nation and heritage of Korea "collapsing right before his eyes," Choe was a robust proclaimer of the new "way" of following Jesus the crucified Savior, who was able to empower both the personal transformation of Koreans and the building of a new Korean society. Making creative use of Confucian terms and concepts to shed light on traditional Christian doctrines, he refused to withdraw "to the inner walls of the church or the inner world of the soul." He nurtured a sense of social responsibility in the life of Korean Christians and in the young Korean church at a time of profound national crisis and never relinquished his hope that the gospel of Jesus would bring about a new Korean identity and a new Korean nation.

For Kim, there are lessons to be learned from the early Christian missionary work of Jones and Choe in Korea. He believes that despite Jones' failure to disengage fully from the worldview that he inherited and carried with him to Korea, he would warn preachers and missionaries today to recognize "the narrowness and particularity of our ethnic and national identities." Choe, for his part, would remind us that the universalism of the Christian gospel does not mean the abolition of a people's cultural heritage and the distinctive gifts of their national life. He would challenge Christians today to account for God's presence in the various cultures, histories, and experiences of people as well as bearing witness to the unique reconciling work of Jesus Christ as God with and for us. In the words of Paul Lehmann, the spirit of Christ is the transforming power in our relationship with God and others that "makes and keeps human life human in the world." For Kim, in important but different ways, the missionary labors of both Jones and Choe opened the way for the "American Christ" to become the "Jesus of Korea."

Daniel L. Migliore
Princeton Theological Seminary

Introduction

This is a story about two men who succeeded in helping the Korean people, with their thousand-year-old faith in Confucian values, adopt a new faith in the American Christ as the Savior who would save their souls and rebuild their nation.

Just over a century ago, in 1910, the Choson Dynasty (1392–1910) on the Korean peninsula came to an end after over five hundred years of rule. It was a kingdom firmly built on Confucian ideals and beliefs.[1] As the longest-lasting Confucian dynasty in history, it tried to create the ideal Confucian state in Choson, from the royal house down to the rural farming family. It resulted in the "height of classical Korean culture, trade, science, literature, and technology." But in the nineteenth century, as infighting, power struggles, foreign pressures, and revolt at home grew, the kingdom weakened rapidly as the century came to a close. Both the government and the people looked for a way out.

American Christian churches began sending missionaries to Korea

---

1. "Korea" and "Choson" are both used in this book. The modern name, "Korea" comes from Koryo, a former dynasty. From 1897 to 1910, the Choson Dynasty was formally known as the Korean Empire. Despite the name change, it was the same monarchy that sat on the throne.

in 1885. There, they started building schools, hospitals, and churches to better the people's lives.

George Heber Jones was an eager twenty-one-year-old working as program staff in an upstate New York YMCA when he heard the voice of God, out of the blue, telling him to go to Choson as a missionary. He had never heard of Choson, and didn't know where it was on the map. Shortly, he was drafted as a missionary candidate of the Methodist Episcopal Church, placed on track to become an ordained clergy, received a little missionary training, and put on a train out of his hometown, Utica, for San Francisco. From there, he caught a steamboat headed for Japan. It took the voice of God less than ten months to land him in Choson! He had been sent by God to be an apostle to the Korean people, without speaking a word of Korean.

Choe Pyonghon was a thirty-year-old Confucian scholar who kept failing to pass the civil service exams to get a government post. Civil service was deemed the ideal career in Confucian Choson. He didn't pass, time and again, but not because he didn't have the brains. What he lacked was the right political pedigree, right connections, and money. By 1888, the civil exam system had become totally corrupt, with offices being sold to the highest bidder. To pay his way while waiting for the next round of exams, in 1888, Choe hired himself out as a Korean language tutor to teach Jones and other American missionaries the Korean language. While he had read a few books critical of the Western religion, this was the first time Choe came face-to-face with Westerners or Christians.

During their five years of close interaction, the men learned a lot from each other. Jones learned the language and became one of the most fluent speakers among the missionaries. But, more importantly, he learned about the Confucian mindset, culture, and longings of the people from Choe. This later helped him speak to the needs of the

Korean people as he preached his American Christ. From Jones, Choe learned about the West and its civilization. In addition, he heard the story of Jesus through Jones and the Bible. After his Christian conversion, Choe became an effective evangelist for the Way of Jesus. He used everything that his Confucian tradition had taught him to tell the Koreans that Jesus was a Savior they could trust. Jesus, he said, would save them and their nation from their plight.

In the following two decades, Jones and Choe helped to build the Korean church with spiritual power, social impact, and cultural warmth. Their initial years together had helped them know how to best present the American Christ to a Confucian society. Together, they saw the deeply-felt needs of the Korean people, who were looking for personal peace and national prosperity. They were able to present a living Savior who knew their suffering and offered a new way to save themselves and their nation. Jones and Choe preached that Jesus would help Koreans find their original goodness and rebuild their nation.

Now, over one hundred years after the end of the Confucian monarchy, nearly 30 percent of South Koreans (population 48.7 million, 2010) identify themselves as Christian[2]—the largest percentage of Christians in an Asian nation, aside from the Philippines. Korea also boasts of having the largest church in the world. It also has the largest Presbyterian, Methodist, and Pentecostal Churches in the world. Its vibrant spirituality, devout church life,

---

2. Of the South Korean population, 29.2 percent are Christian (of which 18.3% (of the total) profess to be Protestants, and 10.9% to be Catholics), 22.8 percent are Buddhist, and the rest adhere to various faiths, including Jeungism, Daesunism, Cheondoism, Taoism, Confucianism, and Won Buddhism. The population figure is from 2010, https://www.cia.gov/library/publications/the-world-factbook/geos/ks.html.Interestingly, according to 2005 statistics compiled by the South Korean government, approximately 46.5 percent of the South Korean population expresses no religious preference. *NSO online KOSIS database.* http://kosis.nso.go.kr:7001/ups/chapterRetrieve.jsp?pubcode=MA&seq=292&pub=3. Retrieved Aug. 8, 2006.

and missionary zeal are well-known around the world; its number of missionaries—17,697—is second only to US churches.[3]

How can we explain this religious revolution in modern Korea? Many people look to the 1970s and 1980s to find the cause of the rapid growth of Christianity in Korea. But to understand the real story behind the growth of the Korean church, we need to rediscover the story of its first 25 years, and that of heroes such as the two men in our story. There, we will learn how the story of the American Christ came to Korea, and gradually, became a part of the Korean people's story. He is no longer the American Christ, but Jesus of Korea.

The story unfolds in four parts.

Part 1 introduces the world of the American missionary and the Korean *sonbi,* or Confucian scholar. We ask, *"Who was Jesus Christ for George Heber Jones as he got ready to leave America for missionary work in Korea?"* and *"What was happening in Choe Pyonghon's life and the Confucian Choson society that made him receptive to the missionary preaching about the American Christ?"*

Part 2 presents the initial encounter between the American missionary and the Korean *sonbi*. We ask, *"What did Jones discover about the realities of Korea that helped him reframe his American Christ as Jesus, Savior of the Korean people?"* and *"How was Choe able to let go of his old Confucian masters' books and grasp the new Book of Master Jesus?"*

Part 3 shows the American missionary and Korean Christian *sonbi* actively engaged in the saving work of Jesus. We ask: *"How did Jesus save the Korean people and society through Jones's missionary service in Chemulpo?"* and *"How did Choe convince the Koreans that the American Christ can indeed save them from their personal sins and national demise?"*

---

3. There are around 17,697 Korean missionaries serving in 168 countries, making South Korea the second largest missionary-sending country in the world, according to a report by KWMC (Korean World Mission Center). http://www.christianpost.com/article/20080729/thousands-of-korean-missionaries-lauded-at-major-conference/.

Part 4 shows the American missionary and Korean Christian *sonbi* engaged in nation-building. We ask, *"What did Jones's Christ promise the Korean people, facing the loss of their identity in the tragic end of their nation, and what would be required of them to rebuild a new one?"* and *"How does Choe's Jesus help the Korean Christians confront the national crisis, and what is demanded of his followers as Korean Christians?"*

The story, in four parts, will show how the American Christ gradually became embedded in the soil of Confucian Choson to become the Jesus of Korea, the Savior of the people and the nation.

PART I

Christian America and Confucian Korea

1

Jones 1867–1887: Experiencing the American Christ

In this chapter, we ask the question "Who was Jesus Christ for George Heber Jones as he began his missionary career in Korea?" We learn how he came to this understanding in his conversion. We look at the many factors that influenced his growing faith and knowledge in Christ and how he went about learning and practicing his faith before he was sent to the mission field.

1.1 The Conversion of George Heber Jones

Throughout his life, Jones looked back upon his conversion experience, at age fourteen, as the foundational event of his life, "the greatest single event of my life."[1] He writes in his autobiographical sketch, "Real Stories from Real Life":

> I attended the services and listened attentively with growing convictions concerning certain things. First, that no man could be saved except

---

1. In his unfinished autobiographical sketch entitled *Real Stories from Real Life*, Jones dedicates the third story to his conversion. George Heber Jones, *Real Stories from Real Life*, ed. William A. Main (Tiburon, CA, 1990), 14. The following sections on his conversion are from this book.

by the Lord Jesus, and second, that I needed to definitely take the step of accepting Him as my Savior…One night, toward the close of the revival, the message took hold of me. I felt I could hold out no longer…Sam Lewis, my chum, was sitting alongside and when the invitation came for those who desired to take Christ as their Savior to come down to the altar – it was before the day of "hold up hands" or singing [[[signing?]]] cards – I said to my friend, "Sam, if you will go with me, I'll go to the altar!" And together we started down the aisle, and then at the altar rail in dear old Fourth St. Church, I knelt, a seeker of life through the Savior. The people crowded around, they prayed, they prayed for me, and by and by there came into my heart a sweet peace; a knowledge and assurance that God for Christ's sake had forgiven me my sins and I began to pray amid my tears, both of grief and joy. I know I was saved that night. I know I entered definitely into a new relationship with God. As we rose from our knees the good people sang, "Take the name of Jesus with you," a sweet blessed counsel, and I have done so through all the years.[2]

Jones described his conversion to Christ in three ways. First, Jesus Christ is the living Savior who opened heaven's door in order to unite him with God for "an inner life" with God. To believe in Jesus was not mainly a matter of knowledge, nor a logical problem about how Jesus was both human and divine, as the traditional doctrines stated. Rather, to be a believer in Jesus was to experience God personally, for himself. It was to have an "experimental," living faith.

> …at that time I was not devoid of knowledge of the teachings of Christianity and the forms of church life. But it was the beginning of my inner life with God, the experience of a new birth of that supreme experience which the Savior declared when he said, "You must be born again"…God has a thousand different ways in which he brings the souls of men [sic] to himself, but though there be a thousand ways, there is but one result: the new birth, being born of the Spirit, born of God.[3]

Jones saw Jesus of his conversion as the expression of God's life

---

2. Jones, *Real Stories*, 14.
3. Ibid., 46.

among humanity. Jesus was a "Savior with whom people must enter into a relationship" since he opened to all peoples a relationship of "sonship" or "filial relationship" with God. It gave them eternal life and a more abundant life here on earth. Jesus' earthly life signaled that God wanted to restore the original unity with the human race. God had created humanity to be his sons and daughters, but that original unity had been broken on the human side by their sin. Thus, salvation in Christ is a reunion with God, with Christ as God's mediator. Sin needs to be overcome because it causes separation, a life of death and destruction, a corrupt and immoral human life, eternal punishment, and a life in search of meaning and truth. When he arrived in Korea, Jones saw the Korean people as needing this same union with God and needing a Savior from their sin, death, and the world. To Jones, Jesus is the Savior of an experiential religion of the heart that meets the spiritual hunger and need of all human beings.

Second, Jones said that the Christ of his conversion was always found in the fellowship and community of the Christian church. Knowing Christ was not a private spiritual experience to be kept to oneself. It was a communal event that placed the new believer in a living community of faith, where Christ dwelt. He writes:

> Thus I came into the membership of the Christian church and began what afterward, in the providence of God, became my life work. I can never adequately express my debt of gratitude to the church for all she has meant to me. I was an unknown and very ordinary lad, seriously handicapped at the start of life by poverty and frail health. It was at the altar of the church that I found God and entered into a conscious relationship of sonship and acceptance with Him. It was the ministry of the Church that brought God and Christ into my life. This is the biggest thing that ever happened to me or that can happen to any boy...The Church opened up to my vision the great and eternal world, the world where God reigns and in which men meet Him.[4]

---

4. Ibid., 61.

Jesus, the mediator between God and humanity, continued his work in the Christian church. The church was the place where Jesus continued his ministry of reconciliation with the people of God. So he says:

> I was assigned to a class, a regular Methodist class. It was made up of about 20 young people and met every Tuesday evening…there was no escape from testifying, and I then learned to examine my own heart life and to express my personal understanding of my own condition and aspiration. Those were blessed days, and that old classroom meant more to me than any School of Theology I ever saw. Listening to older Christians, I learned the true meaning of vital heart life with God. I learned to hate sin as my chief foe, to love God and to trust Him, to value the blood of the Lord Jesus Christ, and to depend on the Holy Spirit. It was personal religion, intelligent heart-searching, expressed in a witnessing life, fired with a sense of human need of Christ, a clear understanding of the perils of worldly life and a desire to bring others into precious faith.[5]

Although his conversion took place in a Methodist Church and he served as a Methodist missionary, Jones never adopted a "sectarian" denominational outlook, even in terms of his theology. Rather, the checkered religious background of his family and his later appreciation of Christian history made him recognize that there is only one great Fundamental, "that the church has no other foundation than that is laid, namely Jesus Christ."[6]

Jones's great grandfather, Edwards of Denhigh, was active in the Welsh Wesleyan Church and personally knew Reginald Heber, the Bishop of Calcutta, from whom the name "Heber" came into the Jones family. Jones grew up in a Welsh-speaking church. His mother was raised as a Roman Catholic, but later, joined the Episcopalian Church, in which Jones was confirmed and attended Sunday school.

---

5. Ibid., 53.
6. Ibid., 59.

In his early teens, he went to a Presbyterian church with his friends. His mother, at first, scolded him for joining the Methodist Church after his conversion in 1881 because it was seen as a "peculiar sect, extravagant in religious things, given to shouting and noise and regarded with feelings of amusement or contempt." But she later joined it herself.

For Jones, the church was an historical body which held within it a great diversity of beliefs, customs, and doctrines. This understanding stopped him from making any culture-based "peculiarity" the identifying mark of the church, such as "matters of dress, specialities [sic] in conduct, forms of creedal doctrine, emphasis upon a single idea, and as Seventh Day Adventist, a rite or a form of government."[7] What mattered for the church is Jesus Christ, whose earthly life is continued through the communal life of the church and believers. He writes:

> The Church made me the heir of a great and glorious history. I have already indicated that the force of heredity made it a natural thing for me to become a Methodist and my heart was thrilled and rejoiced as I have read of the men and achievements of the Wesleyan Revival in Europe and America. But from my earliest Church days I cannot say that I was a good sectarian. And later I came to realize that Methodist was but a convenient form, an auxiliary of the Kingdom of God. The eager quest of my mind has in the years that have followed carried my love out to all organized forms of Christianity and back through the corridors of time until I just gathered into my heart all the splendid history of faith in all the ages.[8]

Third, Christ's key work was to renew and reform the human character. For Jones, the union with God had the purpose of refitting

---

7. Jones tells how he got "interested in a rather emotional expression of Christianity and learned how to shout…but I was repelled by their extravagances. I could not see any connection between their filial relationship with God and cutting up strange antics in meeting; and to claim that to wear a collar and necktie was a sin." Ibid., 18–19.
8. Ibid., 63.

human beings in line with human "filial relationship" with God. Having been born again in God, he was to grow in the "ideals of spiritual Christianity," remain faithful in "personal practical living," stay away from "ways that lead to evil," and be trained "in the virtues of Christian personality."[9] To be a disciple of Jesus meant becoming a better human being from the inside to live a moral and purposeful life in the society.

Jones grew in his faith through an active life in the local Methodist Episcopal church: always being present at all sessions on Sunday, with class meetings on Tuesday evenings, prayer meetings on Thursday evenings, and choir practice on Friday evenings. He began to work for the emerging telephone business and with the Utica YMCA, which was just beginning to be organized—first, as its janitor, and then, as the assistant to the secretary.

Through these, he was able to put his newfound faith into action and came into touch with Christian businessmen who "represent[ed] the highest and best of our American Christian life."[10] Jones saw Christ's work in the human soul being brought to life in the headquarters of a growing business, for these Christian businessmen "helped a struggling badly handicapped lad along life's pathway towards life's best goals."[11] For example, the treasurer of the telephone company, Mr. Woods, helped him learn Latin to prepare him for college. This friendship helped him to appreciate how "true Christian views and sympathies" affected social life.[12] More than the three Rs of the schoolroom, he appreciated how this work trained him for the three Hs: "head, hand and heart."[13] Being a follower of Christ meant living an ethical life in society. Jones did not believe that Christians

---

9. All quotes in this paragraph from Jones, *Real Stories*, 61.
10. Ibid., 27.
11. Ibid.
12. Ibid., 33.
13. Ibid., 34.

should go against the world, nor that the salvation of the soul meant neglecting their life here on earth. He believed that a change in human character would necessarily lead to a change in the larger society.

This was the Jesus Christ of Jones' conversion. To be saved by Christ meant that now, he had become reunited with God as a child of God. As a renewed person, he became a disciple of Christ in the spiritual life of the church community. And Christ continued to work in Jones's life to renew his humanity and personality to make him a citizen in society with a moral core.

1.2 Jones's Early Life

In addition to his unforgettable conversion experience, to which Jones often looked back to regain his life's focus, Jones also regarded his early growing years as a formative time that gave him an openness toward religious commitment, a deep thirst for learning, and a confident perspective toward life. "Local anchorage, which means so much to other men [sin]" was denied to Jones, and his early life was "one of constant change of march and exile."[14] He was born in a hotel in Mohawk, NY, where his parents were staying on August 14, 1867 and lived there the first three years. Then, the next four years were spent in New York City, after which the family moved back to upstate New York to Utica, where he spent his teen years until age 18. The next two years in Rochester were the time of his professional growth and development, along with new religious experiences. It was here that he received the call to be an apostle to Korea, where he would spend a total of twenty-one years. After his return in 1909, he

---

14. Ibid., 1.

and his wife and family settled in Leonia, NJ until his untimely death ten years later, on May 11, 1919.

Jones hailed from the "three national stocks of Britain." His grandfather on his father's side was Welsh through and through, and was of the "gentry" class and a solicitor and a military officer. His grandmother came from the wealthy and prominent Edwards family of Denhigh, who were ardent Welsh Wesleyans. Their home was always open to Wesleyan preachers, as great-grandfather Edwards lived in the time of John Wesley. This tie, for Jones, must have "destined [him] to the Methodist ministry."[15] His middle name "Heber" came from Reginald Heber, the Bishop of Calcutta, who was a personal friend of his great-grandfather Edwards. Jones was often reminded by his grandfather that his name was given "in memory of both the great and good Bishop and of my uncle" named Heber.[16] Jones says, "I seem to be linked up from my birth not only with the ministry and Methodism but with foreign missions."[17] It was his father's generation, educated to be English gentlemen, that came to the United States.

On his mother's side, Jones's great-grandfather was English, George Willoughby Cosser, a businessman and military officer who served in the Mexican War in the Albany Rangers Corp. He was born in England and had come to settle in Albany, New York, via Canada. It was his grandmother on his mother's side who was Scotch, a Murray of the Edinburgh Murrays, which claimed the Duke of Athole as the head of the clan. Some genealogical research later showed him that these ancestors began as cattle "lifters," and later, became respectable cattle "raisers." So, Jones was an American of English-Scotch-Welsh ancestry, which he proudly claimed.

15. Ibid., 7.
16. Ibid., 9.
17. Ibid.

One childhood experience that Jones regretted was attending a Welsh-speaking ethnic church with his mother, which catered to the first-generation Welsh immigrant population. While the immigrants enjoyed the rhythm of Welsh in worship, young Jones's generation only spoke English. He remembers being in the church in his childhood, but not understanding a single word of what they were preaching or teaching. He felt it was a big educational and parental mistake to force children in the "early and imaginative years" to attend church in a "strange tongue."[18] This early experience made him very conscious and perceptive about the uses of language and made him a lifelong student of various languages.

Jones's father became seriously ill, and so, both his mother and Jones worked to support the family from early on. He worked in a variety of jobs after school, such as a cash boy in a big dry goods store at age nine. At age eleven, he came down with inflammatory rheumatism, which nearly killed him. When he recovered, he was left with a damaged heart, "vegetation in the valves of the heart" was the diagnosis of the day.[19] The doctor also said that he might live to be eighteen but never see twenty years of age! He recommended "an outdoor life and warned against dangers of study and sedentary habits."[20] While his family's economic hardship and his health problems gave him "a broken and much interrupted routine in getting a [standardized] education," Jones did so well in his freshman year in high school that within that year, he was promoted three times to the senior graduating class.[21] His end-of-the-year examination exceeded the entrance scores for college, but the school decided it would set a bad precedent to have a student finish four years of high school in one. So, he was told to come back for

18. Ibid., 10.
19. Ibid., 12.
20. Ibid., 13.
21. Ibid., 17.

one more semester, after which he could attend the Academy. He recounts an event in the Advanced School (high school):

> Once in the Advanced School, I recited without a mistake the names of every state in the Union and its capital and every country in the world and its capital. Well, I remember that I was taught that the name of the capital of Korea was King-ki-Tao; so little was Korean known.[22]

But his illness caught up with him, and the good doctor forbade him from returning to school. So, he got a job as a messenger boy in the Mutual Union Telegraph Company. While there, he decided he would need a trade to survive, so entered a vocational school, named the Holbrook School Co. and began learning how to become a shoe-cutter. While earning $3.50 weekly, he spent nearly a year stamping the buttonholes and learned "the deadening process of being a human cog in the living organization that turned out a shoe fit for a lady to wear." Although he only made button-holes for a year, he learned to distinguish between a skilled and an unskilled worker, and "the values and possibilities of a system."[23]

About the same time, he underwent his conversion experience, Jones joined the Utica YMCA on Genesee Street with its new secretary, Glen Shurtleff, who offered him the janitor's job at the YMCA. But Jones became more than a janitor getting $4.00 a week. He became the right-hand man to Shurtleff, who would later become one of the greatest organizers of the American YMCA movement. Under the mentorship of this great role model, young Jones learned many life lessons that would serve him in the future:

> …a familiarity with common place things in life, a willingness to do the so-called drudgery of the kingdom when need be, to keep my mind clear on the dignity of toil, and my heart free from pride, which became a most potent endearment in my work as a missionary.[24]

22. Ibid., 20.
23. Both quotes here from ibid., 21–22.

After six months, in 1883, when Jones was sixteen, he became an office assistant in the Central NY Telephone Co., which shared the same floor with the YMCA. This experience in the growing technology business opened Jones's eyes to many wonders: wonders of electricity, the work of Graham Bell and Thomas Edison and the science of physics, along with an understanding of incorporation, patents, accounting, banking, and the value of integrity. In the two years with the company, Jones estimated that he carried $300,000 to the bank for deposit. He learned about trust and the uses of money: "Money is not a thing for personal use and enjoyment, but is meant primarily as a medium for business and industry, for community service."[25] Later, the telephone company expanded into the first "skyscraper" in Utica, the seven-story Mann Building. Jones loved looking down on his hometown's Mohawk Valley. For two years, Jones worked diligently beyond the call of duty. "What did I get in return? Five dollars a week? Yes, but vastly more than that I received a training for head, hand, and heart, the three H's, as important as the three R's of the school room."[26]

Jones's father instilled in him a love of books from early on, lending books from the City Library that taught American ideals in the stories of Elijah Kellogg, J. T. Trowbridge, Oliver Optic, and Castleman. Later on, he moved on to literature—American, English, French. He read Taine's French Literature twice because it was so interesting to him; he read Gibbon's Rome, Bancroft's American History, Macauley's England, and Guizot's France. He spent "much time in reading always with a book and always with a helpful book."[27] He would never forget reading a book entitled *Filling in the Chinks*, which was given by a neighbor's teenage daughter, Delia Thorn. It

---

24. Ibid., 25.
25. Ibid., 28.
26. Ibid., 34.
27. All quotes in this paragraph from ibid., 35–36.

taught that "life was full of 'chinks'—waste spaces of time—which if filled in would make a completed and beautiful structure of life." This idea caught his "boyish fancy so eager and thirsty for an education and so denied the opportunities for schooling." Jones gives an example of how, early in Korea, when he was living with the Appenzellers, he read through Milman's entire series of works on Christian history while waiting for lunch at 12:30 pm. "Mr. A. would often be detained until 12:45 or one o'clock. This time I spent in reading and in the course of some months finished that monumental history. I can never be grateful enough to Miss Thorn for the help she gave to me in giving me that book."

At the telephone company, he learned to read Latin with Mr. Wood, the president. When he moved to Rochester, he took up Greek so he could read the Gospel of John in the original Greek. He also learned French and German while in Korea. In Korea, his interest in education remained fervent as ever. So, as correspondence education or "non-resident college courses" were starting in the United States, he signed up for an AB degree through Illinois Wesleyan; then, later, changed to the American University at Harriman, Tennessee. He and a colleague missionary, Arthur Noble, studied very hard and diligently for three years for a PhD, earning in turn the AB, AM, and then PhD. Later, Jones repudiated these degrees. But he still appreciated the education he received through "the benefit of intensive work in a wide range of subjects, including mathematics, physics and chemistry, psychology, philosophy, sociology and international law."[28] One can sense the deep and abiding love and practice of self-learning in these words: "Had I my life to live over again, I would force my way through [college], no matter how adverse my circumstances." This habit of study and deep

---

28. All quotes in this paragraph from ibid., 37–39.

self-learning served Jones well, for he not only became one of the most proficient speakers of the Korean language—which earned him an honorary doctoral degree for his translation work on the Korean Bible—he also dug beneath the language, in order to "investigate into the history, traditions, social conditions, the law and the literature of Korea." This enabled him to understand Korea and her people in a special way, opening the way for him to speak winsomely of Christ to them. In Korea, he also learned Chinese and Japanese.

Jones's early life struggles had made him into a solid young man, prepared to face the future unafraid. He had an open and curious mind. But it also was a trained and disciplined mind, perhaps not through a regular standardized school education—but one that was based on diligent self-study of the best literature and culture that the West had to offer. His diverse vocational experiences also earned him a wide vista and wisdom beyond his young age. His family's historic ties to the Wesleyan movement and world missions also lurked beneath the surface as he was getting ready to leave yet another familiar surroundings for a life which was one of "constant change of march and exile."

1.3 Learning the Faith through The YMCA

Jones' newfound faith became tested and nurtured in his work with the Utica and Rochester YMCAs (1883–88) before he went to Korea. It may not be an exaggeration to say that all of Jones's "semi-apostolic" accomplishments in Korea had their roots in the training and skills learned through the YMCA. Jones writes that it was the training class that he led in Utica YMCA that laid the foundation for the "Bible Institute" (*sakyŏnghoe*) "that have so profoundly influenced the life and development of the Korean Church."[29] After his conversion, Jones began to work with the YMCA in Utica

(1883–86), and later, as the assistant secretary of the Rochester YMCA (April 1886–February 1888). These five years in the YMCA were his field training for the missionary work to come. Through YMCA's evangelistic and church work, Bible study and theological study, and social and economic participation, Jones deepened his understanding of the faith and of what Jesus Christ meant for him and the world.

In his YMCA work, Jones was drawn to its "evangelistic side" that was the "chief thing that attracted" him. Called "Religious Work Committee," its aim was to bring young men to "accept Christ as their Savior" and to connect them to the life of discipleship and growth in the local church. Jones records that in one year, 250 young men received Christ through the work of the Religious Work Committee, and were then recommended to the fellowship of a local church. It was here that he honed his skills of evangelistic outreach through his own program of study, the Sunday night evangelistic meetings of the Religious Work Committee, and the Workers Training Classes offered by the YMCA.

> Out of those first experiences in evangelistic services there came to me the abiding conviction concerning religious meetings, namely that the chief purpose of the Church and of all organized religious work is to bring those out of Christ into a living vital touch with him that will mean salvation. It made me a seeker after souls…It has disposed me to question the value of those churches which exist only for themselves…deep in my heart I feel that the Christian who gives no thought to the spiritual need of his fellow men and makes no effort to win men to Christ has missed the real purpose of soulship in Christ here on earth.[30]

It was at the Rochester YMCA that Jones's understanding of Christ became firmly rooted in the Scriptures, in the traditions of the

---

29. Ibid., 23.
30. Ibid., 71–72.

church, and in the life of the society. As a teacher of the Sunday afternoon Bible Study (5 p.m.–6 p.m.), Jones taught about the parables and the miracles of Christ and learned to study the Bible "both analytically and topically." While he lacked formal theological training, his education was eclectic, nonsectarian, and practical. As was his habit, he read widely and wisely, reading "some of the best New Testament literature of the day—French on the Parables and on the Miracles, Taylor on the Parables, Geikie's Life of Christ, and also his Hours with the Bible, Farrer's Life of Christ, and Wesley's Commentary on the New Testament."[31] But most of all, he learned to study the "Book Itself," which gave him a "deep reverence and love for the Word Itself."[32]

In addition, he learned the Christian practice of prayer. Given the centrality of union with Christ in his conversion experience, he saw "the secret of prayer as a key to the opening up of the profounder or the hidden things of the Bible."[33]

> When I would come to a hard place I would kneel and with the Book open at the hard place reverently ask God to enlighten me through his Holy Spirit – and the answer always came…God did not pronounce in my hearing words of interpretation as might a teacher in a classroom – no it was nothing mechanical like that. But light shown in my own heart, my mental powers were quickened and enabled to work with a deeper penetration, my imagination was fired and I saw with an amplitude of vision not otherwise possible. And in that light dark things became plain, hidden things emerged to view and grouped themselves in proper relation to the thing I was studying and helped make them clear and understandable. Thus early I discovered the value of prayer as a primary method of work.[34]

---

31. Ibid., 116.
32. Ibid., 117.
33. Ibid.
34. Ibid., 117. Jones always affirmed that God's communion and communication with humanity was diverse and beyond human control. As we will see below, his call to the missionary service also included using a Wesleyan form of testing God's will: opening the Bible and pointing to specific verses as God's word for that moment. Though he found great assurance from three

Jones's understanding of Christ is rooted in the Bible, in the complex development of the Christian doctrines in history, in personal spiritual experiences, and in practical application in the larger society. In his work at Rochester, the core evangelistic work of bringing young men to Christ included the follow-up work of their education, employment, entertainment, and institution-building. Its goal was to produce the kind of men whom he saw as the best of Christian "manhood" earlier in Utica. In particular, he learned how to participate in the life of the people he was trying to reach for Christ, "the necessity to understand and share in the warm red-blooded life of young men, to maintain interest and keep pace with the aspirations of young life in its first 'drives.'"[35] Just as Christ had come to share God's life with humanity, in his YMCA work, Jones learned the secret of "mixing: that is grounded in a frame of mind which has interest in and hope for all men, to be friendly to a man just because he is a man. I had to meet men on their own ground and in order to be helpful to them, to study and understand their viewpoint."[36] Christ was training him one step at a time so that, one day, he would be able to communicate God's message to a people far different from him. The YMCA, in hindsight, was Jones's five-year course of study in missions, preparing him for the missionary adventures ahead.

1.4 The Triumphant Christ of Nineteenth-Century America

Through his YMCA work, Jones came to believe in a Christ who was active and present in American society, creating it as "the highest Christian culture on earth."[37] In addition, America was given the task

---

verses he chose in this way, he says, "God might have spoken to me in any one of a hundred other ways and it would have been equally conclusive and satisfactory, but in this particular case He spoke to me in that particular way." See ibid., 40.
35. Ibid., 113.
36. Ibid., 114.

of saving peoples and nations through "the Christianization of the people[s]" and "social reconstruction"[38] of nations.[39] This idealistic view of American Christ was the one popularized by Josiah Strong in his *Our Country*, a book which Jones took in with great interest, along with the rest of the nation. With Strong, Jones easily became "very open to the impressions of America's greatness, marked everywhere with the symbolism of power." Strong's Christ is a triumphant, Resurrected Christ whose 1,000-year rule over the world is now about to be fulfilled in America. Soon, all knees would bow and all tongues confess that Jesus is Lord, and all nations would be reborn as Christian nations, like Christian America.

This understanding of a triumphant Christ went hand in hand with a self-understanding of American mission in the world, which had its roots in the colonial theologian Jonathan Edwards (1703–58). According to Edwards, Christ's kingdom was becoming completed in America.[40] To use his terms, God's complex beauty *ad intra* is communicated *ad extra* in Christ and is being made manifest in its diversity in America.[41] By the time of Edwards' grandson, theologian

---

37. In his reflection back on the first twenty-five years of American Methodist missions in Korea, Jones describes the missionaries as "the representatives of the highest Christian culture on earth." Jones, "The Rise of the Church in Korea," Papers, 90.
38. Jones, "Education in Relation to the Christianization of National Life in Korea," Papers, 7.
39. The work of the missions in Korea, according to Jones, "furnishes another proof of Christianity's power to achieve its ideal of transforming the world." Jones, "The Growth of the Church in Korea," Papers, 81.
40. In his MA thesis written in 1902, Jones reaffirms this Edwardsian vision of America as the place where God's will is best fulfilled. George Heber Jones, October 8, 1900. Diary, privately held by family, Tiburon, CA. Entitled "The Influence of Christian Ideas on the Constitution of the United States," the thesis argues "the governments of the world wear an impression derived from the religion which prevails among the people," which is "due to the fact that religious ideas so dominate men that each stage of individual and national development is not without some coloring derived from these. With a change in religion generally comes a change in the form of government." Consequently, "the constitution of the U.S. was a development. It sprung from previous Constitutions and Regulations from governments which have more strongly even the impress of Christian ideas." For Jones, this means that there are many "Christian ideas [that are] traceable in the Constitution," such as "equality of all men, freedom of conscience, responsibility and obligation to moral law, traces of Ten Commandments, justice in the Christian sense, philanthropy, [and] co-operation."

Timothy Dwight (1752–1817), to be a Christian in America was to become a model citizen who would honor the law and obey it practically. So, American Christians came to believe that Christ's work was mainly about making people happy: "All his employments were directed to no other earthly end, than the promotion of human happiness." In nineteenth-century America, Christ was slowly changed "from the promoter of holiness to the promoter of happiness" since it "suited better the demands of a new republic in which the pursuit of happiness was to overtake the pursuit of holiness."[42] Jones would hold on to both Edwards and his grandson—and keep intact the tie between holiness and happiness.

Later in his missionary life, Jones often referred to Horace Bushnell's (1802–76) description of Christ to explain his own belief about the divinity of Christ.[43] Already in the story of Jones's conversion experience, we can hear echoes of Bushnell's effort to rescue Jesus from the exemplary model of atonement that ruled nineteenth-century American theology. Bushnell tried to explain the divinity of Christ by totally separating it from the doctrine of the Trinity.[44] Based on his view of the nature of revelation and the limits of human understanding and expression, Bushnell refused to see Christ through the dry, "incredible" doctrine of two natures. To him, Jesus was simply the expression of God in history: the "organic union of God with human history," which leaves an "impression on the imagination of the individual, making for the development of

---

41. Bruce M. Stephens, *The Prism of Time and Eternity: Images of Christ in American Protestant Thought from Jonathan Edwards to Horace Bushnell* (Lanham, MD: The American Theological Library Association and Scarecrow Press, 1996), 7. "Christ's excellence is the visible evidence that God is a being who consents with our being" while human beings are on "a course of dissent from being." So, in Christ, there is the "conjunction of excellencies."
42. Ibid., 42–44.
43. Jones, July 20, 1900, Diary. For example, speaking to the Russian Prince Count Reinsforf, who denied the divinity of Christ, Jones promised to send him "Bushnell's character of Jesus."
44. This section summarizes Stephens, *Images of Christ*, 156–78.

character." He was interested, not in "investigating the inner mystery of his person," but in what Christ expressed of God.[45]

Bushnell thought deeply about the literal and symbolic uses of language. He noticed that human beings easily misunderstood the metaphorical language of the Bible in terms of logic. He tried to look into the inward mystery of Christ as the expression of God's life among humanity. Calling Christ "God's last metaphor," he refused to see the two-natures doctrine as a scientific problem needing solution. Rather, he called on Christians to accept the mystery and the paradox in faith. He also opposed "self-culture and self-voluntary" salvation for it is "Christ alone not self-culture or education that completes the [human] soul…Christ brings holiness of God which is opposite to humanity, what is not in them." It is this experimental Christ of Bushnell and his tender offer of a dynamic relationship with a living God that Jones would proclaim to the Korean people, not a dry and doctrinaire theory of the two natures of Christ.[46]

1.5 Jones and Nineteenth-Century American Revivalism

Jones's conversion experience—and the ones he would later encourage among the Korean Christians—reflected the revivalism of Charles G. Finney (1792–1875), who brought in many new innovations into the revival movement of the early decades of the nineteenth century. Jones would also turn to these in his own revivals in Korea, which he often compared to the Methodist camp meetings.[47] Like Jonathan Edwards before him, Finney linked

---
45. These three quotes from Jones, July 20, 1900, Diary.
46. This paragraph summarizes and quotes from Stephens, *Images of Christ*, 156–78.
47. Mark G. Toulouse and James O. Duke, eds., *Makers of Christian Theology in America* (Nashville, TN: Abingdon Press, 1997), 131. Finney introduced "new measures" from the Baptist and Methodist revivalist traditions into the mainstream church life: "house to house visitation, inquiry meetings following services, prayer for sinners by name, testimony of men and women in mixed congregation, toleration of emotional excess, call for immediate decisions for Christ."

spiritual conversion to active involvement in social reforms (e.g., temperance and antislavery). But Finney rejected orthodox Calvinism and the emphasis on the autonomy of the human will. Salvation meant the "transformation of the will from selfishness" to what he called "disinterested benevolence" or "selfless love."[48] Like Finney, Jones also made a direct connection between personal holiness and social betterment or "usefulness." From the account of his conversion experience through a revival meeting, his ministry in the YMCA movement, and his call to foreign missions, it is clear that Jones shared the prevalent pietistic Christianity of his day. But he never moved toward premillennialism[49] nor the fundamentalism that prevailed among many American missionaries of the early twentieth century.[50]

On the contrary, Jones also took an element from the new revivalism of D. L. Moody (1837–99) that greatly influenced the young men and women of Jones's era. With Moody, he saw his

---

He also helped introduce the practice of "anxious seat" and "protracted meeting" of four- to five-day revivals, like those in the church where Jones was converted.

48. Ibid., 132–33: "His assertion that a revival is not a supernatural event but the result of human effort under God's influence reflected his belief that the aim of Christian evangelism was not only the salvation of individuals but the shaping of sinful society."

49. In this sense, Jones does not fit the picture of a typical American missionary as a Puritan-type premillennialist that has become part of the traditional view in Korea. Even though Jones grew up in a time of great changes and social crises in America and responded to some of these trends in his YMCA work—urbanization, industrialization, immigrant influx, social unrest, and ecclesiastical confusion, i.e., evangelicalism no longer enjoying cultural dominance—he remained well within the broad tradition of evangelical liberalism with his "own personal religious life" of the "living Christ within" and an indefatigable belief in human potential and did not have a chance to experience first-hand the "pessimism" about the "materialism, capitalist competitiveness and nationalism," which would lead to an erosion of postmillennialist thought in American Christianity in 1865–1925 and pessimism about the world. James Moorhead, "The Erosion of Postmillennialism in American Religious Thought, 1865-1925," in *Theological Themes in the American Protestant World*, ed. Martin E. Marty (New York: K. G. Saur, 1992), 203–19.

50. Jones shares with post-Civil War fundamentalism its adoption of an empirical, scientific method of literalistic interpretation of the supernatural Scriptures that was inerrant and fount of all human knowledge, including ultimate truth and first principles of morality. See George M. Marsden. *Fundamentalism and American Culture: The Shaping of Twentieth-Century Evangelicalism 1870-1925* (New York: Oxford University Press, 1980), 56–61.

new relationship with God as an "inner separation marked by the outward signs of a life free from specific vices" such as alcohol and tobacco. But unlike Moody, Jones kept Finney's emphasis on "God's redemptive work as manifested in the spiritual and moral progress of American society."[51] For Jones, the Christ of the revivals and conversions was not a subject to be studied and debated by scholars. Rather, he was the experimental Jesus, who demanded an urgent decision for an intimate relationship with God. This Resurrected Jesus was still alive in human history, continuing his work of salvation through the church and Christian men and women in society.

Among scholars, it has generally been held that most American missionaries owned a view similar to Moody's premillennial vision that saw an imminent end of the world. Such a vision, they say, demanded a complete focus on the salvation of souls apart from social salvation: "I look upon this world as a wrecked vessel. God has given me a lifeboat and said to me, 'Moody, save all you can.'"[52] Moody's sole mission was to save human souls from destruction and hell. In many ways, Moody's revivalism challenged the American Protestant ethos and vision that had taken root since Jonathan Edwards, one that "did not look upon the world as a wrecked vessel from which people could be rescued, but as the site of the millennium, the locale for the Kingdom."[53]

This premillennial outlook was typical of Moody, who helped to create the Student Volunteer Movement for Foreign Missions (SVMFM), possibly "history's single most potent mission organization." In the 1880s and 1890s, there were only 1/37th as many college students as there are today, but the Student Volunteer

---

51. Ibid., 38.
52. Martin E. Marty, *The Righteous Empire: The Protestant Experiment in America* (New York: The Dial Press, 1970), 184.
53. Ibid.

Movement netted 100,000 volunteers who gave their lives to missions. Twenty thousand actually went overseas.[54] At the same time, the motto of the SVMFM, "Evangelization of the world in our generation" expressed a strong postmillennial vision that had its roots in Edwards.[55]

Despite this seeming difference between Moody and evangelical liberals such as Jones, Hutchison says that both the evangelical liberals such as Jones and the revivalists such as Moody joined in a "world-renovating social emphasis" based on a similar belief in "the conquest of the world not only for Christ but for 'Christian civilization.'" He saw both of the camps sharing the goal of "civilizing," which is based on their belief that America could define for other non-Western civilization what is civilization, "impos[ing] its definition on the non-Western world."[56] Because "they glorified in their identities as Westerners and as Americans…the missionary's problem was, one might say, Christ and culture problem squared."[57]

---

54. Ralph D. Winter, "Four Men, Three Eras, Two Transitions: Modern Missions" found at http://www.uscwm.org/uploads/pdf/ psp/winter_four_men_three_eras.pdf, accessed on Jan. 9, 2011.
55. See Max Wood Moorhead, ed., *The Student Missionary Enterprise* (New York: Fleming H. Revell Co., 1894), 114–15.
56. William R. Hutchison, "A Moral Equivalent for Imperialism: Americans and the Promotion of 'Christian Civilization,' 1880-1910," in *Missionary Ideologies in the Imperialist Era: 1880-1920*, ed. Torben Christensen and William R. Hutchison (Aarhus, Denmark: Forlaget Aros, 1982), 168–76. But in other places, Hutchison denies that he is "reducing American missionary operatives *to* their American identity" and does not argue that "they were more than spokesperson for national and societal values" since "their Christian identity transcended all other." William R. Hutchison, *Errand to the World: American Protestant Thought and Foreign Missions* (Chicago: University of Chicago Press, 1993), 4. Dae Young Ryu, unfortunately, seems to disregard this point and sees their middle-class identity as the core of their religious and missionary identity. "They were converts not only to Christ, but also to the spirit of industrial commercialism." Dae Young Ryu, "Understanding Early American Missionaries," 116.
57. Hutchison, *Errand*, 4. Hutchison hints that it was almost natural to link civilization and evangelization because of "the non-colonial" dimension of American imperialism at this period in American history. But he argues that this is a "moral equivalent" to missional imperialism, given its assertion of the need to civilize others and define their religions and cultures based on American values. Ryu argues that American missionaries were not only "creators" of demand for Western goods in Korea, they were "salesm[e]n for the manufacturers of Christendom" since American missionary movement was largely bankrolled by American middle-class

As Jones begins his missionary career, he is a proud product of American evangelical christianity of the late nineteenth century. But he also takes the new revivalistic spirit of Moody to Korea, with "constant tension and fluctuation between pietism and imperialist ideas."[58] This would become all the more critical as he would stand with the new Christian church in Korea confronted with the demise of their nation at the hands of more powerful foreign nations. Jones also shares Josiah Strong's (1847–1916) ethnocentric belief in "the superiority of Anglo Saxons."[59] He would later agree with James Dennis that non-Christian societies were on the decline while christianity is the motive force in "all noble and worthy moral development" in any attempt to "civilize barbarous races." For Jones, Christian conversion is a means "to an end, namely an improved society."[60]

Finally, Jones's missionary Christ is the social Christ. In his work for the YMCA and for the newly developing telephone industry, Jones came to meet and admire "the highest and best of our American Christian life" in innovative businessmen and their new technologies. In them, he saw the life and example of Christ manifest in the free enterprise capitalism that served the public good and in their moral lives. In this, he shares what church historian Martin Marty calls "a gospel of American economy." One can hear in his generous praise

---

businessmen. Dae Young Ryu, "American Protestant Missionaries," 115n98. On the contrary, Appenzeller's biographer, Daniel M. Davies agrees with Hutchison that "the only imperialism missionaries in Japan (and later in Korea) could rightly be accused is cultural imperialism: the combination of Protestantism and Americanism." Davies, *Appenzeller*, 119. Davies denies that the charge of missionaries serving as the arm of capitalist governments in advancing the cause of imperialism can be applied to Appenzeller. He also denies that Appenzeller held to a manifest destiny notion of Americanism since he rejected using military might to advance Americanism (only religion and cultural influence) although he supported the Spanish–American War. Ibid., 143, 184.

58. Hutchison, "A Moral Equivalent," 7.
59. Gerald H. Anderson, "American Protestants in Pursuit of Mission: 1886–1986," in *Missiology: An Ecumenical Introduction*, ed. F. J. Verstraelen et al. (Grand Rapids: Eerdmans, 1995), 376.
60. Ibid., 379.

of Christian business leaders an endorsement of the new industrial order and economic growth often preached by Protestant preachers in the late 1880s. These preachers used a religious version of social Darwinism to argue that God's providence had made rich people rich and poor people poor:

> In 1876 Protestantism presented a massive, almost unbroken front in its defense of the social status quo...They accepted the idea that God "had predestined inequality"...Bishop William Lawrence said, "Godliness is in league with riches"...Beecher said, "God has intended the great to be great, and the little to be little."[61]

1.6 Student Volunteer Movement for Foreign Missions (SVMFM) and "Evangelization of the World in Our Generation"

When Jones volunteered to go to Korea in 1888 as a young American Christian, he was not alone. In fact, over 20,000 student Christian volunteers would go overseas to serve as missionaries during 1886–1959.

Scholars have long debated why so many young and educated American Christians would leave the comfort of their homes and guaranteed middle-class careers to join this movement for foreign missions. As noted above, the spirit of post-Civil War American culture was one of optimism. It was an active, expansive, enterprising, and growing nation. America was beginning to feel confident about itself and its place in the world, even as the Western civilization as a whole was mounting its empire-building activities around the world. American Protestant churches, in particular, literally saw the world as its parish, as John Wesley had declared a century earlier. It readily credited the success of American civilization to its Christian

---

61. Marty, *Righteous Empire*, 144–50.

basis, while the public considered Protestant foreign missionaries as heroes and heroines. The church had largely adopted the culture of the nation. Thus, eminent church historian Kenneth Scott Latourette wrote: "One of the distinctive tokens of the Christianity and especially of the Protestantism of the United States was the fashion in which it conformed to the ethos of the country."[62] As Josiah Strong said, America was a Christian nation destined for greatness and leadership in the world: "It follows, then, that the Anglo-Saxon, as the great representative of these two ideas, the depositary of these two greatest blessings [civil liberty and pure spiritual Christianity], sustains peculiar relations to the world's future, is divinely commissioned to be, in a peculiar sense, his brother's keeper."[63]

Yet, not all was well in post-Civil War America. Economic turmoil, urbanization, the rise of historical criticism and evolutionary theory, the issue of liberalism versus revivalism—all these complex social problems lay beneath the success of post-Civil War American Christianity. In his book *"Our Country: Its Possible Future and Its Present Crisis* (1885), Strong cited seven crises facing his America: Catholicism, Mormonism, Socialism, Intemperance, Wealth, Urbanization, and Immigration. Some church historians such as Sydney Ahlstrom have argued that foreign missions were emphasized by the churches to avoid confronting these troubling issues on the home front.[64] In a similar vein, church historian Robert Handy suggested that the missions movement helped to dull the self-critical eye of the American church.[65]

It was into this milieu that the Student Volunteer Movement for

---

62. Kenneth Scott Latourette quoted in Sydney E. Ahlstrom, *A Religious History of the American People*, New Haven: Yale University Press, 1972, 858–59.
63. Josiah Strong, *Our Country* (1890), 208–9.
64. Sydney E. Ahlstrom, *A Religious History of the American People* (New Haven: Yale University Press, 1972), 733.
65. Robert T. Handy, *A Christian America; Protestant Hopes and Historical Realities* (New York: Oxford University Press, 1971), 134.

Foreign Missions (SVMFM) was born in July 1886, two years before Jones started out for Korea.[66] In fact, the impetus for the organization of the SVMFM was Luther D. Wishard, the first secretary of the YMCA's collegiate department, who was passionate about foreign missions and guided YMCA students in that direction. In 1885, Wishard encouraged revivalist D. L. Moody to hold an undergraduate student Bible study conference at the Moody-backed Mount Hermon School in Northfield, MA, to be sponsored by the Intercollegiate YMCA. Two hundred fifty-one students from eighty-nine colleges and universities met together for nearly a month. As time went on, the focus of the Northfield Conference slowly moved toward foreign missions, especially after two missionary addresses by famous American Presbyterian preacher and author Arthur T. Pierson and William Ashmore, an American Baptist missionary to China. SCM leader John R. Mott would later reminisce:

> He [Ashmore] knew how to get hold of college men. I will tell you the way to do it, and that is to place something before them which is tremendously difficult. He presented missions as a war of conquest and not as a mere wrecking expedition. It appealed to the strong college athletes and other fine spirits of the colleges because of its very difficulty. They wanted to hear more about it. The number of interviews greatly multiplied.[67]

After ten men from foreign countries spoke about the need for missionaries in their motherland, ninety-nine students signed a paper which read: "We are willing and desirous, God permitting, to

---

66. The following section on SVMFM is based on http://en.wikipedia.org/wiki/Student_Volunteer_Movement and Clarence P. Shedd, *Two Centuries of Student Christian Movements*, New York: Association Press, 1934.
67. John R. Mott, "The Beginnings of the Student Volunteer Movement" in *The Student Volunteer Movement After Twenty-Five Years*, 12–13. Information about the Northfield meeting is also available in the Springfield Republican, August 2, 1886.

become foreign missionaries." This missionary spirit became contagious as two student volunteer leaders from Princeton, Robert Wilder and John Forman, were sent on a missionary recruitment tour of 167 North American colleges and university campuses during the academic year 1886–87. They succeeded in recruiting over 2,200 young men and women who declared their intention to become foreign missionaries.

The foreign missions boom was on. To maintain the excitement and widen its financial and organizing base, the official organization Student Volunteer Movement for Foreign Missions (SVMFM) was formed with its motto, "the evangelization of the world in this generation" in the summer of 1888. When the First International Convention of the Student Volunteer Movement was held in Cleveland in 1891, it was the largest student assembly known in history. Over 6,200 volunteers from 350 institutions had enrolled, and 320 went overseas under appointment of various mission boards. Missions historian Charles Forman writes, "In the new enthusiasm following 1890, mission work was seen by its interpreters as the essential work of the church; no church could be healthy without it."[68] And, by 1959, over 20,000 student volunteers had gone to serve the church overseas as missionaries, just like the 21-year-old George Heber Jones.

1.7 Jones and the American Christ

In many ways, Jones stands firmly in the "Romantic stream in American theology" with its emphasis on a "transformative relation" with a "living, loving and inwardly dwelling God," and not on

---

68. Charles Forman, "A History of Foreign Mission Theory in America," in *American Missions in Bicentennial Perspective*, ed. R. Pierce Beaver (South Pasadena, Cal: William Carey Library, 1977), 83.

impartial literal truth.⁶⁹ Jones breathes and shares the thought world of nineteenth-century American Protestantism with its emphasis on religious experience of God, not doctrinal orthodoxy, its stress on indwelling of God in human souls (Jones's emphasis on "sonship" and "soulship"), its willingness to learn from different points of view (Jones's overt ecumenism from the earliest days, a healthy suspicion of denominational sectarianism, and use of modern educational techniques of debate and discussion), its critique of Biblical literalism and authoritarian ways of thinking (his high view of the Bible but a rejection of bibliolatry), and "its search for relevant ways to apply Christianity to changing world" (his YMCA work, and ultimately, his entire missionary career dedicated to soul redemption and social salvation).⁷⁰

In addition, Jones shares the world-conquering spirit of the growing world missionary movement of late nineteenth-century American church and the enterprising spirit of American capitalism ready to spread its message of hard work, efficiency, and creativity around the world. Because he connects the person and work of Christ to the life of the Christian church and the Christian life in society, Jones regards the progress of American society as a fulfillment of the Christian vision, ideals, and morals. In this sense, Jones is indeed one of the "children of late nineteenth century middle-class Victorian America" trapped in the habits of middle-class America, as Korean scholar Dae Young Ryu says.⁷¹ In his preaching of the gospel of American economy, he shares Josiah Strong's thesis on American greatness and his conservative agenda of supporting free enterprise capitalism. With him, Jones sees "education in Christian morality" as

---

69. Toulouse and Duke, *Makers of Christian Theology*, 127.
70. Ibid., 128.
71. Dae Young Ryu, *American Protestant Missionaries*, 38–39. "More importantly, religion was also an integral part of their culture and hence it was destined to be class-biased."

the second highest agenda, next to preaching the gospel in response to the "new industrial and urban problems."[72]

Most scholars of American missionaries have said that the missionaries basically worked out of an "evangelical-pietist" faith that is world-rejecting and abiding by a strict separation of religion and politics. They were primarily concerned about saving human souls out of the world. But this does not hold true for Jones. While his faith certainly displays elements of the revivalistic pietism of late-nineteenth-century American Christianity, it is also clearly positioned in the mainstream of American Romantic and Edwardsian postmillennial theology. It is strongly social-oriented, looking for ways for the seed of the Gospel to flourish in every arena of the culture. Jones believes that the Christian faith should make one a better patriot, who loves his nation and its lofty ideals. He also believes that the church has a responsibility to spread "scriptural holiness" throughout the land (as Wesley suggested) and throughout the world. It is a living, world-embracing, culture-affirming, nation-building activist faith that Jones brings with him on the trans-Pacific steamer on its way to Korea.

Scholars have also generally held that the American missionaries are simply translators of Western theological concepts. They see the missionaries as those who plant the kernel of the Gospel, its supra-natural essence, in the soil of a foreign country for the purpose of transmitting the "authentic cultural values through their integration in Christianity" and "insert Christianity" in various human cultures such as Korea and other heathen lands.[73] For Jones, the Christian faith is a living, experimental faith in the living Savior, not a set of pure doctrines to be transplanted or embedded in another land. Thus, his goal is not to proclaim a dogma about Christ—like the traditional

---

72. Marsden, *Fundamentalism*, 14.
73. Bevans, *Models*, 43.

two natures model of Jesus' divinity. What matters most for Jones is a living, dynamic relationship with God through Christ that would restore humanity to its rightful place as God's sons and daughters and form a people and a church through which God's work of reconciliation may continue. Anything more than encountering this living Christ is "provincial theology," as Jones would later remark.

On the contrary, it is clear that Jones and the American missionaries shared the values and outlook of his time and generation. Jones, indeed, was an heir of Jonathan Edwards' postmillennial notion that American civilization is the pinnacle of the Christian gospel. So, he shared the liberal tendency to look uncritically at his own understanding of the Gospel or of his evaluation of the West as the bastion of Christian civilization. Being an outsider in Korea provided him with a new set of eyes to see the Korean reality in a way that indigenous Koreans could not see. It is this ability that enabled foreign missionaries such as Jones to help the Korean Christians to become critical readers and leaders of their own culture and society. In the process, the first Korean Christians were forced to ask themselves what their society was lacking in light of the Gospel message brought by the missionaries. On the contrary, foreign missionaries were forced to address the relevance of their message as they were confronted with new realities around them. They were forced to continuously ask themselves whether their message was worthy and useful to the people they were preaching to.

For now, Choe Pyonghon and the Confucian kingdom of Choson waited for Jones's arrival. Armed with his experience of the living Christ, who had transformed his humanity and personality, Jones was arriving with the Christian church through which the living Christ was continuing his work of reforming people and renewing societies to become the Kingdom of God.

2

Choe, 1858–1887: Confronting the Confucian Challenge

"What was happening in Choe Pyonghon's life and the Confucian Choson society that made him receptive to the missionary preaching about the American Christ?" In this chapter, we learn how the internal and external pulls for change in old Choson and in Choe's personal life were bringing them both closer to Master Jesus.

2.1 Choe's Growing Reservations about the Status Quo

In January 1888, thirty-year-old Choe Pyonghon came up to the capital, Seoul, to prepare for the *kwago*, the national civil service exams, which would qualify him for a government position. Many "young m(e)n of patrician ancestry and of the best education of (Korean) schools"[1] had done this for over a thousand years, since the time of the Silla Kingdom (57 BCE–935 CE). This was not the first time Choe had come up to Seoul to sit for the *kwago*. He had come up for the *kwago* in 1875, 1879, and 1881, but had failed to qualify.

---

1. Jones, "The Rise of the Church," Papers, 147.

The *kwago* system began during the late-eighth-century Silla Kingdom by King Wonsong (who ruled from 785 to 798) and continued through the Choson Dynasty. Students fifteen or older were first required to pass a district test, which was held three times a year. The provincial exam (*hoesi*) was held every three years to earn the "beginning degree" or *chosi*. Then, every three years, the *chosi* qualifiers could sit for the exams for the *chinsa* degree in Seoul. The *kwago* was made up of two exams—one in poetry and the other in prose—on a passage from the classics, usually on some historical event. Only 200 persons received the *chinsa* degree, which qualified them to sit for the "great exams," or *taekwa*, held every three years, with only thirty-three being selected.[2]

In 1888, Choe came up to the capital with fire in his belly. During the winter of 1887, he had been unjustly persecuted by the government. He was thrown in jail and publicly flogged on his buttocks with paddles, falsely accused of being a thief and an embezzler. A man named Mr. Song, who had helped his family move down to the country in 1882, had used Choe's name to write a counterfeit note. Choe was blamed for it, and was thrown into jail. A local government official, also named Song, was involved in the conspiracy. Choe had no recourse but to pay 300 *ryang* to gain his release on December 29, 1887.[3] His biographer writes, "Through it, he mourned the corruption of the national law. In his first attempt to enter social life, he had been victimized and shamed by this illegal

---

2. For an informative early account of *kwago*, see H. B. Hulbert, "National Examination in Korea," *Transactions of Korea Branch of Royal Asiatic Society* 14, no. 9 (1922): 9–32.
3. The Kim biography says that he had borrowed some money and had paid it back; but the creditor denied being paid back and threw him into jail. There are two major sources of information on Choe's life: Kim Chinho, "A Short Biography of the Late Taksa Rev. Choe Pyonghon," [K] *Sinhak segye* 12, no. 2 (February 1927); and Choe Chaewon, *A Short Biography of Teacher Taksa* (K), trans. Yi Dŏkju (Seoul: Chongdong Publishing Co., 1998). This recently discovered handwritten biography covers the first forty-eight years of Choe's life. It is surmised that his youngest son is the author. Hereafter, the two sources will be referred in the main text as "The Kim biography" and "The Choe biography," respectively.

act. But this opportunity provided him with a strong determination to reform the evil practices of the society."[4] In prison, he vowed that he would enter politics to set the world aright.[5]

So, in early January 1888, he left his family to go up to Seoul to prepare for the February *kwago* with his friend, Kim Myongjin. His righteous anger did not bear fruit, as his exams were not among those selected.

If Choe's earlier attempts at the civil service exams had been solely to win a government position, this time, another motivation had awakened him to social realities and made his *sonbi* or scholar's blood boil within him. The highest goal for a Confucian scholar was to uphold the vision of *chungkun aekuk,* or "loyalty to the king and love of the nation." The most honored way was to pass the *kwago* and serve in the government.

But little did Choe know that the *kwago* were not what they had been—a fair and equitable method of choosing the best-qualified scholars for government posts. By the latter half of the Choson Dynasty, the exams had become a travesty, with cheating and favoritism openly practiced at the testing site. Homer Hulbert (1863–1949), who had come to Korea in 1886 to teach English at the Royal English School, observed the *kwago* in person. According to him, it seemed anyone could enter or walk about the testing grounds without any problem. He observed one umbrella under which several men were writing together, apparently helping one of the candidates. Thus, "Out of a hundred possible graduates, ninety were probably appointed by favoritism…and perhaps ten out of a hundred would be honestly chosen. It was owing to the possibility of being of this number that the crowds were attracted."[6]

---

4. Kim Chinho, *Biography*, 99.
5. Choe Chaewon, *Biography*, 116.
6. Hulbert, "National Examination," 30.

Choe's sense of anger at social injustice and the illegal use of power urged him on in his studies. He had left his growing family behind in the countryside to focus his mind only on study, but he once again failed to pass the *taekwa* in February 1888,[7] and was forced to make living arrangements so he could continue his studies for the next round of exams. Other times, he had worked as a tutor of younger students.[8] This time, despite his misgivings about Westerners, he accepted his friends' advice to become a Korean language tutor to an American missionary at Paichai Haktang as a side job to support his studies. Little was he to know that a temporary tutoring job would turn him into a permanent worker in the kingdom of eternal life.

2.2 Korea's Great Confucian Experiment Nears its End

As Choe was about to gain a new and life-changing perspective about his place in the world through contact with American missionaries and Western literature, old Choson itself had been undergoing a rapid process of reform, modernization, and foreign intervention in its internal politics.[9] By 1876, when Korea was forced to open up its doors to join the "sisterhood of nations" by Japanese gunboats, and jump-start its modernizing process, the entire society

---

7. It is not clear from the records whether he ever passed the *taekwa*. But it seems he had made enough of an impression on his foster father in the exams to be considered for adoption. In 1895, when he was appointed to a government post by the Kim Hongjip cabinet, he was named a *chusa*, which is a title given to those who had passed the *taekwa*. But by then, the traditional exam system had been abandoned, and so, the titles alone are unreliable sources of information.
8. Choe Chaewon, *Biography*, 114.
9. Beginning with the Treaty of Kanghwa with Japan in 1876, the "Hermit Kingdom" opened its doors and entered into diplomatic relations with major Western powers (US 1882, UK/Germany 1883, etc.), only to lose its sovereignty by 1910. Perhaps the better phrase would be that Korea was forcibly brought into the web of imperialism. "The Komundo incident (1885-7) made it clear that Korea was not the arbiter of its own destiny, but that its fate would be decided by outside powers motivated by their particular selfish interests" Lee Ki-baik, *A New Korean History*, 281. In particular, its fate was decided by the trinity of its three closest neighbors—China, Russia, and Japan—who exercised dominance over the Korean government in successive periods: China (1876–1894), Russia (1895–1904), and Japan (1905–1945).

was under tremendous pressure from within and without. The glue that had held it together was about to come undone. Korean scholar Bruce Cumings defines "the opening" of a country as discovery, enlightenment, free trade and commerce, ideological position, and subjugation, and goes on to say, "In the Korean case, it had all these meanings *for the West and Japan*." For Koreans, it was to be resisted because it threatened to end the "Sinic universe it inhabited, for a way of thinking about the relations between nations, for a way of thought…(it was) the virus that would destroy a unique Korean way in the world and pose for contemporary Koreans a question that absolutely never would have occurred to them before 1876: What does it mean to be Korean?"[10]

The central government, heir to the idealistic neo-Confucian dream of its founding scholar-officials, found itself unable and unprepared both to meet the people's demands for righteous rule and to repel the aggression of foreign powers. The problem with the Choson monarchy, with its "classic agrarian bureaucracy," was its inability to mobilize its ruling partners—the *yangban* or the upper-class aristocracy—who had managed to manipulate the state laws according to their class interests. Their actions completely closed off the central government's control at the local government level. Cumings says that Choson was a "classic agrarian bureaucracy," and not a feudal society:

> Unlike a feudal system, Korea had strong central administration and many officials who ruled through a civilian bureaucracy, not through provincial lords who fused civil and military functions. The system rested upon an agrarian base, making it different from modern bureaucratic systems…In fact, the social elite controlled the bureaucratic structure, kept it relatively weak, and used it to check royal authority.

---

10. Cumings, *Korea's Place*, 95.

At the local levels the elite-controlled officials called *ajon*, often common clerks, worked with important families below the county level.[11]

It looked as if Choson's central government dominated the society, "but in practice landed aristocratic families could keep the state at bay and perpetuated their local power for centuries." Under this structure, the central government's hands were tied. It could not tax the aristocracy, who owned the land, because the reach of the central government extended only to the county level, for below it were "local influentials (meaning strong clans and elders) (who) controlled everything. They pressured (and often bribed) local clerks to keep their lands off the tax rolls."[12] They not only succeeded in keeping the central government from land surveys, but laws kept the *yangban* exempt from most other requirements placed upon commoners, such as most other taxes, corvee labor, and even military conscription. The scheme used by local scholar-officials was the local academy, or *sowon*, which not only was the regional educational center, but also served as the regional center of political power. It was this system of checks and balances (central power and landed wealth) that provided stability over five centuries. "But it was not a system that could be mobilized to keep the imperial powers at bay in the late nineteenth century; instead it fell before them."[13]

The old agrarian bureaucracy managed the interplay of different and competing interests by having a system of checks and balances that tended, over time, to equilibrate the interests of different parties. The king and the bureaucracy kept watch on each other, the royal

---

11. Ibid., 72–73.
12. Ibid., 55.
13. Ibid., 73. "Consort clans, royal censors, a recalcitrant bureaucracy, and an ethic of scholarly remonstrance held the king's power within delimited boundaries." It prevented "the growth of truly centralized power in Choson Korea." Deuchler, *The Confucian Transformation of Korea*, 292.

clans watched both, scholars could criticize ("remonstrate") from the moral position of Confucian doctrine, secret inspectors and censors went around the country to watch for rebellion and assure accurate reporting, landed aristocrats sent sons into the bureaucracy to protect family interests, local potentates influenced the county magistrates sent down from the central administration. In its time, it was a sophisticated political system, adaptable enough and persistent enough to give unified rule to Korea for half a millennium. This civilized order was broken up and laid low by the Western impact in the late nineteenth century, when Korea could not withstand the full foreign onslaught of technically advanced imperial powers with strong armies.[14]

In the nineteenth century, the powerful Andong Kim clan controlled Korean politics and openly sold government offices for profit, which worsened the abuse and corruption at the local level. Their misrule led to major peasant revolts, such as the Hong Kyong-nae Revolt of 1812, as well as the people's search for salvation in messianic religions such as the Tonghak religion of Choe Chaeu. By the 1830s, Choson was clearly aware of the pounding of the West on its doors.

Grayson argues that the activities of the Regent Taewongun (Yi Haung 1820–98) must be seen as the last-ditch effort of the Confucian bureaucracy to revive the received traditions and the monarchy. He tried to strengthen Choson society to face the challenges from the material and spiritual forces of the West at its door. But when he forced over 300 *sowon,* or academies, to close in 1871, leaving only 47 operating, it had an unforeseen consequence, which proved fatal. It ironically signaled the end of the Confucian Choson government. While the closures took place in the name of

---

14. Cumings, *Korea's Place*, 136–37.

controlling regional powers by attacking their political and economic hold, they created a power vacuum across the country. In turn, the ensuing inter-party feuds opened the door for the intervention of foreign powers in Choson's domestic policy.[15]

2.3 Choson's Need for Reform

In the face of these internal and external pressures on old Choson, Korean leaders and people adopted three distinct responses to changing realities after the 1876 Treaty of Kanghwa with Japan: rejection, selective accommodation, or integration with Western civilization, its technology, and religious philosophy.[16]

Anti-Western "Return to Basics" Movements: *Uijong choksapa*

In the open-door era, conservatives wished to revive the old order by bringing back the good old Chinese ways and repelling the Western powers. Most well-known are the anti-Western "defenders of the faith," who resisted the reformist policies of King Kojong, the last monarch of the Choson Dynasty. The Anti-Heterodox Party, or the *Uijong choksapa* (literally, "defend orthodoxy and reject heterodoxy"), was made up of bureaucrat-scholars in and out of the government. They regarded only the neo-Confucian teachings of Chu Hsi (*Songlihak*) as orthodox and considered all other political ideologies and religions to be sectarian or heterodox. As far as they were concerned, the price of heterodoxy was death. To them, the Protestant Christianity of the Western powers was no different from

---

15. Grayson, *Korea*, 171.
16. For a documentary history of this early period of Western encounter, see Peter H. Lee, ed., *Sourcebook of Korean Civilization*, vol. 2, *From the Seventeenth Century to the Modern Period* (New York: Columbia University Press, 1996).

the Roman Catholicism that had entered Korea a century earlier, and was severely repressed. All things Western were seen as a threat to its social order and value system.[17]

In *A Korean Confucian Encounter with the Modern World: Yi Hang-no and the West*, Chung Chai-Sik argues that Yi Hang-no and his radical anti-West, anti-Christian group recognized that anything from the West would destroy the traditional, ideal social order that their version of neo-Confucianism had built. Their answer to the revival and renewal of Choson society was to return to the teachings of the great Chu Hsi and his Korean interpreters, such as Songja Song Siyol (1607–89). The neo-Confucian ideal society was a Sinocentric, value-governed society ruled by a sage monarch under the tutorship of scholar-officials who would also educate people on the way, keeping them from the dangers of heterodox doctrines, such as Protestant Christianity and Catholicism.

Yi linked the threat of foreign invasion to the problem of coping with domestic disorder. He believed that domestic tranquility through the moral leadership of the ruler and the resulting moral rebirth of the people would take care of the threat of invasion from the outside. He explained this threat not as a social, political, or technical problem, but as a problem of moral breakdown. If the neo-Confucian model of nature and its morality were restored and followed, all other problems would be solved. The loss of the Choson's traditional values was much more serious than any foreign intervention. Morality—the soul of the state—was at stake. The political independence of the nation-state was a secondary matter.[18]

---

17. For a discussion of the early Confucian debate on Catholicism, see Kim Hyongchan, *Conflict Among Late Choson Intellectuals Over Importing of Western Learning* (K), in *Understanding Korean Philosophy Through Its Controversies* (K), ed. Hankuk cholhak sasang yonguhoe (Seoul: Yumun Sowon Publishing Co., 1995), 224–47.
18. Chai-Sik Chung, *A Korean Confucian Encounter with the Modern World: Yi Hang-no and the West* (Berkeley, CA: Institute of East Asian Studies, 1995), 76.

By returning the Confucian "principle" to its central place, Yi thought the nation would become morally and culturally renewed. This, in turn, would enable Choson to confront and defeat the foreign powers. As an outside critic with friends in high places, Yi wrote various memorials calling for reforms.

He recommended the following measures: the appointment of worthies to government posts, the elimination of corruption and frivolity, limitations on government expenditure to relieve the people's financial burden, military combat readiness, organization of a militia combining the military and farmers, a ban on luxury goods, the restoration of equity, the promotion of sincerity, and the establishment of legal discipline. Then, Yi repeated the importance of a moral society, stressing the great moral principles in Confucius' *Spring and Autumn Annals*, the kingly way of the Chou, and Chu Hsi's moral teachings. Finally, he presented his understanding of Yi Korean history.[19]

This interpretative framework, however, imprisoned him in his "imaginary ideal order of tradition" and prevented him from making reasonable reforms from within the tradition.[20] However, unlike the idealistic selective accommodationist *tongdo sokipa* (literally, the party of "Eastern philosophy, Western technology"), Yi saw the subversive nature of Western technology. He rejected even Western technology strictly on philosophical grounds and cautioned that it would ultimately ruin the nation. Thus, Chung says while Yi was far more insightful sociologically than the accommodationists, he lacked "a healthy tension between tradition and innovation."[21] Ultimately, Yi's

---

19. Ibid., 81.
20. Ibid., 195. Chung argues that the Chu Hsian dualism of principle and matter-energy (*i - ki* or in Chinese *li - ch'i*) naturally led him to adopt Chu Hsian logic of substance-function (*ch'e - yong*). Chung argues that the downfall of Yi's logic was that he did not see the close correlation between principle and matter (*i* and *ki*), substance and function (*ch'e* and *yong*), and philosophy and ritual (*to* and *ye*).

position also reflected the limits of his own class as a *yangban* scholar with a romantic attachment to the past, but lacking any workable alternative for the people's needs. The conservatives had a particular understanding of the crisis facing the nation.

> They defined the crisis within a polarized, dualistic framework of traditional cultural understanding—*ii and ki*, orthodoxy and heterodoxy, Chinese civilization and barbarian culture, and the like. The emphasis was upon orthodoxy, the axiomatic principle. They regarded creativity, imagination, a critical mind, and an experimental mind as subversive attributes. Such a framework could not cope with the changing realities.[22]

Gradualist Accommodation: *Tongdo sokipa*

More liberal elements in the Choson bureaucracy realized that the West's invasion could not be stopped. They tried to control the speed of the reforms, believing that the West could provide Korea with necessary scientific knowledge and diplomatic connections. This, in turn, would help Korea regain its ancient greatness as well as provide for its people. Following Taewongun's forced retirement, these liberal voices, or "gradualist enlightenment party,"[23] supported the Treaty of Kanghwa with Japan despite its inequitable provisions, such as an "extraterritoriality clause" establishing Japanese settlements on Choson with Japanese residents subject only to Japanese laws.[24]

Under the motto of "*Tongdosoki*" (Eastern philosophy, Western technology), they stood for a selective use of Western technology,

---

21. Ibid., 225 and 228: "They simply dismissed the possibilities of any creative encounter between a venerable tradition and the new values."
22. Ibid., 227. It was not for a lack of creative and innovative reform ideas from within other neo-Confucian factions. But the same framework and intransigent inter-party politics blocked off all other "heterodox" voices, both domestic and foreign.
23. Lee Ki-baik, *A New History*, 275.
24. Ibid., 269.

attempting to limit the reforms to the field of the military and the economy.

Like the reactionary conservative party, however, these liberals regarded Western religions as a great threat that would undo the social fabric. Politicians such as Kim Yunsik (1841–1920), Kim Hongjip (1842–1896), Shin Kison (1851–1909), O Yunjung, and Min Yongik regarded religion and civilization as independent factors. They tried to sift through Western thinking and culture in order to pick and choose what Korea needed. They miscalculated Western intentions, as well as the power of Western ideas that could not be so easily separated from the material goods. Unable to free themselves from the tradition of dependence on more forceful neighbors, especially China (*sadaejuui*), and petty internal politics, liberal-minded bureaucrats and officials were unable to mobilize Korean resources to meet the challenges from within and without.

The Fast Track to Westernization of Korea, the Radical Reformers: *Sodo Sokipa*

"Radical reformers" such as Kim Okkyun, Park Yonghyo, So Kwangbom, and Hong Yongsik[25] saw the advances Japan had made through Western modernization. It was Kim Okkyun (1851–94) who supported Robert S. Maclay's plan to begin a Methodist mission in Korea when they met in Japan in 1882–83. By December 1884, Kim "saw Christianity as key to the Western mind."[26] Earlier generations of scholars such as Park Kyusu (1807–76), O Kyongsok (1831–79), and Yu Honggi (1831–85) had also called for foreign

---

25. All were disciples of Taeji Yu Honggi of the Progressive Party (*Kaehwa-dang*), which included a wide group of people who wanted to follow Japan's path of modernization. They were able to win some reforms through the bureaucratic structure. But it could not achieve the critical mass needed to push through changes as it desired. See Lee Ki-baik, *A New History*, 175–281.
26. Dae Young Ryu, "American Protestant Missionaries," 224. See *A History of Korean Church* [K], vol. 1, 177–82, for a discussion about Kim and Maclay.

trade and enlightenment, but they were unable to push through their agenda because of the strong isolationist stance of Taewongun.[27] Their disciples came to believe that Protestant Christianity would be the key to changing the Korean people's thinking in order to establish a modern nation state on the Korean peninsula.

Thus, many among the Enlightenment, or Progressive, Party called for a policy of officially adopting Christianity as the new state religion. It was not the religious message of soul-salvation, but Christianity's apparent power of nation-building and social reform that appealed to them. They believed Christianity would prepare the Korean people for modernization. In their memorial to Emperor Kojong, they stated their reason in a nutshell, "The West is strong because of their religion, while Korea is weak because of its failing Confucianism."[28] For example, Yun Chiho declared that Christianity is "the sole means of transforming the Korean people's character."[29] Despairing of the declining dynasty's deadening traditions, they believed Korea needed both new ideas and new technologies. So, their motto was *sodo-soki*—Western philosophy and Western technology. They believed that Korea would survive in the modern world only when its sociocultural foundation as well as its material base were reformed by Western civilization, both material and spiritual.

Pak Yonghyo, a leader of the reform movement, told Dr. W. B. Scranton, who was on his first journey to Korea in 1885,

> You can do us a great deal of good...You are so far away that you would not be suspected of selfish designs. What our people need is education and Christianization. Through your missionaries and your mission schools, you could educate and elevate our people. It would be a great aid, and perhaps a tedious work, but your great Republic

27. Ibid., 267–68.
28. Chu Chaeyong, *A History of Korean Theology*, 29.
29. Jong Koe Paik, *Constructing Faith*, 87.

could do this. Your missionaries have already done good work in Korea. Our old religions sit lightly, and the way to Christian conversion is open. An army of Christian teachers and workers should be placed in every section of our country. Our people should be educated and Christianized before they undertake any constitutional reform. Then we shall have a constitutional government and, in the distant future, perhaps, a free and enlightened country such as yours.[30]

However, Ryu Daeyong argues that American missionaries never quite understood how seriously Korean radical reformers took Christianity as a vehicle to Western learning. "They recognized it as an indispensable tool of Westernization, politics, and diplomacy. In retrospect, it does not appear as though American missionaries fully comprehended this."[31]

In 1896, when Philip Jaisohn (Korean name, So Chaepil) returned to Korea from his exile, as an American citizen, he began the Independence Club and published *The Independent* with the idea of modeling the new Korea on Western civilization. It generated great interest among the Korean educated class as well as the masses. The Independence Club carried out massive educational projects through many channels, such as newspapers, newsletters, public debates, and town meetings. It was also able to mobilize the general public to show their political will and intention, such as demonstrating against Russian interference in Korean affairs in February 1898.

However, that same year, the government summarily disbanded the Independence Club due to the pressure of the conservative faction. The Club's experiments in popular government and parliamentary democracy based on American republican and democratic principles were forcibly stopped. Its complete rejection of all things Confucian through a wholesale replacement of the East

---

30. F. A. McKenzie, *The Tragedy of Korea* (London, 1908; reprint Seoul: Yonsei University Press, 1969), 54–55.
31. Dae Young Ryu, "American Protestant Missionary," 230.

with the West and its overdependence on Western nations and their goodwill could not win the common people over to its vision of a new Korea.

Although many historians claim that the Club was a champion of Korean independence and an avatar of democracy and modern civil society, its leaders were as captured by the rhetoric of American progressivism—right down to the denigration of the achievements of their own people—as the 1884 coup leaders had been by Japanese reformism.[32]

2.4 The Persecution of Catholics in Korea (1784-1871)

As Choe stood on the throes of making his decision about the West and its Christian faith, he was well aware of the harsh persecution of the Catholics in Confucian Choson.[33] Over 8,000 Catholic believers, including nine French missionaries, had been martyred in the last and most severe persecution against the Catholics, from 1866 to 1871, under the rule of Prince Regent Taewongun. In neo-Confucian Choson, it was dangerous to entertain nonorthodox beliefs, especially those of foreign origin.

The first foreign Catholic missionary to Korea was a forty-two-year-old Chinese priest named Chu Chunmo (Fr. James Zhou Wen-Mo), who entered Choson on Dec. 23, 1794, and carried out an underground ministry for seven years, until he was captured and killed in the first major persecution of 1801. The first French Catholic

---

32. Cumings, *Korea's Place*, 124.
33. This overview of early Korean Catholicism is based on the following sources: Mun, Kyuhyon. *Writing the History of Korean Catholic Church with the Korean People*. Vol. 1. (Seoul: Bitdurye, 1994); Yu, Chai-Shin, ed. *The Founding of Catholic Tradition in Korea*. (Mississauga, Canada: Korean and Related Studies Press, 1996); Yu Hong-Ryol. *The History of Korean Catholic Church*. Vol. 1 and Vol. 2. (Seoul: Catholic Publishing House, 1962).

priest entered Korea in 1836. But by 1800, Korean Catholic believers numbered well over 10,000. How did this happen?

Korean Catholicism is unique in that the Korean believers themselves formed its first faith communities before any foreign missionary had set foot on Korean soil. Before the missionaries, there were Christian books and religious articles, which came through Korean foreign embassies that made annual trips to Beijing. In the process of these cultural interactions, Western books, tools, and materials were brought back to Choson, including Matteo Ricci's "The True Meaning of the Lord of Heaven" (*T'ien-chu Shih-I*), and other Catholic books and religious articles.

There was a particular group of *yangban* scholars in mid-eighteenth-century Choson, now loosely referred to as the *Silhakpa*, who were interested in expanding the knowledge base in Choson, especially in the areas of science, technology, agriculture, commerce, and philosophy. Their study and research, aimed at improving the life of the *minjung*, the common people, led them to books about the West. Some among them came across Ricci's book and other Catholic writings. Some wished to learn more about the Catholic faith and even began to practice the faith, according to the books. Interestingly, this group of scholars, many of whom were related by marriage, belonged to a faction in the court which was out of power in eighteenth- and nineteenth-century Choson—the *Namin* or the "Southerners." This may have given them the freedom to explore new ideas, including *Sohak,* or Western, philosophy and religion.

When one of their members had a chance to go to Beijing as part of the annual foreign embassy in 1783, they asked Yi Sunghun to visit a Catholic church and receive the sacrament of baptism. Yi presented himself to a surprised Fr. Louis de Grammont and was baptized at the North Cathedral in Beijing. When he returned the following year, he brought back tens of religious books, crosses, rosaries, and other articles. Yi then baptized members of this circle and started religious services at a member's home in Myongdong. He named himself the presiding bishop, and ordained ten priests, including Kwon Ilsin and Chong Yakjon. Realizing that they needed the official church's approval, in 1791, they asked Bishop Gouvea in Beijing to send a missionary. The number of believers quickly grew to 4,000 by 1794.

In 1785, the secret meetings of the Catholic believers were discovered by government agents. Although the government gave out relatively light punishment in the beginning, it made it clear that this Western learning or religion was a heterodox belief and would not be tolerated. When upper-class clans learned that some of their family members were involved in the new religion, they forced many of their family members to recant and leave the faith. It was dangerous, politically, socially, and physically, to belong to a heterodox faith.

As in China, Korean Catholics were taught that as believers, they had to stop the practice of "ancestor worship," or *chesa*,[34] since it was deemed to be an act of idolatry, a violation of the First Commandment. Thus, the act of destroying or burning the ancestral tablets, or *sinju,* became a point of contention with the Choson government. One of the first cases of tablet burning was in Chinsan County, Cholla Province, when Yun Jichung, a *chinsa* who had passed the first round of exams for government office, burnt his ancestral *sinju*. His action was condemned by his family members and the larger society. He was accused of violating the Choson society's foundational value of filial piety. In addition, he had broken his loyalty to the king by violating the edict against the Catholic faith.

---

34. *Chesa,* or ancestral rituals, were quite complicated, especially if your family was responsible for maintaining the ancestral mortuary plates and ceremonial altars. For a short description, see Lee Yeun Ja. "Jongga Ancestral Rituals and Food Culture." *Koreana*. The Korea Foundation. Apr. 7, 2011, http://www.koreana.or.kr/months/news_view.asp?b_idx=558&lang= en&page_type=list.

Thus, the Catholic faith was deemed a threat to the law, order, and values of neo-Confucian Choson. Those involved were put to death immediately. This caused many believers from the upper classes to abandon the faith. But many people were drawn to the message of freedom, equality, and love preached by the Catholic Church.

The initial suppression of Catholicism was based on the church's opposition to ancestral rites (worship) and its willingness to disobey the edict against Catholicism. In addition, the church's acceptance of women and their active participation in the church threatened the patriarchal system of Choson. Later on, when foreign missionaries illegally entered Choson to do their mission work underground, they were often accused of being agents of foreign countries. In turn, the church also was accused of betraying the national interest. The edict associated Catholicism with many serious "crimes": dishonoring traditional custom, destroying morality, stopping ancestor worship, holding false beliefs, using magic spells and incantations, and engaging in anti-state activities. The edict brought about the persecution of 1801, leading to more than a thousand arrests, ultimately resulting in the martyr deaths of 300 believers. Of the crimes against them, it was the Catholic ban against ancestral rites that provoked the harshest persecutions. The persecutions in 1801, 1839, 1846, and 1866 led to the death of about 10,000 martyrs.[35]

The church continued to grow despite the official ban, localized persecutions, and a lack of trained indigenous leadership. It continued to ask the church in China to send a resident priest. Another Chinese priest, Fr. Liu Fangchi, was sent in 1831 and was joined by several French priests during the next five years. In addition, three young Koreans were sent to Macao to study theology and prepare for the

---

35. Currently, Korea has the fourth largest number of saints among the Catholic churches worldwide. Seventy-nine martyrs of Korea were beatified in 1925. Twenty-four more were beatified in 1968. The combined 103 martyrs were canonized in 1984 by Pope John Paul II. Their feast day is September 20.

priesthood, two of whom became the first Korean Catholic priests, Andrew Kim Taegon (1822–46) and Choe Yangop (1821–61). Kim was baptized at the age of fifteen and sent to Macao to study. He was ordained in 1845 and was arrested trying to arrange for foreign missionaries to secretly enter the country by boat. He was tortured and beheaded in Seoul at the age of 25 in 1846.

In 1857, the bishop in Beijing reported to the Vatican that there were 15,206 Catholics in Korea. Despite the persecutions, the Catholic faith was becoming rooted in Korea. The final persecution of 1866–71, under Taewongun, would kill over half of the registered Catholics in Korea, but in the following decades, the church grew by leaps and bounds. The training of native priests was started in 1877, resulting in the ordination of ten priests in 1900. By 1910, the church grew even stronger: 69 churches, 71 priests, including 15 Korean priests, 41 seminarians, 59 sisters, and more than 73,000 members.

Despite Old Choson's changing attitude toward all things foreign, Choe knew that his *sonbi* friends would find it hard to believe in the teachings of Master Jesus. The dangerous memory of the Catholic persecutions would have made them hesitate. Choe was well aware of the Catholic experience and their struggle with *chesa* and Korean culture. Perhaps this is why he would finally end up adopting a strong doctrine of creation. While there was much good in the West and its ideas, the same God who blessed the West has also blessed Korea with much good. He would find a way for Korean Christians to value their cultural heritage while transforming it to be even more vital and life-enhancing. All that was left for him to do now was to taste the goodness of the spiritual food that Jesus, the Western Savior, was offering him and his people.

2.5 Early Life of Choe Pyonghon

Choe Pyonghon was born on January 16, 1858, as the second son of Ŭisankong Ch'oe Yonglae in North Ch'ungch'ong Province. His father sat for the 1857 *kwago*, but failed to pass it. He was an advisor of the third level in the Advisory Body, or the Chungchuwon, to the Central Administrative Cabinet (Uijongpu).

Choe's education began at the age of seven, when he began reading the *Book of Filial Piety* (K: Hyokyong), under teacher Cho Sun. Then, he began to study *The 1000 Characters* at the age of ten. But that year, his mother passed away in an epidemic that hit the region. His education continued with calligraphy and *Korean History* (K: T'ongsa) from teacher Won Sinbo. However, as the family's economic situation worsened, his family was forced to move back to its ancestral home in the country.

When he turned thirteen, Choe began his studies at the Park Chunyang Academy, where he won a poetry contest. It was here that he began reading *The Analects* and other Confucian classics. However, as the family became poorer, like many *yangban* families out of political power, his father was forced to sell the family's last possession, the ancestral chestnut groves. They moved to a smaller house. Likewise, Choe was forced to stop his studies for lack of money. In 1875, Choe turned eighteen and sat for his first *kwago*, which he did not pass. He would return four years later for another crack at the *kwago* in 1879.

When he turned twenty in 1877, Choe became a full-time live-in tutor to a younger student. With the monies earned, he began studying at the Yi Songno Library and studied *The Chwa's Commentary*, a 30-volume commentary on the *Spring-Fall History*, purportedly by Chwa Kumyong, a fifth-century BCE Lo (Lu) historian, one of Confucius' disciples. *Spring-Fall History* is one of the five great classics—the history of Lu from 722 BCE to 481 BCE—which Confucius re-edited and wrote a commentary on between 481 and 479 BCE.

Then, in 1880 (at age twenty-three), Choe was adopted into a more established upper-class *yangban* family in Seoul. He was adopted by Choe Chiknae, a high government official, who had been impressed by Choe's writing during the 1875 civil exams. He moved to Seoul to live with his adopted family, with whom he lived for two years. During this stay in Seoul, Choe first came across books about the West and Christianity.[36] Given the emphasis put on maintaining the family line through the eldest son in Choson society, upper-class families without sons to carry on the family name and ancestral rites adopted qualified men from their clans to continue the family name. Choe's birth family gained financial stability, while he was given an opportunity to study with the upper-class scholars while caring for his foster parents.[37] Unfortunately, his adopted father died a year later, in August 1881.

Choe dedicated himself to study to get ready for the next round of the civil service exams. When the June Military Mutiny shook Seoul in 1882, threatening to turn the city into a war zone, however, Choe decided he had enough of city life and sold the Chongdong home given by his adopted father and moved down to Samak Valley. He hoped to escape outside distractions to focus on preparing for the upcoming *kwago*.

At Samak Valley, he was married to Kim Rodok on Feb. 20, 1884. Their first son, Chaehak, was born in November 1885. As he continued to study for *kwago*, his wife took up raising silkworms, which placed the family on firm economic ground. It was here that he was falsely accused, imprisoned, and flogged in 1887, which only

---

36. Sim, *An Examination*, 143–44.
37. See Choe Chaewon, *Biography*, 114–15 for this event in Choe's life.

strengthened his determination to enter politics to set the world aright. In January 1888, Choe came up to Seoul by himself to take the February exams, but once again, he failed to quality. He continued his studies, while rooming with friends.

On October 18, 1888, through friends' introduction, he became George Heber Jones' language teacher, and received a Chinese Bible from him. When the Methodist Mission opened a Chinese language division at Paichai from 1888 to 1894, Choe was hired as the Chinese teacher in 1889 to placate the Confucian hardliners at the court. For over four years, he lived side-by-side with the missionaries, teaching them Korean and teaching Chinese to the students, while helping translate the Bible into Korean. He prepared for the Kyongmudae (Royal Palace) Internal Exams in 1892, while teaching at Paichai Haktang, but was blocked from even entering the test site to sit for the *kwago*. He finally saw the corruption of the political process and decided to "embrace the Way and wait for the right time," and began to examine religious philosophy, especially the claims of the missionaries that Jesus Christ is Savior of the world. In January 1893, Choe confessed to Jones that he wanted to be baptized and become a follower of Jesus.

2.6 Choe's Life Goal

As a typical Korean Confucian *sonbi*, Choe had grown up believing that the best life for a man was to become properly educated so that he could serve the monarch and guide the people to the True Way. Although his family was typical of many upper-class *yangban* families which had become impoverished and weakened for various political and social reasons in the nineteenth century, he did not give up his educational dream. He pushed himself to pursue his goal of becoming a proper gentleman-scholar. He had taken every opportunity open to him, by being willing to teach children of the wealthy and even becoming adopted into a powerful family as a foster son.

Yet, the social realities did not reflect the teachings of the old Books or the teachings of the old Masters. The only focus of his dreams and determination was passing the *kwago*, but the *kwago* was no longer the sacred path for conscientious *sonbi* and idealistic young men seeking to obey heaven's mandate and serve the people's welfare. It had been bought out by the powerful and the wealthy. It was connections, not competence, that counted.

However, Choe was a true believer of the Way shown by Master Kong. He went back, again and again, believing that it was his fault, his lack of competency and comprehension of the teachings of the old Masters. But reality, sometimes, has to turn cruel before we awaken. When he was unjustly thrown into jail as a victim of a conspiracy by a government official to extort money from him, he finally began to see the writing on the wall.

This traumatic experience did not send him into self-imposed exile, as traditional scholars would have done. Rather, as an active and thinking man, he began to realize the system needed to be changed from the inside. The best way forward was the *kwaço*. The 1888 *kwago* was an eye-opener, as he began to see his reality as if for the first time. He was still a believer, and decided he would give it one more chance to prove him wrong.

That determination to find the truth, serve heaven's mandate, and become a worthy human being would soon find a new channel. A young twenty-one-year-old upstate New Yorker had stepped on Korea's soil and needed a teacher to teach him the language and the culture. Little was Choe to know what great changes and truths he was about to discover. Little did he know that Master Jesus was beckoning to him.

PART II

Encountering the Other

3

Jones, 1887–1892: Going as an Apostle to Old Choson

"What did Jones discover about the realities of Korea that helped him reframe his American Christ as Jesus, Savior of the Korean people?" In this chapter, we see how Jones prepared himself in his first five years in Korea to become an apostle to Old Choson and its people, who were in dire need of a Savior.

3.1 The Macedonian Call to Choson

In his unfinished autobiographical account, *Real Stories from Real Life*, Jones describes how he happened to become a missionary to Choson. Like the story of Apostle Paul, who went to Macedonia because he heard the Macedonian people calling out to him in a dream, Jones says that his call to Choson came out of the blue, literally, as he was trying to decide the next step in his young career. From April 1, 1886, to February 1, 1888, he worked as assistant secretary (director) of the Rochester YMCA under its dynamic secretary, Dean Alvord. He worked tirelessly from 8 a.m. to 10 p.m. for a monthly salary of $40. During that time, he became a member of the Asbury Methodist Church, where Dr. William R. Benham was the pastor. Jones's gift of spiritual and organizational leadership was readily seen by those around him. In particular, Alvord encouraged him to look to lead a YMCA chapter himself, and recommended him to three potential leadership positions, in Middletown, Oneida, and New York City (as office secretary of the NY State YMCA Committee). Jones returned from his 1887 summer vacation to Montreal, ready to tackle one of these three opportunities. God had other plans, and shut the door on each of these places, so he decided to remain one more year at Rochester, learning from Alvord. But another door was opening—a door he had not thought about even in his dreams.

> One day at noon I was on my way to my boarding house for dinner, and as I passed up East Main St. I was very happy thinking how enviable was my lot—busy in a worthy calling, living in awe of the finest cities in the land, and looking forward to another year of friendship and service with those I had come to love very dearly—when I heard a voice in my own soul saying, "Your place is not here, and this is not your work. I call you to be a foreign missionary, to preach my gospel in a distant land and to a strange people!"
>
> It was not an audible voice I heard, but that thought, vivid as though written in letters of living flame, was flashed through my brain. I was startled beyond measure, for the thought was a strange one to me and utterly at variance with the trend and sequence of my thoughts. I stopped for moments on the street to recover my balance for I could not have been more stunned if an angel had appeared and barred my way up the street.[1]

Jones decided that his mind was playing tricks with him, since he had been mulling over the "three-fold open doors that had shut so mysteriously." His rational side told him that this was "of the stuff out of which dreams are made," and he decided to ignore it. But the

---

1. Jones, *Real Stories*, 124–25.

impression and the vision became more vivid as days went by. The more he tried to ignore it, the more it troubled him. "As I look back over the years, I doubt if I have ever put up a sterner, more relentless and determined fight than I did against this call."[2] To settle the matter once and for all, he made a list of all the reasons why his final answer was a definite "No": 1) he could not live his life based on a fanciful imagination; 2) he did not want to be a minister; and 3) he knew he was not qualified to be a foreign missionary. Everybody knew he was born to be a YMCA secretary! His mind was made up, but the peace in his heart disappeared and was filled with turmoil. For three days and nights, he fought the call and the vision, but finally, he got on his knees and surrendered to God, praying:

> Lord, I yield to thee. I cannot yield to the call in my present light. But I will yield to thee. And if it is thy will that I should go to the ends of the earth to find the place in life thou hast for me, and will make it clear to me by opening doors in the way that leads to those distant lands, I will go!" Instantly, there came into my heart such an assurance that all doubt vanished and I knew that it was God's will that I should go to the foreign field.[3]

Jones says that "I had knelt down a YMCA Secretary. I arose a potential foreign missionary."[4] But he had no idea of where he was to go, and as he thought about the possibility of going overseas, he saw a mountain of problems and questions: his youth, inexperience, and lack of qualification, parental dependence as the only child, and the expectations of his YMCA friends. He decided to test the call and trust God to open the doors. He first wrote his parents, who gave their support with the words, "Whatever you decide will be all right for us. If you feel that God calls you to be a missionary, go, and may

---

2. These three quotes from ibid., 126.
3. Ibid., 131–32.
4. Ibid., 133.

His blessing, as will our prayers, attend you."⁵ God had opened door number one. On the following Sunday, he made an appointment with Dr. Benham to see him on Monday morning about a personal matter. At the parsonage, the pastor shook his hand and said,

> "George, who has been talking to you about foreign missions?" I was startled by the question. "Why do you ask me that, Dr.?" I demanded. "Well," said he, "it has come to me that you have been called to become a foreign missionary, and it is concerning this that you have come to see me this morning. Is it not so?" "Yes," said I, "and the only one who has been talking to me about foreign missions is the Lord, Himself."⁶

Jones could not have asked for a better mentor and personal counselor than Dr. Benham. "The ready ringing note of confidence and personal support which Dr. Benham gave me then strengthened me and abides in my heart to this day, fresh and vigorous." Benham said he would speak with the mission secretary in New York City, and asked which field Jones wanted to go. Jones said he would go where God wished to use him. At that point, he thought he should spend "the next four years in college and the seminary" before going to the field, perhaps to India. He expressed this desire to go to India in the application paper that he filled out in September. Dr. John Reid of the Mission Society wrote back, saying that India was out of the question because of his youth. But there was a call for a young man to go to Korea, which was "one of the newest (fields) of the Church and they desired a young man to go there and grow up with the country, master the language as possibly an older man could not, and be trained for large future usefulness."⁷ Dr. Reid asked if he'd be willing to try the experiment!

Jones saw this as another door being opened, "the door to Korea."

---

5. Ibid., 135.
6. Ibid., 136.
7. This paragraph summarizes and quotes from Jones, *Real Stories*, 137–39.

He knew very little about the land, and faintly remembered hearing about it in the geography he'd learned in school. He said yes, either to going immediately or going four years later, after college and seminary. Dr. Reid decided he was ready to go, and recommended him to Bishop S. M. Merrill, in charge of Korea, for appointment to Korea. However, they wanted him to go as an ordained minister, and asked him to get a license. Another door needed opening. With the support of the Asbury Church and Dr. Benham, he requested the Rochester District Conference for a local preacher's license on a trial basis. A long debate occurred, with people expressing much doubt about his age, lack of experience and education, and the rushed process. Before the vote, he was asked to give his reasons for wishing to go to Korea.

> Then one of the ministers said, "Brother Jones, if we decline to recommend you as the Board requests, what will you do?" "I will send immediate word to Dr. Reid and interpret your action as an indication that it is God's will that I remain in America and secure additional preparation for such a great work." I withdrew, believing their action would be unfavorable.[8]

But to his surprise, the District Conference voted almost unanimously to admit him to membership on trial. Once that door opened, other doors started opening. He didn't even have to appear before the St. John's River Conference in Florida, in January 1888, for his appointment to Korea! "It was all of faith and was marvelous in my eyes."[9]

There were those who doubted: his closest friends and colleagues. Dean Alvord "was disappointed and regarded my action as absurd."[10] One of his closest friends, Will Wilcox, was a senior at Rochester

---

8. Ibid., 141–42.
9. Ibid., 143.
10. Ibid.

University. One night, he visited Jones and let him have it, right in the gut!

> He came to my room and labored for hours with me. He emphasized the importance of the work I was doing and my special fitness for it; the tremendous need for work among young men; the high and useful career that awaited me. Then he attacked the whole foreign missionary business; it was built on sentiment; it was an impossible and impractical thing which only fanatics would undertake; in my own case, it was the height of nonsense to take such a momentous step on such an inconclusive experience; it meant exposure to disease and peril of all sorts; it meant association with strange, unattractive and degraded people; separation from friends and from the higher and better things of life. It meant to be buried alive for a few brief years and then failure and death. He begged me, as I loved my friends and hoped to retain their confidence and respect, to give up this wild and absurd notion.[11]

Jones told Wilcox that he was grateful for his love and concern and that he would pray about it. After all, what Wilcox had said were exactly the same things he had thought for three days following his initial Macedonian call. He decided to listen to the Bible. His eyes first fell on John 8:12, which reads, "Then spoke Jesus again unto them saying: I am the light of the world; he that followeth me shall not walk in darkness, but shall have the light of light." The word "again" leaped up into his eyes, for that was what he needed just then. Peace and reassurance came into his heart. God gave him two more witnesses from the Bible, Acts 21:13 and Hebrews 13:13, 14 which confirmed his decision to go.[12]

Looking back on his "call" to the field, Jones says that he did not possess the two reasons most missionary candidates give for going to the foreign field, "a sense of the tremendous need, and a desire

---

11. Ibid., 144.
12. Acts 21:13: Then Paul answered, "What mean ye to weep and to break mine heart? For I am ready not to be bound only, but also to die at Jerusalem, for the name of the Lord Jesus." Hebrews 13:13, 14—Let us go forth unto him without the camp having his reproach, for here we have no continuing city, but we seek one to come.

to invest life to the largest possible usefulness."[13] These came to him later, as he was serving in the field. He says while his call may seem to have a lot of "supernatural elements" present in the beginning, many others may receive a call without them in the beginning. But later, "comes into the lives of the men, who go to the field because of a sense of its need and a desire to invest life wisely, an experience of God's confirming grace and an assurance that they are just where He wants them."[14] On paper, Jones may have lacked everything that a proper candidate for foreign missionary service ought to possess. But he possessed the one thing that would make him into a great missionary for his Jesus in Korea: he knew without a doubt that he was going to a place where God would put him to "great future usefulness."

3.2 Early Years of Missionary Service in Korea

In his September, 1887 application to missionary service, Jones lists himself as "single," "very lightly" in debt, healthy, 5 ft. 3 inches and 128 lbs. He would later be listed as "Rev. George H. Jones," a newly appointed missionary, in the 1887 Korea Mission annual report.[15]

As he had no knowledge of the Korean mission field, he diligently applied himself to learn as much as he could during that time, putting his hands on all known publications about Choson—which wasn't much. The United States had opened diplomatic relations with this "Hermit Kingdom" only in 1885, the same year the Methodist Episcopal mission sent its first missionary, Henry G. Appenzeller.

After bidding tearful goodbyes to his parents, who were losing their only son, he took a long train ride across continental United

---

13. Jones, *Real Stories*, 150.
14. Ibid., 152.
15. *AR*, 1887:22.

States and wondered what the new country would be like, compared to his homeland. He got on an ocean-going ship and accompanied a longtime missionary to China, Dr. H. W. Lowry, on his trip out, and arrived in Japan first to receive his missionary orientation. It was here that he received the latest information about the Methodist missionary efforts in Korea, as well as other data that would serve him well. But it was also here that the missionary prejudice toward Korea rubbed off on Jones. As Japan had modernized one generation earlier, it was progressing at a fast pace. Many of the early missionaries were impressed by the results of its collective and systematic efforts to become modern, especially when compared to the stop-and-go attempts in Choson. Thus, Choson was always viewed as inferior to Japan in terms of its modernization and cultural progress.

After a month-long layover in Japan, Jones arrived in Seoul on May 17, 1888, three months shy of his twenty-second birthday.[16] He arrived in Korea with the idea of staying the initial five years, until 1893, as he stated in his letter to the MEC Mission Secretary A. B. Leonard on February 17, 1888, assigned to teach at Paichai Haktang. As he began learning the language, he became involved in other educational and evangelistic efforts, while taking on responsibility as "statistical secretary" of the Mission, a task well-fitted to his experience in the YMCA and to his personality. His stint at Paichai would continue until 1893, when he was appointed to the Chemulpo (Incheon) circuit. He served as the principal of the school in the last year.

16. He arrived in Korea on May 17, 1888 (May 19, 1888, letter to J. M. Reid). He was appointed as a missionary in 1887, but arrived in Korea in 1888. Most extant biographical notes on Jones, including Price, Noble, Jones Papers, Sachs, and Kim and Pak state or infer that he arrived in Korea in 1887; e.g., Sachs writes, "In 1887 Jones accompanied Franklin Ohlinger, a veteran missionary, to Seoul." There is no record of this. Perhaps the source of this mistake is the three-page death announcement from the Board of Foreign Missions of MEC, which says, "At the time of his going to Korea, in 1887…" He accompanied a long-time missionary to China Dr. H. W. Lowry on his trip out to Korea, not Ohlinger (Jones, *Real Stories*, 47).

In 1890, Jones received his deacon's ordination by Bishop Newman in Japan. The following year, on June 14, 1891, he received his elder's orders by Bishop Goodsell at the seventh Annual Meeting of the Korean Mission, and was assigned as a member of the Seoul Circuit and teacher at Paichai College. He also served as the secretary of the Mission during 1891–1900. At the ordination service, he undertook three lifelong goals: "Unquestioning obedience to God's will; Unswerving devotion to my ordination vows; Complete self-abnegation."[17]

Family and Love

Interestingly, his journal entry on the day of his ordination also includes these feelings, apt for a young man of marriageable age:

> The Bishop was the first to take my hand in friendly congratulation and the brethren whom I love followed. But in that audience there was one hand which lingered in mine just a moment in a loving clasp that meant more to me than any other's grasp that day. Back of it was the noble, pure heart of a woman, who in an act of supreme self-sacrifice of which only a woman is capable has given me the most precious gift of which a man can be the recipient from a woman.[18]

He had found his love in Korea, something that surprised even him, as he writes, "How strange these circumstances all seem to me. To find a wife in the midst of a dark heathenism, here on these Eastern Shores of Asia." She was Margaretha J. Bengel (Aug. 1, 1869–Mar. 7, 1962), who was raised among German-speaking Methodists in Pomeroy, Ohio. She arrived in Chemulpo in September 1890 as a missionary of the Women's Foreign Mission Society (WFMS) of the MEC, to be a teacher at Korea's first school for women, the Ewha

---

17. Jones, June 14, 1891, Diary.
18. Ibid.

Haktang. She went on to teach at the Chemulpo and Kangwha schools.[19]

He proposed to Margaret in the summer of 1891, and they were married two years later, on May 19, 1893, after they were both assigned to the Chemulpo Circuit. At first, the WFMS was not pleased about the blossoming relationship between the two. The marriage took place only after a complicated process of approvals since the WFMS refused to release Ms. Bengel until the Board of Foreign Missions paid the one-way fare that the WFMS had used to bring Ms. Bengel to Korea! It was finally approved, to Jones's relief. Their first daughter, Margaret, was born two years later on Mar. 13, 1895, and the second daughter, Katharyn, on Jan. 18, 1901.

Continuing Education

Jones was a self-taught man and knew the power of knowledge. But, as he would acknowledge later in life, he always regretted that his family's economic situation, along with his health, prevented him from getting a proper education. In particular, he always felt somewhat inferior to colleagues who not only had a college education, but also a graduate theological degree. When the chance came, he signed up to receive a BA degree in 1892 through a correspondence course with the American University at Harriman, Tennessee. Almost every account about Jones's education has this information wrong. The town of Harriman, Tennessee, was founded as a model Christian "temperance" city in 1892, and the "University" opened in 1893. Even his biographers, Kim and Pak, say he graduated from the American University (AU) in 1887, reflecting a general

---

19. After returning to the States in 1909, she worked as "missionary hostess" of the MEC Board of Foreign Missions until 1933; produced a Korean Primer in 1894; and co-authored "The Lure of Korea" in 1912.

notion that missionaries were college graduates. It was assumed that he was a graduate of the American University in Washington, DC.

The American Temperance University was incorporated in July 1893 and began classes on Sept. 12, 1893. The name was changed to American University of Harriman in May 1900. Jones is listed in the 1903 alumni list as belonging to the class of 1900, along with A. B. Noble. AU of Harriman closed its doors with final commencement exercises in May 1908. On Jan. 15, 1914, the AU buildings were sold at an auction, after foreclosure proceedings.[20] As for the 1892 date for his degree, perhaps Jones had begun to make inquiries with ATU in 1893 and received the degree in 1900. But Pulliam says even this alumni list is not in complete agreement with other annual graduation records. Jones writes that he tried "non-resident college courses" and worked through AU for his AB, AM, and PhD in three years. "Later, when I came to better understanding of scholastic requirements, I repudiated these degrees, but I still had the benefit of intensive work in a wide range of subjects."[21]

In Pulliam's account of AU, there is a newspaper clipping of a story in which AU is accused of giving out degrees for money and not academic work. For example, the school's "chancellors" had a habit of holding "exams," after which BA degrees were doled out. Perhaps this was the reason Jones repudiated his degrees from AU. Jones was a lifelong scholar of much caliber and literary production. He writes, "I knew how much I have lost by not having gone through a college, and had I my life to live over again I would force my way through, no matter how adverse my circumstances."[22] One can read the depth of his love for education—a fundamental value that he shared with Choe and the Confucian *sonbi* of Korea.

20. For detailed history of AU, see Walter T. Pulliam, *Harriman: The Town that Temperance Built* (Maryville, TN: M.R. Mangrum Brazos Press, 1978), 253–93.
21. Jones, *Real Stories*, 12.
22. Ibid.

This lack of opportunity for formal education fed Jones's appetite for reading, research, and writing. After receiving three books from the Methodist "Book Concern" in San Francisco, *Gnomon* by Bengel, *Isaiah* and *Hebrews* by Deliztsch, he writes, "How pleased I am! I love books, especially those which may open up a little that one Book of books."[23] He read widely, as his journals are filled with lists of books, both religious and secular, that he ordered from San Francisco, New York, London, Shanghai, and anywhere else he had a connection. For example, his entry for Saturday, Nov. 4, 1899, is as follows:

> Have ordered my periodicals for 1899: The Methodist Review, The Christian Advocate, The Epworth Herald, The Sunday School Journal, The Classmate, The Conference Examiner, The Woman's Missionary Friend, Review of Reviews, St. Nicholas. Books: French: *The Parables* (and) *The Miracles*; Mark Guy Pearse: *Some Aspects of the Blessed Life, Cornish Stories,* (and) *Homily Talks*; Epworth League Reading Course: *Life of Shaftesbury, The Great World's Farm,* (and) *God Revealed;* Hurlburt & Doherty: *Notes on S.S. Lessons.*[24]

He also enjoyed "light reading." Along the top margins of his diary, Jones wrote: "Books read in Jan." (1894). Of the ten books listed in red ink, eight were church-related, such as *Hebrews, Volume I* by Delitzsch, and *Evolution of Episcopacy* by Neely. But two were historical fictional novels by Ainsworth. "For relaxation, Margaret and I have read and finished *The Lord Mayor of London,* by Ainsworth. A pretty little jolly fish of a story as far as plot goes; but most interesting in the glimpses it gives of the early years of George III."[25]

He also became actively involved in literary societies, such as the Christian Literary Union—for which he prepared his article on the

---

23. Jones, Dec. 13, 1893, Diary.
24. Jones, Nov. 4, 1899, Diary.
25. Jones, Feb. 11, 1894, Diary.

1592 Japanese Invasion of Korea—and especially, the Royal Asiatic Society, of which he was the president for nine years from 1900 to 1909.

Given his enormous appetite, diligence, and enterprise, just as he was beginning his work in Chemulpo in 1893–94, he also moonlighted as a correspondent of the *London Times* and the *NY Times*. In 1899, he was writing occasional news articles from Chemulpo for the *Nagasaki Press*. He also wrote occasional articles about the Korean Mission and culture for many mission-oriented magazines, such as the *Gospel in All Lands*.

His theological education continued under the guidance of senior missionary Appenzeller, who had a full theological degree from Drew Seminary. Appenzeller and Scranton took the younger Jones under their wings. Jones was a quick learner, and extremely insightful and wise for a person of his age.[26] As a single man, Jones shared housing with the Appenzellers for three and a half years. It was through Appenzeller and his Confucian teacher, Choe, that Jones received his real education to prepare him to work for Jesus in the Kingdom of Choson.[27]

Initial Evangelistic Work

As public preaching and open evangelistic activities were still forbidden by the government, Jones's home was used to hold private worship services for those interested during the summer and fall

---

26. In his Diary entry for Feb. 15, 1893, Jones has a list of 37 books, divided into five sections: Admission, First Year, Second Year, Third year, Fourth Year. Most of them are theological books, while a few cover general subject areas such as *Psychology* (Hill), *Introduction to Political Economy* (Ely), and *History of Rationalism* (Hurst). While it doesn't state its purpose clearly, it seems to have been a schedule of reading for theological self-study, based on Appenzeller's theological study at Drew Seminary.
27. Jones, Dec. 12, 1891, Diary.

of 1889. Then, as evangelism was silently sanctioned by the government, a building was secured to hold regular worship services.

The first Quarterly Conference was organized in December 1889, and so, the Methodists finally had one church or society that was organized on Korean soil. It was a church with nine members, thirty-six probationers, and one hundred sixty-five adherents, with an average attendance of fifty-five. There had been twenty-nine conversions and twenty-seven adult baptisms in 1889.

After he was ordained as an elder on June 14, 1891, at the Annual Meeting of the Korean Mission, Jones was assigned to the Seoul Circuit, with F. Olinger. The work of evangelizing was difficult, given his still minimal proficiency in language. He writes in his journal entry of June 21, 1891:

> I found the charge at Aogi embryonic. It is situated on the road from Chemulpo, about 20 minutes walk from the Seoul wall, and is on the top of the ridge from which you gain your first sight of the City Gates approaching from Chemulpo. Formerly it was occupied as a dispensary, but medical work has been abandoned by our doctors now. My chapel was a room in the Gatehouse, 8 x 8, and used now by a native apothecary. It was filled with the fragrance of drying herbs. There were 25 hearers gathered in and around the room. I spoke concerning the true doctrine, the method of approach to God. No visible effect. I am convinced I must redouble my efforts to master this language. I am still in charge of our Sunday School here. Reviewed the lesson on the death of John. This evening I began Services in the chapel; there were only 1/2 dog present. Spoke from Luke 5:5.[28]

Now that he was an ordained minister and appointed to a circuit, he was preaching almost weekly, both to the Koreans at his small chapel as well as to the compatriots at the Foreign Church. Preaching to small and larger crowds, he began to find his preaching voice. He

---

28. Jones, June 18, 1891, Diary.

wanted to be a good preacher of the Word and tried hard to improve himself. He writes in his diary,

> A sequel to my first sermon on "Seeing Jesus." John 12:21. It was almost extempore, as I left nearly 3/4 of the manuscript on my desk and referred but little to what notes I did take. The Lord blessed me greatly, and I had a profitable time, for my own soul, at least. I am anxious indeed to become an extempore preacher, and if I had had a charge of my own these past three years and a half might now be on the high road to it. But, as my Bro. Ohlinger says, "A man preaching but once in 8 or 10 weeks and then to a congregation of clergymen, he is excusable if he falls back to a great extent on manuscript." At my suggestion, we now preach one month at a place instead of changing every Sabbath on the circuit. This month, November, I have the Chong Dong Charge and Bro. O. is at Aogi.[29]

Jones was an untiring preacher—preaching at every occasion, to anyone who would give him a hearing. He wanted so much to become a great preacher so that he could fulfill his mission to the Korean people. He writes on Aug. 18, 1891, "Yesterday, Sunday, I preached at my old stand, the Great East Gate, and had two men, strangers, to listen; one was a neighboring blacksmith and became much interested. I had a long hot hard walk to reach the place, chiefly on account of the mud which was very deep." In another place, he writes after his preaching at the Foreign Church: "I was very weak and exhausted in the pulpit, but under the influence of the Spirit preached with much freedom. M[argaret] was pleased, wrote me a note that it was 'splendid' and sent me a bouquet of flowers as a reward."[30] "Last Sunday I preached before the foreigners on 'Growth.' A poor sermon, poorly delivered and which I fear did more harm than good."[31] He preached an English sermon on October 25 and administered his first Communion.

29. Jones, Nov. 12, 1891, Diary.
30. Jones, July 5, 1891, Diary.
31. Jones, Sept. 28, 1891, Diary.

His journal contains an interesting entry about the difficulties of starting a new church, especially in the early years of missions in a foreign country:

> Sunday evening last (13th inst.) I had a new experience; I went to the Chapel to preach and found only three present: Kang, Han, and Nam Sani. I was thoroughly discouraged and concluded I had better give up the meeting entirely. The thought, however, would come that such a course would be a virtual surrender to Satan, so after a talk to the brethren, I suggested that we go out on the street and see what we could do. We stopped at our gatehouse and invited the gateman to come. We then went to the Union grounds across the way and found an old man guarding the lumber; he could not leave his ward, but Brother Han gave him a short exhortation, crowding a great sermon into a few pithy sentences, and then we went to the corner; there is a store also a restaurant and some houses there, and always a crowd of men. I must confess I approached them with trepidation; for Christianity is a proscribed thing, and the Legation would rise in a prohibitive attitude before me; but consigning the whole thing to God, I spoke to some rough coolies waiting there, and asked them, "Are you not coming to the Church?" Kang and Han were right by me and explained that they would be welcome; rising and stretching themselves, they turned their backs on us and shouted out in mocking tones, it seem to me, "Aye, we are coming!" and walked off in an opposite direction. This dampened all my ardour and I turned and went back to the Chapel. A native who had been listening to the conversation with the coolies was standing in the road, and I spoke to him and invited him, hoping he would come in. He was a scholar who has just taken his second degree at the National examination, and after Kang and Han had urged him, turned just inside the gate, and then saying he had a friend from the country at home and would go and get him, walked rapidly out of the gate and disappeared in the darkness. Then my heart went down into my boots. We went into the Chapel and sat down, unconsciously awaiting what the Lord would do. Soon some of the boys came in, and thus to my great surprise, some of the neighbors and some of my coolie friends. It seems when they turned their back on us, they went to the neighboring houses and called the people to come. And last of all, the scholar came back, though without his friend from the country, and I had a congregation of 13 and a glorious time declaring salvation through Christ Jesus. The bye-ways

and hedges are still fruitful sources from which to find guests for the wedding feast in heaven."[32]

Yet, he steadily improved his language and constantly worked on translation, especially working with Ms. Rothweiler on hymns. On June 23, 1891, he writes, "I have so far translated 'Jesus, Lover of My Soul,' 'All Hail the Power of Jesus' Name,' 'Jesus, Where in Thy People Meet.' We hope someday to have a Korean Methodist Hymnal."[33] As a result of his joint work with Miss Rothweiler, a hymnal (*Chanmika*) was published in 1892, which contained thirty songs. It was to go through many editions.[34] As traditional Korean singing was different from the Western style, Jones also taught hymn-singing to his students and church members.

He also wrote curriculum for the Sunday School and the Tract Society, such as Studies in the Old Testament, and translated other denomination-related materials such as "Our Catechism," which he translated with Choe. He also wrote and translated diligently for the Korea Religious Tract Society, and in the process, became a good student of the Korean language:

> Had the pleasure of seeing the first material results of my Enmoun idea. Four boys read the entire M[ethodist] E[piscopal] Catechism thro to me in two sittings. My plan is to make our course cover our entire Enmoun literature. I do enjoy my Korean work. Spend five hours dictating to Bro. You on the O.T. Studies; one hour in hearing the boys read the Catechism; three heard Misses Bengel & Lewis read John, and Nam Sani read the Peek a day.[35]

Along with fatigue, misgivings, and setbacks, came illness. Jones

---

32. Jones, Sept. 15, 1891, Diary.
33. Jones, Diary.
34. Kim and Pak say 1892; the first had 30 songs; the third edition of 1895 had 81 songs, the fourth (1898), 90; the fifth (1899), 176, and the sixth (1902), 205. Ryu Tongsik, *The History of Korean Methodist Church*, 273–74.
35. Jones, Jan. 6, 1893, Diary.

seems to have suffered everything that his Korean native colleagues, students, and members suffered. He was kept in bed for days at a time by strange diseases. For example, his entry for July 5, 1891 read, "I have been quite weak and sick during the week. A combined attack of diarrhea and biliousness has rendered me miserable. Both my teacher and Kang have also been sick, and as a result, I have not done as much work as I had hoped to accomplish."

The First Missionary Trip

The most eye-opening experience of his early years was the thirty-two-day trip up the Korea–China border region to "Wechu," covering more than 750 miles and over 30 large cities and districts in April 1891. Travelling with his faithful co-worker, he preached where he was accepted and sold 329 copies of Scriptures and religious tracts. They met small groups of recent believers and made friends with those who were open to the gospel. This trip made him realize the difficult road lying ahead of him, yet he also realized more and more that the Choson soil was ripe for planting the seed of Christ.

Jones and His Teacher, Choe Pyonghon

Early on, Jones' love of books, history, culture, and education met a match in Choe Pyonghon. As soon as he learned the basics, Jones took on a heavy research project with Choe: the 1592 Japanese Invasion of Korea. "My information is derived entirely from native sources, which, written in Chinese, give me many a pleasant hour with my teacher, for he translates them into Korean for me, and I am thus getting the language in both a pleasurable and practicable manner."[36] With Choe's assistance, he also translated many other texts he needed for his training sessions, such as "Our Catechism" in 1890.

Language wasn't the only thing Jones learned from Choe. If Appenzeller and Scranton were in charge of Jones's theological education in the field, it seems Choe took it upon himself to educate this young Westerner in all things Korean. Both the Methodist Board of Foreign Missions and the Korean Mission were wise in calling for "young men" to come to Korea in order that they may "grow up with the country" and learn the language so well that they can be useful for a long time. Jones had the capacity, ability, and willingness to fulfill these requirements. Even before Jones landed in Chemulpo, God had been at work, opening and closing many doors, in order to bring Jones and his "inestimable" teacher together. There may have been many other qualified teachers for Jones—Koreans who knew the West or spoke English, for example. But Jones needed a particular kind of a teacher: one who could open his mind and heart to feel the heartbeat and the pains of the Korean people pining for a Savior.

Choe provided that, and more. In Choe, Jones met a genuine and conscientious scholar, *sonbi*, who was not afraid to speak his mind. The *sonbi* were also referred to as the party of the axe. When the society of the scholars or the literati would protest against a government policy they considered to be egregious and harmful to the entire society, they would get on their knees in front of the royal palace and call out the king and his advisors. They would also have an axe in front of them as a sign of their resolve. They were willing to lay their life on the line for their opinion. They would speak the truth, no matter the cost. Thus, the *sonbi*—or the scholarly class—was held in high esteem in Old Choson. It seems Choe was such a *sonbi*. He knew who he was. He was a solid personality. He

36. Jones, July 15, 1891, Diary.

was not afraid to ask questions or even challenge Jones. Learning from such a teacher made a big impact on Jones. He learned his Korean. He also learned to feel the heartbeat of the Korean people through his teacher, Choe, and that made all the difference in how Jones presented his precious Savior, Jesus, to the Korean people.

3.3 Three Discoveries about the Korean People

As Jones neared the end of his initial period of service as a teacher to begin his missionary work in earnest in Chemulpo (Incheon), he was ready to approach it with a clear awareness of three fundamental factors that affected the life of the common people: 1) the Korean people possessed a religious heritage of belief in *Hananim,* the one sovereign ruler of the heavens; 2) the Choson society, which was organized around ancestral worship, was not geared to serve the common people, but neglected and mistreated them; and 3) the Korean people were living through a time of unprecedented changes and upheavals, which would result in its humiliation at the hands of its historical enemy, Imperial Japan.[37]

Jones saw the potential to use these religious and political realities to frame his message of salvation in Jesus in three dimensions. His initial missionary strategy was to begin to preach about a Christ

---

37. The fate of Old Korea would be determined in the ten years of critical events between the Sino-Japanese War (1894–95) and the Russo-Japanese War (1904–5). Many volumes have been written about this turbulent period: the two wars fought on Korean soil, the Tonghak Revolution of 1894–95, the Reform policies of 1895 and Korea's forced march into modernity, the murder of Queen Min by Japanese assassins in 1895, the flight of King Kojong into the Russian embassy in 1895, opening a decade of Russian intervention in Korea, the proclamation of an independent "Empire of Korea" in 1897, the emergence and repression of the civil society (Independence Club) in 1897–99, the Anglo-Japanese Alliance treaty in 1902, Korean immigration to America in 1902–7, and the Korea-Japanese Treaty of 1905, giving Japan almost full control of Korean politics. For a general history of Korea, see Lee, Ki-baik, *A New Korean History*, trans. Edward W. Wagner with Edward J. Shultz (Cambridge, MA: Harvard-Yenching Institute and Harvard University Press, 1984), and Bruce Cumings, *Korea's Place in the Sun: A Modern Korean History* (New York: W.W. Norton & Co., 1997).

who came to reveal again the living God, *Hananim*, about a human Mediator with *Hananim* who would deal compassionately with the suffering masses, and a Savior who offered hope for a dying nation.

In other words, Jones wanted his Korean hearers to see Jesus centrally for what he expressed of the Living God. After all, Jones himself had entered into a relationship of sonship with God through his conversion experience. Jones's first sermon at Chemulpo on Sept. 24, 1892, was entitled "Seeing Jesus," taking as his text John 12:21.[38] Earlier, he had written in his journal, "(I) have already begun on my long proposed complement to my sermon on 'Seeing Jesus.' It is to be entitled, 'Jesus Seen,' on Heb. 2:9. I have carried it in mind for 3 years now, but have never until the present had the courage to attempt (it)."[39]

Having seen Jesus himself, Jones had looked for ways in which the Korean people could be invited and persuaded to see Jesus for themselves. As his knowledge of the land, people, language, history, culture, and religion increased, and as he continued his one-on-one tutoring sessions with Choe Pyonghon, his mind had slowly shaped a strategy to help the people see Jesus so that Jesus would be finally seen by the whole nation of Choson.

These and other entries show Jones paying close attention to what he said about Jesus, for he wanted the new believers to probe the inward mystery of Jesus as the expression of God's life among humanity.

For Jones, Christianity was not a religion about a system of truth, salvation, or redemption. Rather, it is about Jesus, a Divine Person from God. In so doing, Jones was implementing what Robert E.

---

38. "They came to Philip, who was from Bethsaida in Galilee, and said to him, "Sir, we wish to see Jesus" (NRSV).
39. Jones, October 25, 1891, Diary. Hebrews 2:9 reads: "But we see Jesus, who for a little while was made lower than the angels, now crowned with glory and honor because of the suffering of death, so that by the grace of God he might taste death for everyone" (NRSV).

Speer, Secretary of the Presbyterian Board of Foreign Missions, would advise thousands of students gathered in Detroit in 1894, as the keynote speaker at the Student Volunteer Movement for Foreign Missions' second convention:

> Fellow students, that is our Gospel. Don't preach a system of truth. What good is a system of truth anyhow? Don't preach salvation; don't preach redemption. Preach the Savior. Preach the Redeemer. What is wanted the world round is not more truth; it is a Divine Person. What is wanted is not a larger doctrine; it is the advent of the Divine life…we shall never fail if we go preaching the simple, the omnipotent, the irresistible Christ.[40]

3.4 *Hananim* and the Christian God

As he preached about Jesus, Jones came to realize that the Korean people had a robust concept of a monotheistic God, or a Transcendent Being called *Hananim* (literally, The Great or One Being or the Heavenly One), and that all people had an innate sense of relationship to this *Hananim*. He also came to recognize the inherent spirituality and spiritual yearning of the Korean people. In 1894, he writes in his journal, "The great truths of pardon, peace, assurance, regeneration, and sonship are very dear to their hearts…We have felt that God is indeed the God of all the earth and Christianity is God's own remedy for all ill."[41]

In 1894, Jones drew up a rather controversial document in favor of the traditional *Hananim* "as the term for God, and signed it, intending to use it to secure signatures and thus obtain an expression from the community of a preference. This paper I hope will settle the term question in Korea."[42] The issue became critical for Jones because

---

40. Max Wood Moorhead, *The Student Missionary Enterprise*, 12.
41. Jones, May 10, 1894, Diary.
42. Ibid.

he felt that the alternative terms—*Sangje* (The Sovereign Lord) and *Chonju* (The Heavenly Lord)—were too Chinese and Confucianist, and would also confuse the people with Catholicism, which used both terms for God. He sensed that in *Hananim*, there was already an indigenous term that they could use from their daily life to speak about the Living God of Jesus, but without the shamanistic overtones and absolute transcendence of the traditional belief.

By seeing Jesus, the people would see the central truth which Jesus revealed about the true *Hananim*; He is the living God who desires humanity to be in relation with him and would ultimately lead the human family into union with God. While Jones did not yet fully understand the religious dynamism of Asian religions in their fundamental desire to reach unity and harmony between the trinity of heaven (God), earth (Spirit), and humanity,[43] he clearly recognized the fundamental desire of the Korean people to communicate with God and to be in union and harmony with *Hananim*. While he did not yet fully comprehend nor appreciate shamanism (given his evolutionary bias of it as the lowest and the most primitive form of religion) nor its highest goal of reaching a religious ecstasy in order to become lost in the Spirit, which would transform its followers from the inside, Jones recognized that the people were hungry for God, and so, offered the Koreans his "experimental religion,"[44] which was marked by experiential worship, exorcism of demons, and fervent prayer. Throughout his journals and writings, there are descriptions of the people being filled with the Spirit and experiencing[45] the

---

43. See, for example, Jung Young Lee, *The Trinity in Asian Perspective* (Nashville: Abingdon Press, 1996) for an interesting discussion of this issue.
44. Jones, November 14, 1894, Diary.
45. As he was getting ready for a theological class, Jones met Noble to work out certain translations, one of them being "experience." "So we searched for a term but none came forth. To us is the honor of being theological pioneers in Korea and possibly as a result we may get our names into the footnotes of history. But the situation is a trying one to us." How can you describe what you are trying to do when you cannot find the word to describe it; experimental faith!

presence and action of God in their lives, much like the revival meetings of his youth. "The prayer meeting tonight was one of blessed power and influence to us all. God was in our midst and we all grew warm. The testimonies were ready and hearty."[46]

3.5 Jesus and the Korean Demons

Along with these early experiences of the Living God through his Revealer, Jesus, Jones demanded from the people a denunciation of false gods and idols. His proclamation of Christ was accompanied by a strong emphasis on the complete extrication of the new believers from all forms of "heathenism." For Jones, heathenism was the "bondage to ceremony and rites in Confucianism," which he claimed had a human origin, while Christianity had a divine origin.[47] For Jones, the religious state of the Korean people was "pitiable" at best, for in their "spirit worship," the people were dominated by fear from a "multiplicity of inferior deities and spirits."[48] Jones described Confucianism's function as a state religion, and Buddhism's broken, corrupt, and decaying power[49] as disobedience to God, or sin. In his lectures on early church history at various theological classes (e.g., Seoul Theological Class, held Nov. 10–28, 1909), Jones spoke on the need to rid Korea of "heathenism and idolatry," since "Christianity and heathenism cannot exist together." Since Christianity introduces a "new, spiritual life" to the people, they have no need for heathenism or shamanistic spirit worship. *Hananim* of Jesus is a living presence

---

But Jones found that there was something even more fundamental and basic than words: the direct and intimate "God-experience," which preceded its understanding. He found the Spirit had opened the door of experience before he could explain it! Jones, July 20, 1900, Diary.
46. Jones, November 13, 1901, Diary.
47. Jones, November 9, 1900, Diary.
48. Jones, "The Christian Missions," Papers, 2.
49. George Heber Jones, *Successes and Opportunities in Korea* (New York: The Missionary Society of the Methodist Episcopal Church, 1906), 3.

who fills the people with "love, mercy and enlightenment." Jesus comes to bring the Korean people back to the knowledge of the living *Hananim*.

In the face of unbridled idolatry and the widespread presence of fetishes and ancestral rites, Jones preached the divine Christ, who is able to overcome and conquer these spiritual forces. In Korea, even shamans were seen casting out demons. So, in the earlier years of missionary evangelism, it was important to show that Jesus is stronger than the demonic forces, and that he is the conqueror of evil forces. Jones, therefore, preached often on the power of Jesus to defeat the Devil and deliver the people from its hold. After recounting how Choe Pyonghon was converted, with many others following his example, he writes:

> The Devil has been badly stirred. In fact, I should esteem it rather a reflection on us if the number now in Korea could not make him feel anxious about the welfare of his kingdom. My gates have been placarded twice, one of them giving me notice to quit within 20 days.[50]

The exorcism of demons and the Christian practice of destroying or burning the ancestral mortuary plates and altars after conversion was a sure sign that Christ was conquering the kingdom of the devil in Korea.[51] Jones saw idolatry as a signs of the devil's firm hold everywhere. "These objects of worship (straw fetishes) may be found everywhere and show how this nation lies prostrate in the dust before huddles of straw and pieces of paper."[52] There was much work to

---

50. George Heber Jones to A. B. Leonard, April 12, 1893, Missionary Collection, Letter Books 209–13, (General Commission on Archives and History of the United Methodist Church, Drew University, Madison, NJ).
51. For description of an exorcism and Korean heathen superstition, see Jones, December 12, 1893, Diary. Also for an example of Christian rejection of idolatry, see Jones, December 29, 1893, Diary.
52. Jones, April 15, 1894, Diary.

be done, for Christ has come to deliver the Korean people from the Devil.

> These poor Koreans can't do anything without running a risk of the displeasure of hell. God is gone from their thoughts and the Devil has inserted himself instead. He sits in ugly tyranny on the center of their beings and rules their life in all its outgoing, to their ruin and sorrow and his own fiendish pleasure. May God hasten the day when he shall be bound forever in his own place.[53]

Putting away "ancestral rites" became an important part of the people's conversion experience. A probationer was first required to burn various fetishes, especially the wooden panels with the names of the ancestors. They were also told to stop holding or taking part in all forms of ancestral rites.[54] It was not only a statement of religious purity against idolatry; it also defined their relationship to the society as an outsider, belonging to a new society, the kingdom of the Living God, the *Hananim* of Jesus. Often, new converts paid dearly for these acts of faith. In Jones's eyes, becoming a Christian sometimes meant becoming completely non-Korean. The choice was stark: either "Christ or Belial," the false god who dominated the Koreans and their whole culture.

> And as I have seen them braving devil and man, boldly breaking away from every superstition and vice, reforming their lives until hardly a

---

53. Jones, March 8, 1894, Diary.
54. There were many kinds of ancestral rituals and ceremonies that a typical family observed. If a person happened to be the oldest son in the family, he had the burden of keeping the family's name alive by maintaining the tablets and keeping up with the ceremonies. See the following article about the many types of ancestral rituals being kept in modern Korea by "jongga" families. "Jongga" families are those families which claim to have maintained the ancestral tablets for tens of generations, going all the way back, in some cases, to the founder/s of a clan or a surname such as Kim. A typical "jongga" family would have well over 30 ancestral and seasonal rituals they have to perform every year. Lee Yeun Ja. "Jongga Ancestral Rituals and Food Culture." *Koreana*. Korea Foundation. April 7, 2011 <http://www.koreana.or.kr/months/news_view.asp?b_idx=558&lang=en&page_type=list>.

vestige of the old Korean mode remains, I have felt "God surely is in this place."[55]

Thus, Jones's Korean Jesus was a continuation of his Experimental Christ in a new land and for a new people. By "seeing" or experiencing Jesus as he had done, Korean believers would reclaim their relationship to the great and singular "Sky-God" *Hananim* of their ancestors. Through Jesus, they would gain the true knowledge of the Living God, who seeks to be reconciled with them and call them His sons and daughters, but it also demanded a complete break with the old gods of shamanism, Confucianism, and Buddhism who were, in reality, already "dead" to the people's lives. And so, only after two years of work at Chemulpo, Jones could write proudly:

> And as Mrs. Jones and I have made our weekly rounds we have found in these mud huts and extreme poverty, hearts as warm and loving and devotion to Christ as sincere as can be found anywhere amid the grander surroundings of Christian civilization…Our Koreans have hearts susceptible to high affections and their souls, when made alive by the life-giving Spirit, turn with as strong aspirations for God as any whose Christian heritage has come down through many generations…The great truths of pardon, peace, assurance, regeneration, and sonship are very dear to their hearts…We have felt that God is indeed the God of all the earth and Christianity is God's own remedy for all ill.[56]

Had he exchanged the word *Hananim* for God, he would have not been amiss, for Jesus revealed to the Koreans that the *Hananim* of Jesus is indeed the Living God—not to be equated with the dead idols, demons, and the spirits of Korea's old religions.

---

55. Jones, May 10, 1894, Diary. Part of "Report on First Six Months, Chemulpo Circuit."
56. Ibid., 457–58.

3.6 Called To Be an Apostle from Birth

The initial five years in Korea prepared Jones well for the "apostolic" work waiting for him. He became nearly fluent in the language—thanks in no part to his excellent teacher, Choe Pyonghon. More important, Choe had instilled in him the dreams, hopes, fears, and longings of the Korean people, as he shared his own story and life with him for the five years. It had allowed him to quickly and intuitively sense the felt needs of the people and the nation. Once he gained these insights, his YMCA-trained organizational skills were ready to be put to good use.

In reality, these first five years were years of missionary training and preparation, done in the field, immersion style. It was far better than the four years of college and seminary he may have received if he had not been sent immediately. He not only learned the language, but had one of the most qualified teachers in Korea teaching him its history, culture, and politics. His lack of formal theological training was addressed by older colleagues, who shared their knowledge with him liberally. Perhaps it was this theological education in the field that helped Jones develop his unique perspective that was thoroughly Korean in its outlook. More important, he applied himself constantly to fulfill his calling: writing, translating, publicizing, reporting, organizing, and preaching. He knew his limits, yet he had no fears and kept trying to improve himself and the life of the new people he had met. Like a young man, he fell in love and nurtured a caring family. He had not only survived, but thrived in the challenges of living in a new land.

Now awaited a future wife, a mission to fulfill, and the Jesus of experimental faith to share. Here I am, Lord, send me!

Years later, when he started his autobiographical account, *Real*

Stories from Real Life, he opened it with a story about an incident that foreshadowed his apostleship in Korea:

> Mother has often told me the story of how in the first winter of my life, she went to visit friends in the hills, somewhere back of Remsen NY. She rode in an open sleigh with me as a baby in arms. The snow lay deep and it came on to storm. They lost the road and had great difficulty in reaching the farmhouse to which she was going, almost perishing in the attempt. For several days she was storm-bound in a blizzard which was historic in its violence. I came down ill and nearly died. Thus did winter and Jack Frost almost nip my young life, and put me to sleep until the resurrection morning amid the Black River hills. My early escape from death was but the beginning of a series of escapes from the Ring of Terrors, and was as much due to my mother's prayers as to medical skill. Long afterward, when I had determined to become a minister and a foreign missionary and told my mother of it, she gave me the story of my first winter and said that when the doctors gave me up and said I could not live, she fell on her knees beside me and promised God that if He would save my life, she would gladly give me to His service in any way that He might will. And so my first winter passed, marked by a historic blizzard, my own visit to the portals of death, and my return, and my mother's prophetic dedication of my life to God's service.[57]

He had been born and saved as a baby to become an apostle—a messenger—of the Lord Jesus Christ to a people pining for the good news in the land of Master Kong (Confucius).

---

57. *Real Stories,* 1.

4

Choe, 1888–1892: Drawing Near to Jesus the Western Savior

"How was Choe able to let go of his old Confucian masters' books and grasp the new Book of Master Jesus?" In this chapter, we follow Choe as he increases his knowledge of Jesus and the West while serving as Jones's language teacher for five years. These years turn out to be a time of preparatory training for Christianity.

4.1 The Initial Contact with the Missionaries

When Choe's friendship with George Heber Jones, known as Cho Wonsi (the name Jones put in Korean syllables), and other American Methodist missionaries began, Choe had to filter out all kinds of frightful rumors floating about the foreign missionary "devils." It was said that the missionaries kidnapped and ate little children. The first American missionaries had only officially come in 1885, so Choe shared the general public's fears about the strange-looking Westerners. In "My Language Teacher," Jones also recalls how Choe revealed to him his secret fear of the missionary diet that supposedly included "roasted Korean babies," and the cookies that contained secret ingredients that would change their guests' hearts and magically turn them into Christians.

The Paichai Haktang, where Jones taught and met frequently with Choe, was "the first building ever erected in Korea for educating men on Christian principles." Measuring 76 by 52 feet, it was a brick building in the Renaissance style, one story high. It contained "a chapel, four lecture rooms, a library, the principal's office, and a basement under half the building" for the "industrial department." The first Methodist missionary sent to Korea, Henry G. Appenzeller was the principal. The Methodist educational work had started almost immediately in the fall of 1885, after the first missionaries landed in Chemulpo (Incheon) on Easter Sunday, April 5, 1885. By mid-1886, the academy received governmental sanction. Appenzeller describes the events in his 1887 Korea Mission report:

> Official recognition and endorsement by the Government. His majesty, having our school represented to him by the president of the Foreign Office, gave it the name of *Pai Tjai Hak Dang*; "Hall for rearing useful men." This name, written in large Chinese characters, has been properly framed and now hangs over the large front gate, the silent guardian of our education work.[1]

As Choe met with Jones and Appenzeller almost every day, he was given a Chinese New Testament as well as other books in Chinese about the West and the Christian religion. Choe continued to prepare for the civil service exams, but he was also greatly curious about the West and Christianity. Earlier in 1880, when he had moved up to Seoul,[2] his friends had given him a book from Shanghai,

---

1. Annual Report of the Board of Foreign Missions of the Methodist Episcopal Church, Korea, 1887. Found on 23 of IKCH collection.
2. The Kim biography says Choe came up to Seoul for the first time in 1880 and received this book. But in the Choe biography, it is clear that he had come up to Seoul even earlier, in 1875, 1879, and then, in December, 1880. Perhaps it was when he came up to live with his foster parents that he made new friends among the *yangban* families in Seoul through whom he received this and other books about the West.

Short Compendium of World Geography, which talked about the great civilizations of the West and Christianity's place in it. Whenever Choe had a question about the Christian Scriptures, he would bring his questions to the missionaries, who tried to answer them as best as they could. His biographer notes,

> Whenever he had a question about a Scriptural passage, he asked about each of them and gradually came to the realization of the truth. Although he could almost taste the sweetness of the way of the truth, he was unable to let go of his personal dream (of passing the civil service exams). So he read many religious materials and prepared for the faith for five years.[3]

As time went on, Choe was retained as a teacher in Paichai's Chinese language department in 1889. In addition, as Jones's teacher, he was often asked to translate sections of the Christian Bible in Chinese into Hangul, the vernacular Korean. As he picked up the language, Jones would try his best to persuade him to become a Christian and join him in the work of giving the Koreans "the knowledge of the true God and the better way of life."[4] But Choe remained loyal to the "faith of his fathers" and resisted the many attempts of the missionaries to evangelize him. Throughout his contact with the missionaries, Choe continued to prepare himself for the *kwago*, but found success hard to come by. He didn't realize that the results of the exams did not depend on a person's abilities, but on his political connections and wealth.

In the fall of 1892, Choe tried to take the Kyongmudae (Royal Palace) Internal Exams[5] with his friend Oh Yangson, but the proctor

---

3. Kim Chinho, "Biography," 100.
4. Jones, "My Language Teacher," Papers, 1.
5. Kyongmudae was a building on the grounds of the Kyongbuk Royal Palace—the modern-day Korean Presidential Blue House complex. It was built in 1868 during the fifth year of Kojong's rule, when the Kyongbuk Palace was repaired, and was used as a site for the *kwago*. "The History of the Blue House." Jan. 10, 2011, <http://kr.blog.yahoo.com/hoonso.o/13951>.

refused to certify their exams on time. So, their exam books were deemed incomplete and thrown out. From then on, Choe abandoned his lifelong dream of passing the *kwago*, saying, "The scholars are the foundational force of a nation. But what is the use of trying to pass the *kwago* when you live in a world that treats you so shabbily? The best thing to do is to stay put and embrace the Way and wait for the right time."[6] He decided to examine religious philosophy.

The Kim biography gives further details about this final straw that broke Choe's back regarding the viability of trying to change the system from within, as he had vowed to do after his imprisonment experience in 1887. According to Kim, Choe saw through the corruption of the entire system, especially the class-consciousness of the *yangban,* or the upper-class, Koreans who so nonchalantly broke the law to maintain their power and gave no thought to the love of the nation or service to the people. He writes:

> The Teacher observed all of these things and was greatly saddened that the current situation was so corrupt. Not only that, the so-called "people of the great families of power" judged people only according to their class status. In other words, you had to be someone's son or someone's grandson to be counted as anything. If you were of the lower classes, your skills or virtues counted for nothing. Your knowledge or intelligence meant nothing. The Teacher was greatly angered by the state of affairs and would have nothing to do with the families with wealth and power. Never again did he sit for the civil service exams. But he never stopped thinking about how to right the wrongs of the nation and to improve the life of the *minjung*.[7]

Choe had studied for the exams for five long years so that he could help reform the nation and serve the people. Now, he realized that the system itself had become very corrupt. It had lost its ability to correct itself when it closed its doors to reform-minded people such

---

6. Choe Chaewon, *Biography*, 116.
7. Kim Chinho, "Biography," 100

as him. As many Confucian scholars had done for centuries, when the system became irrevocably corrupt and would not heed the voice of the honest *sonbi*, the best thing was to wait for the system to collapse on itself by the weight of its own corruption. Meanwhile, the *sonbi* would resign completely from the world, try to purify and prepare himself even further, and wait for the time when his views and judgments would be valued.

Choe did not make the typical turn to ascetic retirement in the mountains while ignoring the entire corrupt scene below. Rather, his love for the nation and loyalty to the king (*chungkun aekuk*) remained steadfast, and his desire to serve the people by bringing peace over the land did not waver. But how did he react?

The Choe biography contains an interesting phrase that may explain Choe's next steps. Choe decided to "embrace the Way" and "examine religious philosophy." The five years of preparing himself to work in the government to serve the people had also been a period of enlightenment. As he read new books and reflected on the Christian books he was helping to translate, and as he conversed with Jones and Appenzeller, his outlook and perspective slowly changed. New books, along with the Christian Bible, were changing him once and for all: "*World History, New History of the Great West, Book of Western Politics, A Compendium of Geography, Examination of The Origin of All Things, Search for the Origin of the Heavens, Psychology*, and *Pursuing West, Looking for East*."[8]

While he had held onto the old books of Master Confucius and the venerable teachers of the East, he had begun to read and learn from the new books, as many reformed-minded Koreans had begun to do. These Chinese language books on Western geography, civilization,

---

8. Kim Chinho, "Biography," 100. Their names in Korean are as follows: Mankuk tonggam, Taeso sinsa, Sojong yangso, Jiri yakhe, Kyokmul tamwon, Chondo sowon, Simryonghak, and Jaso Jotong.

and science brought new knowledge and information. More important, they opened his eyes to a new way of thinking—a new worldview. The geography book he obtained in 1880 had opened his eyes to the world and taken him out of the China-centered worldview of the Confucian Choson Dynasty and had opened his eyes to see that "Christianity was at the center of the civilization of the great nations of the mighty West."[9]

Now, these new books had further expanded his horizons and given him a global perspective that included the East and the West in his understanding of reality. In addition, these books showed him a different and wondrous civilization of science and industrial progress that could only enhance his new vision of patriotic nationalism. They helped guide his path toward active participation in the movement for cultural enlightenment toward the creation of a new Korea. But most of all, these books convinced him intellectually that the Great West had its roots in Jesus the Savior and his new great way.

The Old Masters had taught him volumes about becoming a complete person and building an ideal society: doing good always, obeying heaven's mandate, following destiny, obeying parents, reflecting on oneself, living within limits, following one's heart, fulfilling one's nature, desiring to learn, teaching the young, knowing oneself, fulfilling life's goals, building the just society, nurturing a happy family, living ethically, building relationships, speaking rightly, enhancing friendship, and becoming a virtuous

---

9. Kim Chinho, "Biography," 99.

man.¹⁰ The missionaries and their Savior, Jesus, seemed to profess no less of the truth than the Old Masters.

But what finally persuaded him to faith was the way the missionaries lived out their faith. It is one thing to preach something and another to walk the talk. As he lived, ate, and breathed with these foreign missionaries, Choe was able to determine what kind of people they were. A traditional proverb says, "Over a long distance, you learn about the strength of your horse; over a long period of time, you get to know what's in a person's heart." Character is revealed by time.¹¹

But a 500-year-old tradition is not something you can set aside easily or without second thoughts. Its hold on the Korean people—including Choe—was tremendous. Jones tells an interesting story about how Choe remained loyal to the "faith of his fathers" and resisted his many attempts to convert him.

> One day, I remember, I pressed him a little too earnestly. Turning to me he said, "*Moksa* (pastor), you are very zealous in inviting me to become a Christian like yourself. I want to tell you how it all seems to me. Here is a man who has a book and its binding is broken, its covers dilapidated and its pages soiled and torn; and along comes another man who has a book, a new book with strong, handsome binding, and clean white pages, and he says to the other man, "Throw away your old book and take this new book instead." "But, ah, Moksa," said he, "that old book was the book of my fathers. Those stains upon its pages and the rents in the binding have been made by the passage of the centuries and the caressing of fingers that have long since turned to dust. No matter how much I like your new book, I cannot, for the sake of the sacred

---

10. These are the 19 chapter headings of a collection of over 200 wisdom sayings and proverbs from old Masters, including major Confucian, Buddhist, and Taoist teachers, called *Myongsim Pogam*, lit. "A priceless mirror to illumine the heart." It was widely used in the homes and schools of the Choson Dynasty since the mid-sixteenth century. For over 400 years, young and old lived by these sayings, which captured the ethical, cultural, family, and social values of the Confucian world. It is still a perennial bestseller in Korea. *Myongsim Pokam,* ed. Ahn Byonguk et al (Seoul: Hyonamsa, 1996).
11. Ibid., Friendship, Proverb 7, 273.

memories that cluster about the old book and the thought of those who have gone ahead of me, give it up. No, no, Moksa, keep your new book, I must hold onto the old one."[12]

4.2 Choe's Conversion to Christianity

Korean history had taught Choe that his Choson ancestors in the fourteenth century had adopted the neo-Confucian teachings of Chu Hsi of the Song (Sung) Dynasty. The ancient Koryo Dynasty also had accepted the teachings of the Buddhist scriptures from China. Choe began to think that the new religion of Christianity with its new book might hold the key that would help him honor his ancestors by truly serving the king and loving the people, as well as bring peace in the world.

After much thought, reflection, and focused study of both Western books and Asian religious texts, Choe made the hard decision to believe in Jesus and his religion of love. He came to believe that the religion of Jesus Christ was a new way that would save the Korean people and nation, as the missionaries had preached. He believed that Jesus would help transform them into true lovers of God, truth, and humanity. He would enable them to fulfill their human destiny and build a new, enlightened Christian nation, as strong and righteous as America and Europe.

There are several accounts of Choe Pyonghon's conversion, especially in George H. Jones' writings.[13] In the story of Christian beginnings in Korea, Choe's conversion was something of a legend, in that he was one of the first prominent *yangban* (person of the upper

---

12. George Heber Jones, "My Language Teacher," Papers, 2.
13. Jones to A. B. Leonard, April 12, 1893, Missionary Collection; Jones, "Obstacles Encountered by Korean Christians," 148–49; Jones, "The Rise of the Church in Korea," Papers, 147–49; Jones, "My Language Teacher," Papers, 1–3.

class) or educated Korean *sonbi* to become a Christian. His conversion was big news among the Confucian upper class. In his letter to A. B. Leonard at the MEC Board of Foreign Missions, Jones rejoices that three men from the "scholar class" became converted.

> One of them is my personal teacher who has been with me for four years, and while ever favorable yet had no courage to take the step. But the Spirit aided him at this time, and he crossed the line amid much tribulation. On the day fixed for his baptism, he was forcibly detained at his home by members of his class. While threatened severely, however, he remained firm and later on received baptism at my hands. Since then much persecution has followed him, but he has stood firm throughout it rejoicing that he is counted worthy to share in these tribulations. The result of these new men coming among us has been most beneficial, especially in the school, which is immediately under my supervision. A number of the students have been quickened and energized; and some who have held out long have been led to surrender.[14]

Jones was ecstatic when he heard the news. "You have been with me for five years. You've read the Bible many times and heard many sermons. Why should you wait any longer? Why don't you get baptized this coming Sunday?"[15] So, Choe began visiting his old friends and acquaintances and told them of his conversion to Christianity and his upcoming baptism.

> I went to each home where they had received me with welcome in days gone by, and told them I had become a Christian and wished them to know the fact; that I trusted this would make no difference in our friendship; but if it did, I wanted them to tell me frankly…In every instance, they greeted my confession with ridicule and sneers and insults. They told me that my action had placed a gulf between me and my friends which could not be bridged. They told me that I had betrayed the ancestors. They said our friendship was over.[16]

---

14. Jones to A. B. Leonard, April 12, 1893, Missionary Collection.
15. Choe Chaewon, *Biography*, 116.
16. Jones, "My Language Teacher," Papers, 3. In recent years, some scholars have begun to surmise that Choe turned to the Wang Yang-ming School of Confucianism in his critique of the

The following Sunday morning, dismayed and angry friends physically prevented him from going to church in his full *yangban* attire. So, while the church waited for him at the morning and evening services, Choe did not show up. After meeting him the next morning and learning about his situation, Jones decided that Choe should be baptized more discreetly at the mid-week prayer meeting. So, on February 8, 1893, he was baptized. That fall, he was made an exhorter (*kwonsa*), a lay preacher.

In explaining his conversion, Jones believed that Choe did not mean any disrespect in "laying aside the 'old book' that had served its purpose so long and taking the newer and better book." After all, it was not such a new book, but was the "oldest of all books and which alone contained the truth without which no true and victorious life was possible." Choe came to him later and said,

> *Moksa* (Pastor), I think very differently about it. Now I know that if my ancestors could speak to me out of the unseen world, their message would be, "Follow Christ, follow Christ. We had no knowledge of him when we were on Earth, but if we were living today, we would be His followers; you must follow Him."[17]

His ancestors would be *sonbi,* or Confucian scholars, who would not have adopted a new religion or accepted new sacred text for selfish purposes of financial gain, honor, or personal safety. Confucian scholars often criticized the Buddhist doctrine of salvation from hell because it was regarded as a selfish motivation for seeking the truth. For a *sonbi* to seek a new religion simply to save his own skin would

---

ruling Confucian school. However, there has not been enough textual evidence to warrant this claim. But it seems clear that Choe was following the method of critical scholars who hoped to save Choson's corrupted neo-Confucianism by going back to the "classic" texts of Confucius and Mencius. See Yi Juik, "Taksa Choe Pyonghon's Theology and Thought" (K), in Choe Pyonghon, *Mongyangwon: A Collection of Speeches*, trans. Yi Juik (Seoul: Taksa Publishing Co., 1999), 84–107. See also Pyon, "Taksa Choe Pyonghon and Eastern Thought," 91–151.

17. Ibid., 2.

be the height of egotism and selfishness.[18] Truth was to be sought for truth's sake. As a Confucian scholar, Choe would have examined himself thoroughly about his motivations for becoming a Christian.

One of his first public Christian writings is "The Famous Words of a Scholar,"[19] which tells the story of an elderly scholar from his hometown. This gentleman scolds him for his lack of social finesse in not using the Westerner's influence to land a high government post. Instead, he says Choe has fallen for their religious mumbo-jumbo, which he called "religion of the 'Chonju;' Catholicism." Choe scolds him for his dishonest trick of using the foreigners for personal gain and for seeking such an improper path of power, like political hacks. He was not interested in Christianity as a way to advance his own career or for personal gain, be it material, intellectual, or spiritual. He had decided to believe in Jesus the Savior because his Confucian method of truth-seeking had convinced him that Christianity contained the principles of the Great Way of Truth (*taedo chili*).

Elsewhere in "The Great Disease of Humanity," a teacher finds that a student in a Christian school had been absent for three days. On visiting the student's home, he finds that the parents were fearful that the child was becoming a believer, a Catholic. In light of this incident, Choe says humanity suffers from two kinds of diseases: pride and ignorance. Pride makes people think that their own self-knowledge is all there is, and leads them to scorn others' words. Ignorance, on the contrary, makes people susceptible to lies, which make them doubt the true principles. While he found the parents to be ignorant for believing rumors about Catholicism being evil, he found that many of his Confucian contemporaries suffered from

---

18. See early neo-Confucian critique of Buddhism in Pak Kyonghwan, "Buddhist-Confucian Controversy: Conflict of Worldly Values Versus Transcendental Values." in *Understanding Korean Philosophy through Its Controversies* (K), ed. Hankuk cholhak sasang yonguhoe (Seoul: Yemunsowon Book Publishing, 1995), 71–110.
19. Choe Pyonghon, "The Famous Words of a Scholar" (K), *KCA*, April 5, 1899.

pride. The latter thought that Confucian scriptures were so much better than other scriptures that they adopted an "uncompromising position." It became easy for them to promptly reject other teachings without even examining them, by calling them "heterodox" and "heretical." He said such a reaction was against Confucianism itself, since the search for the "truth" is one of its fundamental principles.[20]

His reading of the Christian Scriptures obtained through his seasoned Confucian custom of textual study had led him to Master Jesus. According to Chu Hsi, the father of neo-Confucianist schools in Choson,[21] to truly understand a sacred text, a person needed to practice inner mental attentiveness to grasp the principle that was present in the text and in the world.

> In reading, we cannot seek moral principle solely from the text. We must turn the process around and look for it in ourselves…people simply have sought it in the text, not in themselves. We have yet to discover for ourselves what the sages previously explained in their texts—only through their words will we find it in ourselves.[22]

Ultimately, experiencing the text fully would help the reader gain full self-understanding, for the same principle that existed in the text also existed in human nature. Reading the texts correctly would lead to spiritual enlightenment and self-transformation. Given this neo-Confucian immersion method of Bible reading, Kil Sonju, the famous Presbyterian revivalist of Pyongyang, is said to have read the entire Bible several hundred times, the Gospel of John over five hundred times, and the Revelation of John over ten thousand times.[23]

---

20. Choe Pyonghon, "Great Disease," 510.
21. Neo-Confucianism of Chu Hsi (CE 1130–1200) used Buddhist and Taoist ideas to further develop Confucian theories about the relationship between *li* (principle) and *chi* (matter) and the theory of the nature of the human mind and how it can be nurtured properly.
22. Chu Hsi, *Learning to Be a Sage*, trans. Daniel K. Gardner (Berkeley, CA, University of California Press, 1990), 149.
23. Ryu Tongsik, *Vein*, 70.

Choe's knowledge of Master Jesus also increased as he engaged the missionaries with his many questions, translated the Chinese Bible into vernacular Korean, and listened to the preaching of the missionaries. In his later writings, he wrote frequently about the initial attraction of Christianity, as well as the natural resistance of his internalized traditional values against it, but the person and work of Jesus was the center of his conversion story.

The Kim biography contains an interesting phrase that provides a window into Choe's thoughts as he considered Christianity as his newly adopted religion of the Book. Although he knew beforehand that his *yangban* friends and the larger Confucian *sonbi* community would reject and even ostracize him, he decided to follow Master Jesus. "The Teacher tried to reach the goal of his heart's great desire through Christianity." Kim had earlier defined Choe's desire and dream as "the concern of how to right the wrongs of the nation and to improve the life of the *minjung*,"[24] the common people.

As he read about Christianity and the West, he saw Christianity as a new way, or *tao,* a new philosophy of life, since it promised a new civilization based on a new vision of being human, just as in Confucianism and Buddhism. Choe apparently came to believe that the message that Appenzeller and Jones were preaching to him offered a new path for becoming a true human being (evangelization) and creating a new spiritual and material civilization as its consequence.[25]

Initially, Choe came to believe that the advanced and powerful civilizations of the West and their modernization were due to their

---

24. Kim Chinho, "Biography," 99–100.
25. Yi Dokju, *Formation of Indigenous Church*, 43–47. Yi Dokju argues in reverse that "Both the Roman Catholic Church and Protestant missions played a part in hastening the collapse of the social order of Korean feudal order." Protestant missionaries and their church were seen as a party of the modernization movement, leading to various reactions from the conservative party (Baby Riots of 1889, Pyongyang Persecution of 1894, 1900 secret edict to annihilate all Christians, etc.).

Christian religion. He saw their initial attempt at education[26] (the most trusted and tried way of self-cultivation and national power in Confucianism) and medicine (in its care for the suffering people) as a proof of its truth, as well as its practical and beneficial nature.[27]

Choe's conversion to Christ, however, was not a typical emotional experience such as the ones Appenzeller or Jones had experienced in their youth at revival meetings. His conversion process took over four years. Yet, like Appenzeller and Jones, Choe also had to make a dramatic and binding decision to accept Christ as the Lord and Savior of his life. His decision did not come from a revivalist's call to walk down to the mourner's bench or to the altar of prayer, but his soul heard a clarion call as he spoke frankly with Jones and Appenzeller, listened carefully to the sermons in the first Christian church in Seoul, read the Bible carefully and methodically, and delighted in the books that opened new vistas and horizons to him. It was the voice of a person, "Yesu-ssi" (*Master Jesus*), the universal Savior of the world, atoning for human sin on the cross for humanity, calling him.

Choe was not interested in any Savior. His sense of despair at his own society and the unfulfilled needs of the nation demanded a Savior who would be able to truly save the Korean people and the nation caught in a desperate crisis. The people were caught

---

26. It must have been a relief to Choe that the Protestant missionaries, unlike the Catholic mission, gained favor with the Royal Court and received the names for their first educational institutions from the king and the queen directly, Paichai Haktang and Ewha Haktang. BFM-MEC, *Annual Report*, 1887: 23.
27. James Huntley Grayson, *Korea: A Religious History* (Oxford: Clarendon Press, 1989), 198. Paik Jong Koe also argues that missionaries in China and Korea taught that Christianity had beneficial social impact (e.g., W.A.P. Martin and Ernst Faber, whose books American missionaries in Korea used as part of their theological curriculum) and presented the Ten Commandments as Christian ethical norms plus their evangelical-pietist ethics. They also viewed traditional ethics both positively (e.g., monogamy, sincerity, and filial piety) and negatively (e.g., sexual discrimination and slavery). He says that early American missionaries emphasized the idea of Christianity as a creator of new civilization and culture (*munmyong kaewha*), introducing the concepts of human rights and sexual egalitarianism in Korea. Paik Jong Koe, *Constructing Christian Faith in Korea*, 130–34.

between a rock and a hard place. They were in danger of losing their own identity (in the loss of the nation), and at the same time, they knew they were not ready to ride the wave of modernity that was crashing on the shores of their culture. The nation was in moral disarray, with the leading families and upper classes breaking the laws indiscriminately for their own profit and self-interest. They had no concern for the people's welfare or the nation's future. Its doors had been battered down from the outside by foreign powers. Now, it faced an uncertain future of change and reform, renewal and modernization, and the suffering of the people continued to grow unabated.

Choe himself had suffered at the hands of corrupt and dishonest men who controlled the government and its legal system. He had seen how inter-party feuding among the ruling classes had so deformed the *kwago* system that it only promoted those who would only further impoverish the people and flaunt the laws of the land for their own stomachs and families. He had seen the desperation in the frightened eyes of the people fleeing from the capital during the 1882 Imo Military Mutiny and the 1884 Kapo Rebellion—people seeking to flee to a place of safety and refuge. Luckily, he and his family owned some land in the Samak Valley of Poun County in North Chungchong Province—historically, one of the "ten best places to flee" in times of war or national crisis.[28] They found temporary refuge there before he was rudely thrown in jail as a victim of an extortion scheme by government officials. He believed Jesus would be such a Savior for the Korean people. He would offer them the Great Way of Truth as the true salvation for the people and the nation caught in a storm from within and without. He believed Jesus would give the Korean people a new heart and a new home.

---

28. Choe Chaewon, *Biography*, 115.

No doubt he had many unanswered questions about this Western Jesus, and whether he would be able to save an Eastern people such as the Koreans. He had to overcome his initial fears as well as the cultural shock of the Western missionaries, but he found them to be genuinely concerned for the people as they tried to educate the Korean children, heal the people, and offer the good news of Jesus to everyone. As a *sonbi*, he placed the highest premium on the unity of word and action, belief and practice. For over four years, he had watched and observed carefully what they said and what they did, how they lived and how they loved. He was genuinely touched by their compassion and sacrifice, and impressed by their courage and insight. Through the witness of their words and life, he came to see Jesus as more than just a Western Savior. He believed that Jesus was the Savior of the whole world, who came to show "the Great Way of Truth," in which is revealed the universal God.

4.3 Jesus, the Self-Sacrificing Savior

In Choe's eyes, the most amazing fact about this Savior was that he was a self-sacrificing Savior, unlike the founders of the three major Korean traditional religions: Confucius, Buddha, and Lao Tzu. While the latter three were considered saints sent by God to bring order and conscience among the people of the East, they could not be compared to Jesus. In "Conversation among the Three," he writes that as *Hananim,* or God himself, Jesus is different from the Asian sages.

> Savior Jesus is not a sage like Confucius, Mencius, or Lao Tzu, but is actually *Hananim* (God) himself…When we look at his activities on this earth—resurrecting the dead, healing the sick, opening the eyes of the blind, making the deaf hear, making the lame walk, cleansing the lepers, feeding the 5,000 with five rice cakes and two fish—we know these

wonders and miracles cannot be done by a sage. Of them, the greatest thing is that he was crucified on a cross and died, and atoned for the sins of all people of all nations. Originally as the Third Person in the Trinity, God became incarnate on earth. But he possessed the power of God; thus he cannot be compared to a holy saint. He is the sole Savior of all nations of the West and the East, past and present.[29]

Jesus' superiority over Asian sages springs not only from his divine personhood, but his death on the cross, which was Jesus' self-sacrifice on behalf of the world's people and their sins. Later on, Choe's initial understanding would become deepened through theological training and Biblical studies, such as in the "Doctrine of Sin" (K: Choedori) and *Reflections on the Holy Mountain* (K: Songsan myongkyong). But from the beginning, Choe recognized a central difference between the religions of the East and Jesus' salvation. In "The Birthday of the Savior," Choe again emphasizes the difference between Jesus and the founding sages of the Eastern religions:

> In our opinion, the teachings of the ancient sages had much benefit for their followers, but none of them atoned for the sins of the world's people like the Savior. If the Savior did not have the power to atone for the sins, then he would not have become incarnated, nor would we have believed nor rejoiced at his birth. But through Jesus' coming, he saved myriads of people from their sins.[30]

If the main difference between Jesus and the Eastern religious founders is his saving work on the cross, it also points to a new discovery about God that the religion of his ancestors had missed.

---

29. Choe Pyonghon, "Conversation Among the Three" (K), *Korean Christian Advocate* (K), March 21, 1900, 68. Hereafter, *KCA* will be used for the *Korean Christian Advocate*.
30. Choe Pyonghon, "The Birthday of the Savior" (K), *KCA*, December 16, 1899, 293.

In each of Choe's biographies,[31] the centrality of the love of God in Choe's theology is highlighted, encapsulated in Matt. 5:44–48:

> But I say to you, Love your enemies and pray for those who persecute you, so that you may be children of your Father in heaven; for he makes his sun rise on the evil and on the good, and sends rain on the righteous and on the unrighteous. For if you love those who love you, what reward do you have? Do not even the tax-collectors do the same? And if you greet only your brothers and sisters, what more are you doing than others? Do not even the Gentiles do the same? Be perfect, therefore, as your heavenly Father is perfect. (*NRSV*)

For Choe, these verses described the broad, universal, and unfathomable love of God, which was so different from the image of God that was found in other Eastern religions. Noble describes an early encounter of Choe with Christianity in action, in which he saw many Koreans walking by and ignoring a poor sick woman by the side of the road. Then, a foreign missionary came by and took pity on her and took her to the hospital, treated her for free, and cured her. He saw in this action the love of Christ being poured out for the people of Korea and the internal dynamic of the Christian *tao*.

In his understanding of Jesus' self-sacrificing atonement on the cross, which he learned through his reading of the Gospel and the entire Bible, Choe had come across a critical key for understanding the new faith: the Christian Creator is not like all the other gods. Jesus' God is beneficent and kind, merciful and compassionate, long-suffering and full of joy. This Creator is not angry or vindictive. This was a major discovery about Jesus and his God that would influence

---

31. Both Noble's and Kim's accounts of Choe's life mention the centrality of the text from the Sermon on the Mount (Matthew 5:44–48) as a key to understanding Choe's initiation into Christian faith. Choe saw these words as defining the inner core of Christianity as a religion of love. Mattie Wilcox Noble, *Victorious Lives of Early Christians in Korea* (Seoul: Christian Literature Society, 1933), 116–17. Kim Chinho, "Short Biography," 100.

his future spiritual experiences and color his later theological development.

In "The Birthday of the Savior," Choe describes how the mercy and compassion of this God of salvation is to be understood.

> When the sins of the earth's people increased, God could have sent floods like the time of Noah, or sent fire from heaven like Sodom and Gomorrah. But God looked with pity on the total destruction of the billions of creaturely life and sent a Savior to atone for the sins of all people. Then heaven's door was opened, and he became the mediator of the way of life, making the dead to live again, healing the sick, enabling the lowest sinner to come near the most high God. When we think of such grace, how can we not be thankful and rejoice?[32]

Choe saw this as the "love" of God that had been extended to the entire human race and the created world, and came to adopt this law of love as the primary rule of his life.[33] When he came to the end of his long examination of the Christian religion, he decided to "taste" for himself the "way of salvation" in Jesus Christ, to experience the law of love in his own life, and to set out on a new path of national renaissance and enlightenment.[34]

The God of love had sent such a Savior of self-sacrificing love to the world. In time, this Savior would save the Koreans from their sins and bring them back to a right relationship with God. If this was true, then it was urgent for the whole nation of Korea to turn to this God and his Savior. Here was the Savior who would enlighten and edify the Korean people, and through them, establish a new nation. Choe did not understand the salvation of the Korean people in a dualistic way: saving the people's souls for heaven, but letting their bodies suffer below. Rather, he saw the saved souls as those who were being

---

32. Choe Pyonghon, "Birthday," 293.
33. Mattie W. Noble, *Victorious Lives*, 122.
34. Kim Chinho, "Biography," 100.

changed by the sacrificial love of God into a new people. They would imitate the love of their Savior in their life with others.

In his conversion, there is a clear sense of the power of Jesus' salvation to influence the destiny of the Korean people and the Korean nation. In the first edition of the *Korean Christian Advocate* (K: Choson Kuristoin Hoebo), which Choe edited with Henry G. Appenzeller in 1897, they editorialize:

> How sad, our compatriot brethren. Do not favor only Eastern books, nor consider only our ancestors' deeds righteous. When we look at Eastern history, we notice that the Ha nation celebrated loyalty, the Un nation venerated respect, and the Chu nation respected civilized politics. Their gradual change was wrought by God and not by human strength. As we encounter all the nations of the world in this era of mutual interaction, the people of the East must not read only Eastern writings nor venerate only the Eastern Way (*tao*) or only keep up with the news of the East. Read our *Advocate* and you will naturally learn useful information about the world and interesting historical events of each nation.[35]

Choe makes a strong connection between the Christian message of Jesus and the mighty Western civilization. In response to the Korean people's search for a new path of survival in the modern world, Choe pointed to the sociopolitical implications of the missionary preaching about Jesus' saving power. Jesus would help make Korea a Christian nation with the necessary scientific, technological, and philosophical support needed to build a strong nation, just like the homeland of the missionaries.

In his first publicly preached sermon in Korea, on Christmas Day, 1887, Henry G. Appenzeller, the Methodist Episcopal Church's first missionary in Korea, preached from the text, Matthew 1:21: "Thou

---

35. Choe Pyonghon and Henry G. Appenzeller, "We Publish the Korean Advocate" (K), *KCA*, February 2, 1897, 1. The author is unnamed, but since they were co-editors, we can assume that both had their input in it.

shalt call his name Jesus, for he shall save his people from their sin." Appenzeller's message from the very beginning had been a simple one—believe in Jesus, the Savior of the Korean people from sin, and the creator of a Christian nation like the modern, powerful, and wealthy Western countries that believe in Jesus.[36]

Likewise, Jones writes in 1894, after he began his work at Chemulpo, "We have felt that God is indeed the God of all the earth and Christianity is God's own remedy for all ill."[37] What Choe heard from these two missionaries initially was the message that Christianity is a religion of salvation and that Jesus is the Savior, not only of the Western people, but also of the Korean people and the entire world. The benefits of his salvation, won through his sacrifice and death on the cross, were applicable both to the Korean people and to the nation, which was being pushed onto the path of industrial modernization and political liberalization.

4.4 Can a Western Savior Save the East?

In his five-year sojourn toward the truth of this Savior of love, this central question held his attention: "Can a Western Savior save the people of the East, including the Koreans?" If he had entertained inner doubts about the wisdom of turning away from the books of his ancestors, the Jesus he found in the new Book had quieted his anxiety and assured him that salvation was available to him and his people. Adopting the new Book was not a betrayal of the "faith of his

---

36. Davies, *Life and Thought of Appenzeller*, 144–50. "The Appenzellers believed the bringing of civilization and progress (i.e., Western technology and American culture) to Korea part of their responsibility as missionaries…and worked in Korea for the Kingdom of God on earth patterned on the United States." Although he recognized that the United States failed to live up to the standard of the Kingdom of God on earth, it was still a standard for other nations. He believed that God had commissioned the Anglo-Saxon race to spread Protestantism throughout the world to "remove all forms of corruption from human life."
37. Jones, May 10, 1894, Diary; part of "Report on First Six Months, Chemulpo Circuit."

fathers" nor was there any disrespect intended in "laying aside the 'old book' that had served its purpose so long and taking the newer and better book." After all, the Christian Bible was not such a new book, but was the "oldest of all books and which alone contained the truth without which no true and victorious life was possible."[38]

At his conversion, Choe came to see Jesus as the universal Savior, preaching not a "Western" *tao,* or way, but a universal way. He would later name it "the great way of truth" (*chili taedo*). He recognized "the great way of truth,"[39] which revealed the universal God, so that he could profess, "The eastern sky is the western sky, and the Sovereign Lord (*Sangje*) of the West is the Sovereign Lord of the East. The people there are also ruled by God (*Hananim*)."[40] From the very first, Choe came to see Jesus not as a foreigner, but as the universal Savior, whose salvific power extended to the Korean people and their situation. He came to understand Christianity and Jesus as the Savior who will save the national community by meeting the historical demands of reform and enlightenment as well as the religious and spiritual needs of the Korean people.

In summary, at his conversion, Choe affirmed his faith in Jesus, the world-saving Savior. First, in Jesus, he saw a different kind of a Savior, unlike the sage-founders of Eastern religions. He was a Savior who gave himself up for the people's sin and took their sins upon himself. Second, in Jesus, he saw the love of God the Father, who came near to the people and opened the door for the people to approach his majesty, unlike the transcendent Sovereign Lord (*Sangje*) of the East, who remained lofty and demanded the people's

---

38. Ibid. For a historical-sociological reading of this encounter, see Chai-Sik Chung, "Confucian-Protestant Encounter in Korea: Two Cases of Westernization and De-Westernization," in *Confucian-Christian Encounters in Historical and Contemporary Perspective*, ed. Peter K.H. Lee (Lewiston, NY: The Edwin Mellen Press, 1991), 399–433.
39. This phrase first appears in Choe and Appenzeller, "We Publish the Christian Advocate," 1.
40. Choe Pyonghon, "Great Disease of Humanity," *KCA*, August 30, 1899, 510; Choe Pyonghon, "Eastern Sages Also Worshipped God," *KCA*, June 14, 1899, 452.

fear and respect. Third, in Jesus, Choe saw the Christian faith as opening the way for a new humanity to be born on the Korean soil as the people were transformed by the Spirit of Jesus, and as they imitated his way of self-sacrifice in their relationships. This faith would ultimately lead the people to become true human beings (*kyohwa*), which would naturally lead to a new civilization (*kaehwa munmyong*). Fourth, Choe began to see Jesus not as a foreign Savior, but as the universal Savior of the universal God. He himself overcame the pull of his traditional education and tradition—"the old book." As he picked up the "new book," he recognized it not as a Western religion, but as the universal, great way of truth (*chili taedo*).

Choe's faith at his conversion was thoroughly based on the stories of Jesus found in the Bible. Having met Jesus primarily in the Bible through his Confucian reading of sacred texts, Choe interpreted Jesus as the Savior sent by the universal God of the world who ruled the eastern as well as the western sky and peoples. He saw Jesus as the embodiment of God's love that was universal, a love that was primarily seen in the self-sacrifice of Jesus on the cross. This made him different from all the other mediators in Asian religions. By defining Jesus and his God as the universal Savior and universal God, Choe placed Jesus into the circle of East Asian mediators who brought about reconciliation between heaven, earth, and humanity. He was now ready to become an evangelist for his Master Jesus, the loving Savior of the world and the Hope of the Korean people and nation.

PART III

Part 3: Jesus the Savior of the Korean People

5

Jones, 1892–1903: Witnessing God's Power to Save

"How did God save the Korean people and society through Jones's missionary service in Chemulpo?" In this chapter, we see Jones at work, building the church of Jesus the Savior at the busiest meeting point of the East and the West during a decade of great social upheavals in Korea.

5.1 Overview of the Missionary Work at Chemulpo

During the eleven years of missionary service in Chemulpo (modern Inchon), Jones established forty-four churches and baptized over 3,000 believers. He became an apostle of Jesus the Savior to the people of Korea. In 1910, Jones reviewed his work at Chemulpo with the following words, "The work at Chemulpo has maintained its evangelistic and educational character from the first. It has resulted in the founding of an influential self-supporting church in Chemulpo, which is a fountainhead of aggressive evangelistic activity reaching to all the neighborhoods in the vicinity of the port."[1] These carefully chosen words by Jones reveal how he carried out the work of

---

1. George H. Jones and W. Arthur Noble, *The Korean Revival: An Account of the Revival in the*

spreading the message of his American Christ to this new area. The work at Chemulpo had five clear foci: 1) carrying out an aggressive evangelistic outreach; 2) forming self-supporting local churches; 3) organizing schools, Sunday Schools, and youth organizations such as the Epworth League; 4) organizing theological and leadership training of local church pastors and lay leaders; and 5) publishing literary and religious books.

The quality and quantity of work that Jones did in Chemulpo can be seen in the description of his accomplishments, found in his death announcement,

> There were no Christians in all that region. Ten years later there was a presiding elder's district with 44 organized churches; 22 local preachers and exhorters; 100 class leaders; and 2,800 Christians (members, not probationers); and Dr. Jones had the unique honor of being the presiding elder of a district, every church of which he had himself organized; every preacher and class leader was a son in the Gospel to him; and he had personally baptized every church member in the district. There are today (1919) seventeen members of the Korean Annual Conference who were won to Christ by Dr. Jones, and all of these men have records as soul winners.[2]

5.2 How Jesus, the Incarnate Mediator, Saves the Common People

As noted earlier, American missionaries used the shorthand, "Christianize and uplift" to express the two main directions of the missionary task in Korea. Central to this task of preaching the Gospel

---

Korean Churches in 1907 (New York: Board of Foreign Missions of the Methodist Episcopal Church, 1910), 29.

2. Board of Foreign Missions of the Methodist Episcopal Church, "Death of Dr. George Heber Jones," Writings and Photographs, Mission Geographical Reference Files 1880s–1960, Folders 1466-4-7:22, General Commission on Archives and History of the United Methodist Church, Drew University, Madison, NJ.

of Jesus was the proclamation of the divine Jesus who became a human being to be their Mediator and Savior. In the first decade of American missions in Korea, the earliest missionaries carried out their missionary task through a three-pronged approach: medicine,[3] education,[4] and evangelism. But in all their activities, their primary focus was always aimed at starting and nurturing a vibrant, indigenous church for Jesus the Savior.[5]

When they began their public and open evangelism, starting in 1890, it was natural for them to turn to these images of Christ connected with their initial missionary activities: Christ the Teacher, Christ the Healer, and Christ the new Savior, promising eternal life and heaven. As the Gospel spread among diverse classes of people, Jesus was described and called by other creative and colorful names and images. In addition to Savior, Healer, and Teacher, Jesus was the Protector and Brother of women; for the working classes, he was the Co-laborer; for upper class dissidents, the *Sonbi*; for the elderly population, the Giver of Eternal life; and for the lower castes and social outcasts, the Liberator and Friend. Thus, in the process of becoming rooted in Korea, Jesus became all things to all people. Jones

---

3. "Korea was opened by the lancet of the physician." Jones, "The Christian Impact on Korean Life," Papers, 3; see also, George Heber Jones, *Christian Medical Work in Korea* (New York: Board of Foreign Missions of the Methodist Episcopal Church, Korea Quarter-Centennial Commission, 1910), 7.
4. It wasn't that Koreans were not devoted to education. That they were. However, missionaries wanted to introduce modern education fit to bring Korea into modern civilization, especially education of the sciences. By 1909, more than 1,400 of 2,000 schools, from elementary to college, were maintained by the church and under Christian control. Jones, "The Christian Impact," Papers, 4; and Jones, "Education in Relation," Papers, 8.
5. At Paichai Haktang, they would begin to describe Jesus Christ as the "greatest Teacher of mankind." Board of Foreign Missions of the Methodist Episcopal Church (hereafter, BFM-MEC), *Annual Report*, Korea Mission 1884–1943, collected and bound as *Annual Report of the Board of Foreign Missions of the Methodist Episcopal Church, Korea Mission 1884–1943*. Compiled by Hankuk kidokkyo yoksa yonguso (Seoul: Institute for Korean Church History, 1993), 1896: 116. At medical centers and hospitals, they would begin to dispense Jesus Christ as the Healer, "But we do tell them, often for the first time, of the One who can cure them of their soul's disease, and who can cleanse them from all sin and give pardon, peace and purity." BFM-MEC, *Annual Report*, 1897: 137.

knew that Jesus' power and might were infinite, and his arm was not too short to save all peoples of all nations.

Hwamok: Christ the Reconciliation

But a challenge awaited them. How were they "to teach Korea that Jesus Christ is its only Savior and hope?"[6] It was a question demanding a solution. Twenty years later, as he began his new appointment as the first president of the Biblical Institute of Korea (renamed Methodist Theological Seminary of Korea in 1911), Jones made it a rule of thumb to throw out all Western theological texts because of their "theological provincialism."[7] Jones argued that the Korean church would not benefit from Western texts that address theological issues mainly out of "philosophical doubts and intellectual debates." The Korean church he had helped grow was grappling with practical issues related to life, such as, "What's wrong with ancestral rituals? What's the matter with polytheism? Why is it wrong for a man to own slaves and have three wives?"[8]

For Jones, Western texts necessarily bore a kind of theological provincialism because of their "racial and civilizational limitations, and thus cannot occupy the place of primacy in the Korean church which is accorded them in the West. That place is filled by only one book—the Bible."[9] The Koreans proclaimed the good news of Jesus as they encountered him in the Bible, and through their own spiritual experiences and practices of faith. Especially in these early years in Chemulpo, Jones recognized that Jesus must be proclaimed where the common people lived. The people also needed to learn

---

6. BFM-MEC, *Annual Report*, 1888: 28.
7. Jones, "The Transformation of a Nation," Papers, 15.
8. Ibid., 14.
9. Ibid., 15.

new concepts of the Bible—a new language, as it were. Thus, the missionaries focused on simply telling and retelling the Jesus story to the people. This became the content of the good news of Jesus that Jones proclaimed, and which the Korean church accepted.

As the message of Jesus began to spread, it became known as the *Yesukyo* (Religion or Teaching of Jesus) or *Kusekyo* or *Kusechukyo* (Religion of Salvation or Religion of the Savior). Their preaching became more and more centered on Jesus as the atonement for human sin, who, through his own suffering and death, defeated death and brought salvation to humankind.

In November 1900, Jones, William B. Scranton, and W. Arthur Noble, as leaders of the Methodist Episcopal Mission in Korea, met with leading Korean church leaders to reach a consensus on major theological terms. For atonement, they chose the term *hwamok,* with *sokyang* (redemption) and *sokchoe* (forgiveness of sin) as alternatives favored by Noble and Scranton, respectively. *Hwamok* is made up of two Chinese characters meaning harmony and friendship. *Hwa* has various connotations of fittingness, peacefulness, unity, lack of conflict, and responsiveness; *mok* literally refers to "kind eyes" and connotes friendliness, closeness, softness, and accessibility.

All three terms describe the result of Christ's act of atonement: reconciliation, redemption, and forgiveness of sin. In selecting *hwamok,* the early Methodist leaders chose a word that held great meaning for the neo-Confucian religious tradition of Korea, which saw "cosmic peace and harmony" as the highest goal of all religious and intellectual pursuits. For example, in *The Great Learning* of Chu Hsi, a clear line of progression and mutual influence is seen in the work of the Great Learning in human society. It covered all of reality, stretching from the investigation of reality (intellectual pursuit) to cosmic harmony. The goal of cultivation of the self (*susin*) is to bring order to the family (*cheka*), which leads to righteous rule of the nation (*chikuk*) that establishes peaceful harmony over the entire universe (*pyong chonha*).

Jones and the early Methodist missionaries quickly recognized that the aim of all Korean religious traditions was to answer the question, "How can I live the good life as a good person?" All of them claimed that true humanity is achieved when there is a union or harmony with heaven, or *Hananim,* the One God of Heaven. The missionaries sought to answer the central question being asked by the Korean people by focusing on Jesus as the mediator, reconciling humanity to God and to each other.[10]

5.3 Jesus of the Bible Seen in Chemulpo

We see Jones's understanding of Jesus most clearly expressed in the accounts of Incarnation that are given in the *Sinhak Wolpo,* or *Theological Monthly*, which Jones began publishing in late 1900. Because of a lack of written materials geared to the emerging Korean church, the published articles in the *Sinhak Wolpo* became the textbook as well as the newsletter of the early theological training of ministerial candidates and lay leaders in the Korean Methodist circle. When Jones returned to Korea in June 1906, after a three-year furlough, he found that the journal had been discontinued. As the official seminary opened in 1907, using the Jones's training class model, Jones resumed the *Sinhak Wolpo*, publishing the theological lectures given at the training sessions.

The first major theological piece in the *Sinhak Wolpo* is J. S. Gale's "Thoughts on the Incarnation,"[11] which largely reflects Jones's

---

10. Jones, November 21, 1900, Diary. See this diary entry for a list of other words.
11. James S. Gale, "Thoughts on the Incarnation," *Sinhak Wolpo* 1, no. 1 (December 1900): 16–20 (Hereafter, *SW*).

perspective on Jesus and his work of salvation. While the Christmas issue of the *Sinhak Wolpo* is naturally focused on the Incarnation, Gale's thoughts capture the "Jesus" emphasis of the Christian Gospel being proclaimed in Korea by American missionaries.

First, Gale focuses on the fact that Jesus was sent by God to share the suffering of humanity and become the mediator between God and humanity. Second, he argues that Jesus is both God and human, using several examples to prove the New Testament paradox that in and with Jesus of Nazareth, humanity encounters the living God, and yet in and with Jesus of Nazareth, humanity encounters one of its own kind. He does not try to explain this paradox, but tries to present this story as he finds it in the Scriptures. Thus, Jesus sleeping on the boat is a sign of his humanity, and his calming the seas is a sign that he is of divine origin. His suffering on the cross is a sign of his humanity, while his promise of eternal life to the thief on the cross reveals that he is the "omnipresent, omnipotent God." Third, Gale lays stress on the moral of the Incarnation story. It is imperative for the followers of Jesus to imitate and embody the righteousness and love of God shown by Jesus.

Finally, he offers a modern parable to illustrate the Incarnation of Christ in the story of Peter the Great (perhaps given the dominance of Russia in Korean politics at that time). He tells how Peter the Great looked at the sad situation of his nation and people and took on the form of a common citizen to learn the skills of military training and shipbuilding in order to strengthen his nation and serve his people.

Mirroring the aim of this article, Jones teaches the early Korean Christians to adopt a simple understanding of Jesus, based on the Bible. He teaches a commonsense unity of the person of Christ, claiming that the philosophical basis of the historical understanding of classic Western Christology is part of the "provincial theology" of the West. He holds together the divinity and humanity of Jesus, without trying to explain the intricacies of the Chalcedonian two-natures doctrine.[12]

Like Gale, Jones gives weight to the very example of Jesus as the model for human life in his 1899 Christmas sermon. Jesus is the moral example because he shares our humanity, but is at the same time, from God and is God. It is both Jesus' identity with the human situation and also his discontinuity—his divinity—that qualifies him to be our Savior. This, in a nutshell, is the Chalcedonian definition of the two natures that are not to be confused or switched or separated, although he does not offer any explanation of it. While Jones's sermon tries to retell the sense of the New Testament witness to Jesus' incarnation as historical, his chief concern is focused on the salvation of humanity.

This salvation emphasis comes out clearly in "Jesus' Birth and Its Purposes"[13] in which Jones explicitly states that the purpose of Jesus' incarnation was to die on Golgotha for human salvation. Then, he uses a series of metaphors to explain the meaning of the redemption wrought by Jesus' incarnation and crucifixion. Heaven's door is opened; humanity can now look upon God's face; there is a now

---

12. The doctrine of the "hypostatic union," or the two-nature doctrine of Jesus, was determined at the Council of Chalcedon in 451 CE. It reads in part, "Therefore, following the holy fathers, we all with one accord teach men to acknowledge one and the same Son, our Lord Jesus Christ, at once complete in Godhead and complete in manhood, truly God and truly man, consisting also of a reasonable soul and body; of one substance with the Father as regards his Godhead, and at the same time of one substance with us as regards his manhood; like us in all respects, apart from sin; as regards his Godhead, begotten of the Father before the ages, but yet as regards his manhood begotten, for us men and for our salvation, of Mary the Virgin, the God-bearer; one and the same Christ, Son, Lord, Only-begotten, recognized in two natures, without confusion, without change, without division, without separation; the distinction of natures being in no way annulled by the union, but rather the characteristics of each nature being preserved and coming together to form one person and subsistence, not as parted or separated into two persons, but one and the same Son and Only-begotten God the Word, Lord Jesus Christ; even as the prophets from earliest times spoke of him, and our Lord Jesus Christ himself taught us, and the creed of the fathers has handed down to us."For the full text in Greek and English, see "The Chalcedonian Definition." Early Church Texts. <http://www.earlychurchtexts.com/main/chalcedon/chalcedonian_definition.shtml>.
13. George Heber Jones, "Jesus' Birth and Its Purposes," *SW* 1, no. 12 (November 1901): 483–86.

mediator between God and humanity, who reconciles humanity to God; and the way to heaven and eternal life is opened. Rather than looking at what Jesus is reported to have done and said or meant, Jones emphasizes what it all adds up to.

Again, in "The Love of the Brethren,"[14] Jones explains the significance of Christ's incarnation: Jesus shows us the Father's love so that we, too, may love others. Jesus' example of love shows his infinite patience and humility, so that in "following Jesus' example, we may not live only for ourselves but for others, according to Christ's will."[15] Jones's understanding of the Incarnation always includes both a redemptive and an ethical focus. At the same time, it is not our humanly-manufactured love for others, but the indwelling Christ who enables us to love others—once again hearkening back to Bushnell's teaching on Christ as the divine presence in us.

From early on, Jones preached often on the topic of Christ's sacrifice on behalf of humanity. When the workers at Chemulpo asked him to train them in the faith, his first Worker's Training Class, in 1893, centered on the Book of Hebrews, on the topic of Jesus, our High Priest, as the fulfiller of Old Testament prophecies of Isaiah and the prophets. He held fifteen sessions on Hebrews, helping them to interpret the Scriptures by Scripture, especially the relationship of Old Testament to the New Testament.

His goal was to "to thoroughly embue (*sic*) them with the mighty truth of the atonement and the priestly character of Christ's relation to this sinning race."[16] Working out of this framework, Jones turned to the Old Testament system of sacrifices as the first covenant to explain Jesus as the sacrifice of the second covenant. As he taught them, Jones was aware of the system of sacrifices that held the Korean

---

14. George Heber Jones, "The Love of the Brethren," *SW* 2, no. 5 (May 1902): 112–18.
15. Ibid., 16.
16. Jones, May 10, 1894, Diary, 464–65.

people together and the presence of many mediators in their religious traditions. For example, the founding "father" of Korean nation, Tangun, is known as a shaman-priest-king, a mediator between *Hananim* and humanity. He offered yearly sacrifices on behalf of the people. Buddhism also is filled with mediators, especially the Maitreya Buddha, whose compassion for suffering humanity knew no bounds. It was natural, then, that Jones added Jesus to this pantheon of Eastern mediators, using the salvation history framework of the Bible—creation, fall, redemption, and heaven—to provide a cogent and powerful narrative of Jesus as the Final Mediator.

Jones describes the result of the training of the lay and clergy leadership, who, during the developmental period (1894–1906), attended semi-annual training classes and Bible conferences that were held typically for ten days, with daily sessions running from nine in the morning to midnight. It produced pastoral leaders who have "…an humble and invincible faith in the Deity of our Lord and in His atoning work upon the Cross. They are men of one Book and their preaching is marked by a thorough saturation of Bible matter."[17] What Jones had planned in terms of theological education was bearing its rightful fruit: an indigenous church leadership who saw Jesus as the divine Mediator, who transforms the traditional notions of sacrifice and mediators with his own self-sacrifice on the cross on behalf of a sinful humanity.

5.4 Jesus and the Common People

Finally, the Incarnated Mediator came to bring salvation to a people in sin, especially those who suffered the most from the effects of sin. Jones found the people flocking to the Gospel because, "the people

---

17. Jones, "The Growth of the Church in Korea," Papers, 30.

were tired out, weary, and disheartened with the barrenness of pagan beliefs and religions,"[18] which resulted in numerous social diseases: polygamy, slavery, women's oppression, outcaste class, absolute monarchy, and oppressive power of the ruling classes. As he came to know the Korean people, Jones personally came in contact with the life of the *minjung,* or the masses, and their troubles as well as their long-suffering perseverance. He quickly realized that the message of Jesus was indeed "the Good News" with "its radiant promise of better things"[19] for a people living in such dire situations. At times, Jones despaired of the people's sinful situation. After one year of work in Chemulpo, he wrote:

> Margaret and I were talking today of the awful scene Asia presents and how it afflicts us. It seems as though I have spent the last six years in a disguised hell. I long to go home to morally recuperate, for it seems as if I can hardly bear these sights and sounds longer, nor endure a knowledge of more evils. It shakes the very foundations of one's moral nature.[20]

Jones did not need to be convinced that humanity is sinful. Nor did the Koreans, for they lived in sin and suffered the consequences of sin: alienation from the true God, hostility among peoples according to class and status, the repression of women and children, polygamy, slavery, corruption in high places that corrupted every other relationship in the society, the deadly stupor of alcohol, a fear of death, and the hordes of spirits that haunted every corner of the land.

In his 1899 Christmas sermon, from Luke 2:10–15, Jones declares:

> The gospel was first preached, not to the learned scholars, the wealthy aristocrats or the King of the land, but to lowly shepherds. This ought to fill those of us who are learned with humility and empty us of the

---

18. George Heber Jones, *Korea: The Land, People and Customs* (Cincinnati, OH: Jennings and Graham, 1907), 105.
19. Ibid., 105.
20. Jones, November 3, 1893, Diary.

pride of learning; empty those of us who are aristocrats of our pride of birth and position; and fill those of us who are lowly born with love and humility in God's sight.[21]

For Jones, Jesus—the Incarnated Mediator—came to announce "new personal values for humanity," including human dignity and full acceptance for every ordinary human being. He turns to the example of Korea's tattered "*yangbanism*" to tell the story of the freedom which the Incarnated Mediator offered to the Korean masses.

> One day a Korean nobleman, on my invitation, attended divine services, and after it was over he came to my house as my guest and discussed frankly his impressions. Among other things he said, "I notice that you preach and offer Christianity to our low class people. This is a great mistake on your part, for they can never become Christians. They are too inferior and ignoble. Do you know how we regard them? We say that society is organized on a basis of big fish, little fish, shrimps and mud. The big fish eat the little fish, the little fish eat the shrimps and the shrimps eat the mud. These people are but mud beneath our feet. They exist but for a day and pass away forever. Why waste time upon them?" That was the general attitude (of the *yangban*) toward the masses. They were regarded as mud beneath the feet of the super-man of the times, and they had no defender. Then came the Son of God, who identified Divinity with their humanity, selecting their class as the vehicle of the divine incarnation, and thereby putting the stamp of the divine interest, God's confidence, and God's high value upon the common ordinary folks…He created a new sense of personal dignity and worth, and thereby made possible all future democracies.[22]

5.5 "Ancestor Worship" = Old Korea

On his first "unauthorized" exploratory trip out of Seoul into the interior in 1891, Jones came across the familiar sight of a Korean

---

21. Jones, December 24, 1899, Diary.
22. Jones, "The Release of Power through Sacrifices;" Sermons and Addresses.

family mourning at its ancestral burial grounds. After watching them, he penned a poem called "Ancestral Worship":

> Far from all scene where Christian men
> Are found God's will to do
> Where naught is known of hope or heaven
> Nor of things pure and true.
>
> Beneath the sunlit smiling sky
> Amid fields fresh and green
> Where one would start to hear a sigh
> So glad did Nature seem.
>
> I saw the forms of heathen men
> Bow on the hillside fair
> In worship which had shackled them
> To hopeless, dark despair.
>
> Their white clad forms at altars knelt
> The wind their praises bore
> Praises wrung from souls that felt
> Grief unrelieved sore.
>
> Their altar was the new made grass
> The men bowed to its dead
> No ray of light came thence to save
> Or guide through realms of dead.
>
> Those sounds of praises were cries of grief
> Bewailing loved ones gone
> Yet vainly sought those hearts relief
> In funereal song.
>
> Ancestral worship! Naught of bliss
> Thou bridle the soul of Man
> What pride! Apotheosis
> And man bows down to Man.
>
> Ancestral worship! Awful fate
> When to that dark abode

> The plunging soul comes
> Finds in the grave its God. [23]

While this poem was written relatively early in Jones's missionary career in Korea, it marks the beginning of Jones's progressively profound reflections on this peculiar ritual of Choson's neo-Confucian society, called the *chesa,* or ancestral rites.[24] Later, ancestral worship would become a central object of attack in his sermons, theological education, and political analysis. In this poem, ancestral worship symbolizes the religious idolatry of Korean people, who worship their dead parents as their gods (apotheosis, "man bows down to man"), which is tantamount to an excessive observance of the sixth commandment that violates the first commandment. In his youthful eyes, the funereal cries, the dirges, and the ceremonial bows of ancestral worship amounted to a liturgical dead-end.

For Jones, ancestral worship was the single most important cultural key to understanding what made the Korean society tick. Jones came to the same conclusion that modern scholars of Choson Confucianism affirm: ancestor worship is the symbol of the Korean version of neo-Confucianism that revolutionized the Korean society in the fifteenth and sixteenth centuries. Like these scholars, Jones did not see ancestral worship simply as a religious ceremony or as a mark of heathen idolatry. Nor did he interpret it as an excessive form of filial piety, which he sincerely appreciated in his Korean members. Rather, he came to see it as the central symbol of the political and religious structure of the Korean society. One can see the move that

---

23. Jones, April 22, 1891, Diary.
24. For a discussion of neo-Confucianism, see William Theodore De Bary, *Neo-Confucian Orthodoxy and the Learning of the Mind-and-Heart* (New York: Columbia University Press, 1981) and his *The Message of the Mind in Neo-Confucianism* (New York: Columbia University Press, 1989). For Korean neo-Confucianism, see Martina Deuchler, *The Confucian Transformation of Korea: A Study of Society and Ideology* (Cambridge: Harvard University Press, 1992).

he would make later, when this simple act of a family grieving at the gravesite—a scene very reminiscent of an American funeral—is rightly understood as civil religion.

By 1895, he was able to express himself more clearly and critically. In a *Korean Repository* article, "Obstacles Encountered by Korean Christians,"[25] Jones identifies ancestor worship and shamanism—spirit worship—as the two major influences on Korean personality.

> Ancestor worship…is the State religion… (having) the Confucian Code as its ethics. The hold which this possesses on a Korean can hardly be overestimated; a hold which cannot be loosened without shaking the very foundations of his mental and moral being. The State religion, it enjoys all the sanctions which such an alliance can give it. But more than this it has its roots in the most sacred soil of human life, the family, and entwines itself about the tenderest of human relations, that of parent and child.[26]

Here, Jones recognizes how ancestor worship is formed in the family itself and reinforced in the educational system, with filial piety as "the center and circumference of all virtue,"[27] and parental authority deemed almost sacrosanct. But his central critique is that Confucianism is non-religious because it "ignored the divine side of religion and reduced it to a series of regulations to govern the relations of man with man."[28] Jones sees ancestral worship for what it truly was—an act of national identity, a loyalty oath.

This insight is very different from what other missionaries in his day or modern scholars often write about "ancestral worship," which is usually portrayed as an innocent religious ceremony or an effort at adding religiosity by the nonreligious Confucianism of Choson

---

25. George Heber Jones, "Obstacles Encountered by Korean Christians," *Korean Repository* 2 (Apr. 1895), 145–51 (hereafter *KR*).
26. Ibid., 145.
27. Ibid., 146.
28. Ibid., 147.

Korea. For example, Henry G. Appenzeller saw ancestral worship as a part of the Confucian ethical system that is a purely a religious act without power, and was the source of all Korean problems, since it worshiped human beings instead of God. Likewise, Horace G. Underwood interpreted it as idol worship in *The Call of Korea*. Some missionaries, such as James S. Gale, wanted nothing to do with the issue. Clark treated it as an ineffective, false religion.[29]

Jones saw it otherwise. In this sense, he did not take the same approach toward Choson neo-Confucianism as the first Korean Catholics, like Yi Pyok and Chong Yakjong had taken a century earlier.[30] They saw Christianity as complementing what was lacking in Confucianism, whereas Jones saw them as antagonistic. Cultural historian Choe Chunsik argues that the eighteenth-century Roman Catholic hierarchy did not realize the social significance of ancestral worship in Choson society when it prohibited the Korean Christians from observing this ritual.[31] It was the central communal act that reaffirmed the collective identity and the social order, based on social relationship of familism, expressed through *hyo* (filial piety) and *chung* (political loyalty).[32] When the Korean Catholic Church followed the directive of the Vatican and attacked the practice of ancestral

---

29. Appenzeller in Song Paikkol, *A Study*, 142. *The Call of Korea* (New York: Fleming H. Revell, 1908), 98. Gale in Yi Dokju, *Formation of Indigenous Church*, 80. Charles Allen Clark, *First Fruits in Korea* (New York: Fleming H. Revell Co., 1921), 240.
30. For Chong Yakjong's theology, see Hector Diaz, *A Korean Theology: Chu-Gyo Yo-Ji: Essentials of the Lord's Teaching by Chong Yak-Jong Augustine (1760–1801)* (Immense, Switzerland: Neue Zeitschrift Für Missionswissenschaft, 1986); for Yi Pyok's theology, see Yi Songbae, *Confucianism and Christianity: The Korean Theological Principles of Yi Piek (1754–1786)* (K) (Waegwan, Korea: Bundo ch'ulp'ansa, 1979). Both of their theologies reflect the positive view of classical Confucianism taken by Matteo Ricci in his book *T'ien-chu Shih-I* (The True Meaning of the Lord of Heaven), trans. Douglas Lancashire and Peter Hu Kuo-chen, ed. Edward J. Malatesta (Taipei: The Ricci Institute, 1985).
31. Choe Chunsik, *Understanding Korean Religions through Their Culture*, vol. 1, *Shamanism, Confucianism, and Buddhism* (K) (Seoul: Sagyejol, 1998), 186–209.
32. For a helpful discussion of Korean familism, see Pak Hyojong. "Confucianism and Korean Communitarianism." Nov. 15, 2002 <http://aped.snu.ac.kr/cyberedu/ cyberedu1/eng/eng24-01.html>.

worship, its mission suffered a tremendous setback. In today's terms, such an attack was not a simple rejection of a social custom. It was tantamount to a call for an upheaval of the social order, an anti-state revolutionary call.[33] Catholic theologian Mun Kyuhyon concedes this point.

> The absolute nature of Catholic authority caused the authority of the monarch and of the parents to become relativized. The fellowship (in the church) that united the yangban, chungin, and pyongmin (upper to lower classes) into one was regarded as an act that disturbed the Confucian social order based on a strict caste system.[34]

Put simply, in using the term "ancestral worship" to criticize Confucianism, Jones was fully aware of the sociopolitical connotations, for it meant "shaking the very foundations of (the Korean) mental and moral being."[35] After all, it was only twenty years earlier that Prince Regent Taewongun had undertaken organized attacks (1866–72) against the Catholics, which decimated nearly 10,000 Catholics because he considered them "immoral" for "teaching Koreans to dishonor their parents by forbidding ancestral worship" and challenging the monarchy by forbidding royal concubines. Because the continuation of a family bloodline was of paramount value in Choson, it was permitted for men to have concubines in order to propagate the family line. Also, it was expected that the king would have several consorts in order to protect the royal lineage and guarantee its succession through sons.[36]

On the surface, the Methodist mission's critique of "ancestral worship" sounded very much a part of the Scriptural injunction against idolatry in the first chapter of Romans and the First

---

33. Choe Chunsik, *Understanding Korean Religions*, 206.
34. Mun Kyuhyon, *Writing the History of Korean Catholic Church with the Korean People*, vol. 1, *From Its Beginnings to 1945* (K) (Seoul: Bitdurye, 1994), 27.
35. Jones, "Obstacles," 145.
36. Jones, April 24, 1891, Diary.

Commandment. Since Jones fully recognized the bloody history behind the critique of "ancestral worship" in Korea, why did he persist in using the term? Protestant missionaries realized that they would not receive the same fate as the earlier Catholic missions because the international situation had now changed, with Korea on the cusp of reform and forced modernization. In addition, American missionaries had been able to win the Royal Court's permission and apparent approval for their missionary undertaking.

However, Jones clearly saw the Court and its ruling superstructure, with ancestral worship as the central symbol, as the source of Korea's overall social decay, despair, and distress. In order to lead the people toward a new social vision, a clear understanding of the source of its problems was necessary. Thus, while attacking individual social ills such as alcohol, polygamy, women's oppression, and the "atheism" of ancestral worship, Jones used the term "ancestral worship" as his signal for a radical critique of the Korean government and its societal arrangement and governance as a whole.

While some missionaries may have misinterpreted it as a purely religious idea, the Korean government (especially its conservative ranks) and thinking people, in and out of the government, recognized that the Protestant mission was no friend of the ruling ideology. Thus, despite its strong anti-Western ideology and occasional threats against the Western missionaries, the *Tonghak* peasant revolutionaries, in general, were quite sympathetic toward the Christians because they saw the believers as being on their side again. During the *Tonghak* Revolution, the insurgents would stop anyone who had on Western suits as supporters of the government. But then, they would question them to see if they were Christians because they considered the latter to be sympathetic to their cause. Because of this, even non-Christians began carrying Bibles in the *Tonghak* regions.[37]

The critique of "ancestor worship" sounded innocent enough as a religious critique. But in reality, Jones was mounting a serious political critique of the Korean government, its ideology, and its social arrangement that blinded the people in their spiritual life and denied them their rightful place in the society as human beings. Jones's critique of Confucianism took on a double-edged form with his metaphor of ancestral worship: its lack of true spirituality, i.e., worship of a transcendent being or God, and its bankrupt polity that resulted in the oppression of the people. In this light, Jones frequently quoted from an article by a leading Korean Christian liberal Yun Chiho,

> (Confucianism as) a system of ethics yielding the fruit of agnosticism, selfishness, arrogance, despotism, degradation of women, cannot be pronounced a good one. If other countries can make a better use of it, Korea is or ought to be willing enough to part with it—the sooner the better.[38]

Jones also criticized the ruling Confucian system for its "agnosticism" that opened itself to a lower form of religiosity in shamanism, one of the three traditional religions in Jones's understanding of Korean religious history.[39] He believed that "a religious system is a normal and essential factor in every evolving society."[40] However, he regarded the religious tradition in Korea as a syncretistic "confused

---

37. Jones has an interesting story about this phenomenon. George Heber Jones, "In the Camp of the Insurgents," Papers.
38. Yun Chiho, "Confucianism in Korea," KR 2 (November 1895): 404. The author is not named in the article, but in his diaries and writings, Jones names Yun as the author of this article.
39. Here, Jones asserts the view that the three religions of Korea are Confucianism, Buddhism, and Shamanism, and not the traditional three religions of Asia—Buddhism, Confucianism, and Taoism. He understands Korean shamanism as *Sindo*, or "Spirit Way," and asserts that Koreans confused this with *Sondo* or Taoism, and states that Koreans have not adopted Taoism. Because of this misunderstanding, Jones misdiagnoses the rightful role of shamanism in Korean religious history. See chapter one in Choe Chunsik, *Understanding Korean Religions through Their Culture*, vol. 2, *Taoism, Tonghak and New Religions* (K) (Seoul: Sagyejol, 1998).
40. George Heber Jones, "The Spirit Worship of the Koreans," *Transactions of the Korea Branch of the Royal Asiatic Society* 2, no.1 (1901): 38.

jumble" in people's minds, filling their existence with spirits and demons.⁴¹ Jones defined shamanism as the spirituality underlying Korean history and personality and its pantheistic belief system, marked by divine immanence, divine capriciousness and human insecurity. In that sense, Jones was critical of those who thought Korea was agnostic or nonreligious. Even as late as 1894, F. Ohlinger, speaking at the Second International Convention of the Student Volunteer Movement for Foreign Missions (SVMFM), reported that Korea is "without a religion."

> In Korea we have to deal with a people that is *almost* without a religion. I do not say that this will prove either an advantage or a disadvantage to the work, but simply state the fact. In India religion is a mania, in China a problem in domestic economy, in Japan a fad, in Korea an accident. In India it raves, in China it respects the multiplication table, in Japan it rants, and in Korea it has a holiday."⁴²

On the contrary, while he made the initial discovery of shamanism, Jones was not able to explain its long-lasting presence nor disclose its "religious genius."⁴³

> The Korean is born under their influence or even may think himself to be their offspring or incarnation…They lie in wait for him along the wayside, in the trees, on the rocks, in the mountains, valleys and streams. They keep him under a constant espionage day and night…It certainly

---

41. Ibid. For Jones, it is a matter of determining the level of its religious evolution, which can be judged by three standards: the sense of dependence on a transcendent being, a belief in communion and relationship with this being, and a soul seeking freedom from "annoyance and pain."
42. Max Wood Moorhead, *Student Missionary Enterprise*, 266.
43. What is it in Korean shamanism (*sindo* or later *mukyo*) that draws the people in? What is significant about the fact that Tan'gun, the Korean progenitor, is known to be a shaman-king? While these questions were probably asked, the lack of written materials stumped his effort (most likely, Jones was not privy to the oral history and communal stories which form the basis of the shamanistic system). Nor did he have a wide range of observations of actual shamanistic practices to draw informed conclusions. His opinions would have reflected the negative view of shamanism that was prevalent among Confucian scholarly circles, including his colleague Choe Pyonghon.

must be a most uncomfortable condition of mind in which he passes his days, for they are all about him, they dance in front of him, follow behind him, fly over his head and cry out against him from the earth. He has no refuge from them even in his own house…Their ubiquity is an ugly travesty of the omnipresence of God.[44]

5.6 Jesus the Savior in Chemulpo

In the second phase of his missionary service in Korea, Jones preached Jesus as "the Good News" for people suffering in sin. They were separated from God because of a religious system that kept them from the true knowledge of God while pulling them down into the pit of idolatry and heathenism. The same religio-political system that created so much separation between the classes led to the hatred, mistreatment, and oppression of the poor Koreans who made up the vast majority of the population.

Jones's two images of Jesus as the Revealer of the Living *Hananim* and the Incarnated Mediator who saves the common people emerged out of Jones's immersion and ministry in the Korean social reality, circumscribed by the metaphor, "ancestor worship." By delving deeper into the inner structure of "ancestor worship," Jones was able to uncover the social reality which it obscured—a deadening religion of shamanism that exploited the people's fears and a sociopolitical oppression that brought about suffering and oppression of the common people. For Jones, ancestor worship was the key to unlocking the secret of the social reality. It was into this social reality, unlocked by the key "ancestor worship," that Jones preached the Good News of the Living God and his Liberating Savior who makes the common people rejoice.

Thus, at the height of his missionary service in Korea, Jones

---

44. Jones, "The Spirit Worship," 58.

became a powerful preacher and teacher. God indeed had a purpose in sending him to a strange land to work with a people he did not know. By becoming fully embedded in Chemulpo, just as Jesus had done in his Incarnation, Jones was able to become God's tool to free the Korean people with the life-giving message of the Gospel of Jesus. His preaching reawakened the people to *Hananim,* to whom they had been praying for millennia without real knowledge. His witness to Jesus enabled the people to repair their relationship with their heavenly Father and reclaim their true humanity as God's sons and daughters, called now to rebuild God's garden on the Korean peninsula.

6

Choe, 1893–1903: Preaching the Great Way of Truth

"How did Choe convince the Koreans that the American Christ can indeed save them from their personal sins and national demise?" In this chapter, we see Choe becoming an evangelist of the Great Way of Jesus, the Savior of the world, in God's work of salvation and reform in Choson.

6.1 Overview of Choe's Work as an Evangelist

Upon Choe's dramatic conversion and baptism, the missionary community immediately set about to train him to become one of the first "native preachers" and leaders of the infant church in Korea from the *yangban* class. Unlike other "high-level" converts who later disappointed them greatly, Choe was a man they could trust. They had lived with him for five years and had found him to be a genuine and conscientious human being. Moreover, he was a true believer and practitioner of the way of Master Kong, deeply concerned for the welfare of his people and his nation. In the 1892 Missionary Report for the Seoul Circuit, Franklin Ohlinger shares this story about a convert gone bad.

> One of these (bad news) is the continued backsliding of our oldest converts and leading men. Adultery, gambling, drunkenness, and theft in various forms have been depleting our classes. Year by year, for half a decade, these crimes have deprived us of men on whom we had spent much labor, and possibly more money, and left us a mere remnant of what we had hoped would soon become our first class of native preachers. This year we have lost but one, the first Korean baptized by a Methodist missionary in Korea, and he is now suffering the penalty of a most daring and deep-laid plot to rob our (printing) press.[1]

Jones's "inestimable" teacher, Choe, was almost immediately assigned to the Chongdong charge in Seoul—the oldest charge in Korea—to assist Appenzeller as an evangelist and a Sunday School teacher in early 1893. As a *yangban* and a Confucian *sonbi*, or scholar, Choe would have drawing powers in the capital, and he didn't fail them. His conversion sparked a great interest among the scholarly circles in the capital, and many were drawn to the faith because of him. A decade later, after Appenzeller's unexpected death, Choe would become the first Korean pastor of this mother church of Korean Methodism, sometimes called the *yangban* church. He continued to teach in the Chinese language division of the Paichai Haktang and helped with the translation work on the Korean Bible until it was finished.

When the *Tonghak* Revolution erupted in the countryside where his family still lived, he decided to bring them up to safety in Seoul in 1894. As he readied for the move, one major issue worried him. As the carrier of the family name, he was the keeper of the ancestral plates and the family altar. Some of the Confucian converts had publicly burnt these familial items as a show of their newfound faith. Some of the missionaries had demanded that new converts should destroy these articles of their old religion as a sign of a complete break with their pagan past.

---

1. MEC-BFM, Annual Report, Korea Mission, 1892, 286.

What Choe had learned on meditating on the books of his ancestors and the new books of the West together was that the God of the East and God of the West is one. Somehow, these religious artifacts, even with all their historical baggage, had helped his ancestors to connect with the One God of the Heavens, however dimly or weakly. Though he may have closed the old books in order to open the new Book, he believed they were still part of his identity and deserved respect. So, after offering his final respects, he carefully buried the ancestral plates and altar pieces in the family cemetery, before moving his family up to Seoul.

In Seoul, he and his family moved into a large house in the Chongno district in central Seoul that Appenzeller had bought from Choe's friend Oh Sangyon. It was also to double as the Great East Bookstore, the first private library in Korea. This provided Choe with an open space where he could meet the public, especially the *yangban* and learned classes, and share his newfound faith, along with the necessary literature. Appenzeller would report in 1897 that "we conducted a street-preaching service every Sunday afternoon at our bookstore at Chongno. We stopped when the cold weather set in. Most interesting were some of the meetings. They may not result in many direct conversions, but they keep Christianity before the people and stir up thought."[2]

Appenzeller also made him the co-editor of *The Christian Advocate*, a new publication, aimed at sharing the news of the growing Christian community with the society at large while informing and encouraging the new Christians. Years later, in December 1900, he began publishing *Sinhak Wolpo,* or Theological Monthly, with Jones, which continued until 1910. Choe also attempted to publish another newspaper, the *Chekuk Shinmum.* He also wrote for the *Hwangsong*

2. AR, 1897, 240.

Sinmun, a newspaper published by Confucian reformers. In 1901, he published "The Doctrine of Sin" (K: Choedori) in the *Sinhak Wolpo*. This was the first theological article written by a Korean convert.

Choe's name would make its first official appearance in the Korea Mission Annual Report in 1895, as a local preacher at Chongdong,[3] where he was named an evangelist and became the superintendent of the Sunday School. As time went on, Choe's workload and leadership roles progressively increased at the Chongdong church. He helped to raise funds among the members to build the first church building. He became the Korean language secretary of Chongdong in 1898 as its *chondosa* (evangelist or candidate for ordained ministry), while Jones became the English language secretary. He moved into the Chongdong parsonage in 1898.

In September 1900, when Appenzeller went on a furlough, Choe was put in charge of the Chongdong church for one year. It grew to a church of 244 adult members and 120 Sunday School children.[4] Then, in May 1901, when the Sangdong Church was dedicated, he was made the head *chondosa* there. On May 20, 1901, he went to Chemulpo to break ground for the Naeri Church with Bishop Moon. He would continue, and was appointed as *chondosa* when the first district meetings were held in 1901.

In addition to his evangelistic and literary work, Choe started to act on his belief that the new Savior would help the Korean Christians rebuild their nation. Consciousness-raising and public education became an important goal. At Paichai, he helped organize the *Hyopsonghoe*, or the Mutual Assistance Society, with Appenzeller, who had invited American-educated liberal Philip Jaisohn to speak. It would later develop into the Independence Club, of which Choe was a major sponsor and promoter. He organized a Western-style debate

---

3. Hyangchongdong or Upper Chong Dong in the Choe biography.
4. Song, "Taksa," 45.

series at Paichai to raise awareness of important social and political issues facing the country. Appenzeller reported in 1897,

> The minister of foreign affairs and the minister of education and other high officials have at various times attended the meetings. The society is probably the first really deliberative body in the country. The meetings are held in the chapel every Saturday afternoon, and questions, political, economic, and religious, are discussed with profundity and zeal characteristic of students in other lands. There is hope.[5]

Then, in October 1895, the government appointed him as a *chusa* or an entry-level official in the Bureau of Agriculture, Commerce, and Manufacturing, from which he tried to resign in 1896. He was finally able to resign two years later, when he refused to perform the ritual of ancestral worship at the Bureau. He had achieved his childhood goal of landing a government position to help the people. But now, he had found a new and a better way, which would help him meet the deep-seated and desperate needs of the people and the nation.

In 1897, the Annual Conference appointed him an evangelist, or *chondosa*. Believing that the most important way to share the Good News was to go out and win new believers, since "no church will grow if it sits and waits for the world to come to it,"[6] Choe carried out his task as an evangelist faithfully and fervently. He went on evangelism/preaching tours every year after he was appointed. He also went on an evangelism tour to his old hometown, where he was well-received. He also accompanied Appenzeller on a nationwide evangelism tour in 1898. Later, in November that year, he went on an evangelism tour to the central region of the country. He also went to the Kangwha Island for an evangelism tour. Given his status, he would often be asked to accompany the missionaries when they went to meet government officials, as he did with Jones to meet a

---

5. AR, 1897, 246.
6. AR, 1897, 241. H. B. Hulbert of the Baldwin Chapel wrote this in his 1897 report.

provincial governor. In May 1902, he accompanied Bishop Moon and Jones to Chinnamp'o and engaged in debate with Confucian scholars there. Through these tours, he preached the Good News of salvation and saw much success through his efforts.

In 1898, when the Mission needed new typefaces to print the Korean Bibles, Choe accompanied Bunker to buy them in Japan. This tour to Japan opened Choe's eyes to the possibilities of modernization and the backwardness of Korea when compared to Japan.

On his return, he found that many of his colleagues and students had been arrested and imprisoned in the Independence Club incident. He helped to organize support for them. On September 1, 1898, he supported the Independence Club's commemoration of the national founding day (*Kiwonjol*). The following year, he helped Appenzeller organize an All Nations Prayer Meeting on behalf of the welfare of the nation and the people on New Year's Day, 1899.

Early in 1899, Choe had a profound spiritual experience, which he described as a spiritual rebirth and "slaying in the Spirit." While he was not given to emotional ecstasy—like most Confucian scholars—he found these spiritual experiences to be helpful and life-giving. Later, in May 1900, he had another encounter of God's presence and began to focus on Bible studies.

In 1901, great tragedies visited his family. On April 17, three-year-old baby Songbaek died suddenly. A week later, his wife gave birth to a baby girl, on April 29. Unfortunately, his wife died a few days later, on May 2. A week later, the infant girl also died, on May 10. Previously, in 1897, he had lost another son, Songman. These tragedies affected him so much that his eyesight was badly damaged. Yet there were also joy in the family, as Chaehak, his eldest son, who attended Paichai English division, got married in 1899 and graduated from the school in 1900.

Choe became an ordained minister (deacon) on May 18, 1902, at the annual conference at Pyongyang, presided over by Bishop Moon. Bishop Moon then appointed him to be the senior pastor at the Sangdong Church, which was the largest church in Seoul at that time, with 316 baptized adult members. After he repaired the Sangdong parsonage, he moved into it from the Chongdong parsonage. Then, on June 11, Appenzeller drowned in a shipwreck on his way to a missionary meeting. Because of this sudden change, Choe's appointment was also changed. He was named the first Korean pastor of the Chongdong Church, where he would serve for ten fruitful years.

Thus, nearly ten years after his conversion, Choe became the pastor of the "mother" church of the Methodists in Korea, and an influential leader of the nation. He had become a committed disciple of Master Jesus and his Great Way.

6.2 Jesus and the Founders of Eastern Religions

As Choe Pyonghon began his work as an evangelist of the new faith of Jesus, he began preaching Jesus as the world Savior, and of his great way of truth. As a Confucian scholar with his fingers on the pulse of the nation, Choe recognized the burden placed on him to speak hope and courage to his brothers and sisters in the deepening crisis of the nation, now caught between modernization and imperialism. In this difficult period, Choe preached the great way of Jesus as the true way of new humanity. Jesus comes and proclaims a new humanity by revealing true human nature and showing the way back to recovering their original nature as the children of God. Choe proclaimed Jesus as the transformer of human nature, and the maker of a new people under God.

As Choe began preaching his newfound Savior, he quickly faced the challenge of responding to the hesitancy of the people in embracing *sohak,* or Western religion. The effect of Taewongun's bloody massacre of the Catholics in the 1860s lingered long, especially with the obstinate presence of the anti-Western *choksapa* in the Court always presenting memorials against the evils of the *sohak*. Many of Choe's earliest writings try to meet this challenge by arguing that Jesus is the universal Savior of the universal God.

One strategy he uses in his writings is to point out that all the so-called traditional religions of Korea—Confucianism, Buddhism, and Taoism—are of foreign origin, with none being native to Korea. He also makes the positive argument that Jesus was also born in the Asian continent, and thus, has every right as any of the other three to be embraced by the Korean people. In "Conversion among the Three," the Christian evangelist tells the Confucian scholar,

> Confucianism, Buddhism, Taoism, the three religions (tao) all came from foreign countries. How can you call them "our native religions?" Confucius was born in the state of Lo (Lu)…none of the founders of these religions was born in the land of Taehan (Korea)… but you say, "They are our national religions." But the *Kusechu* (the saving Lord) was born in west Asia in the land of Judea; thus it is in the same continent as Taehan. So why must you write it off as a "foreign religion" and not heed its teachings? Is that logical?[7]

The center of Choe's argument focuses on identifying the Christian God with the Sovereign God (*Sangje*) of Korean tradition and mindset by calling Jesus the universal Savior sent by the universal God. In "Disease of Humanity," he makes an astounding claim about the universal Savior, which he would repeat many times. After describing a parent who refused to send a child to school because he was afraid it might make him a Catholic, Choe comments on the closed-mindedness of the parents:

---

7. Choe Pyonghon, "Conversation," 62.

> They do not even look at the books of other religions, but condemn them as heretical. This is a great disease! But isn't the Eastern sky the same as the Western sky? The Sovereign Lord of the West is the Sovereign Lord of the East. The people there are also people whom God rules.[8]

Choe goes on to argue that under the one God, there is one world, and one people-family.[9] With his premise of one God and one heaven, he was able to gain a perspective that helped him maintain a critical distance from his own cultural heritage as well as from the Western civilization that was pouring into his own. By claiming that the East is one with the West, he declared that the East is as independent as the West. By claiming that the West is one with the East, he also claims that the Korean people must adopt what is good from the West, for its own sake.[10]

After arguing that Jesus is not a foreign Savior, but an "Eastern" Savior, born in Asia, Choe then goes on to differentiate him from the other founders, based on his divine nature and his saving work of self-sacrifice on the cross.

> Savior Jesus is not a sage like Confucius, Buddha, or Lao Tzu. He is actually *Hananim* (God) himself...Of all (wonders and miracles) he did, the greatest was that he was crucified on the cross and died and atoned for the deadly sins of world's people (*mankuk manmin*: literally, all people of all nations).[11]

For Choe, Jesus is definitely the most worthy Savior. He stands at a level higher than the other three because he himself is God come

---

8. Choe Pyonghon, "Disease," 510.
9. Choe Pyonghon, "Conversation," 62. "The world is like one house and the people of the four seas are brothers/sisters." For Choe, all the people are created by the One God. His doctrine of creation has many implications for human identity and political existence.
10. In "Diligent Study," Choe calls on the Koreans to learn both civilizations. This principle still holds true as contextual Christology must become intercultural theology, as Küster and Schreiter claim. Choe Pyonghon, "Diligent Study," *KCA*, April 26, 1899. 404.
11. Choe Pyonghon, "Conversation," 68.

down from heaven. When compared to other sages and religious figures, Jesus is different in a big way: Jesus died on the cross to save humanity from sin because he loved them.

Thus, Choe mobilizes all his mental capacities to prove the superiority of Jesus the Savior over the other sages. For him, Jesus' greatness overshadowed not only Korean sages, but also all sages and saviors found around the world. Having identified Jesus with *Sangje*, the "Sovereign Lord who saved all people of all nations,"[12] Choe concludes that Jesus is a non-Korean, just like all three founders of Korea's traditional religions. At the same time, he claims that Jesus is the most universal and most powerful of the three, since he is the only mediator who sacrificed himself to atone for the sins of all people, including the Korean people.

6.3 Jesus and the Human Problem in "The Doctrine of Sin"

"The Doctrine of Sin"[13] is important for several reasons. First, it is the first Korean attempt to explain the doctrine of humanity and atonement. Second, it is an original, Korean telling of the Christian story, out of the Korean Confucian worldview. Third, it creatively applies the Biblical doctrine of sin and atonement to the social demands of Choe's time. Choe wrote this essay in 1901, eight years after his conversion.[14] It is generally acknowledged to be the first theological essay by a Korean Protestant Christian. This was written one year before his ordination as a deacon of the Korean Methodist

---

12. Choe Pyonghon, "Birthday," 293.
13. "The Doctrine of Sin" (K: Choedori) was written in response to a contest run by the *Sinhak Wolpo* for original theological essay on any theological theme. While Choe served as an editor, he also wrote for the contest and won the contest.
14. Choe wrote two essays on the same topic in the *Sinhak Wolpo*. The first was a shorter outline; "Doctrine of Sin 1," *SW* 1, no. 8 (1901): 309–14. The second was a more fully developed theological essay with his customary poetry summarizing each section: "Doctrine of Sin 2," *SW* 1, no. 11 (1901): 446–55.

Church, and several months following the tragic deaths of three members of his family (noted above).

Human Sin and Its Consequences

Choe's essay follows the outline of the salvation history found in the Bible: creation, fall, redemption, and completion (earthly Garden of Eden and heaven). He defines human sin as disobedience to God that breaks the original bond of love and communion formed between God and humanity at creation. Yet, sin provides the occasion for God to take the initiative of love to save humanity, which ends with Jesus as God's final act of salvation. This is the salvation that had been foreshadowed by the sacrificial system, human conscience, and the law. In "The Doctrine of Sin," Choe sees Jesus in terms of his two roles—mediator and atonement. Jesus restores and reconciles the broken relationship between God and humanity; he becomes the perfect atonement for human sin through his self-giving sacrifice on the cross.

Adam is created in God's image, which means he has a free will as an autonomous being. Original sin arose out of a conflict between God's law and human autonomy that broke the commandment of the Lord of Heaven, *Chonju*. Through original sin, Adam, as the father of the human race, forever distorted human destiny and human nature.[15] The effect of Adam's act was enormous. It caused the "separation of holy love and life" between God and humanity and opened the door to all kinds of misery on humanity: misfortune, disease, suffering, and death.[16] Adam's descendants participate in his original sin by sharing the same nature, or tendency to sin, and so, disobey God. Through

---

15. Choe Pyonghon, "Sin 2," 439–41.
16. Ibid., 440.

their sinful acts, they, too, disrupt the original relationship of love with God.

Choe turns to various metaphors to describe the notion of human "participation" in Adam's original sin—a strong tree with strong branches and a diseased tree with sickly branches, or a rich man and his prodigal son, or a contagious disease, or seed and plant. The point of these metaphors is to show that individuals commit "actual sins" using their free will (*chajujang*; capacity for self-determination), now distorted by the original sin to commit real sins.

What is surprising in Choe's storytelling is that he pictures both God and his now estranged human children as both desiring the reunion and revival of true life. On the one hand, God is pictured as an involved participant in this process of human self-destruction and sinfulness. God does not stand aloof, but desires to restore his relationship with humanity and to save them—"the desire of the Heavenly Lord to revive our life is greater than our own desire."[17]

On the other hand, Choe makes a curiously positive interpretation of human autonomy[18] and human sinfulness. First, Choe says it is not sin that kills the human race; rather, it is humanity that gives sin the opportunity to kill it by committing sin. "Thus it is not sin which kills me but truly it is I myself who kill myself."[19] He says that human beings could keep their hearts from moving toward sin's temptation and could grow and draw near to God with the faculty of choice and will (*chajujang*). But that is possible only if we are "strengthened by God" to defeat sin. Thus, the occasion for sin has become the opportunity for life; sin can be a "good source" of life.

---

17. Choe Pyonghon, "Sin 2," 443.
18. Choe Pyonghon, "Sin 1," 312. "Even those who are under the control of sin are able to approach God by putting one's faith in the Savior who is the only Mediator. By believing in Jesus Christ, you are reconciled with the Holy Spirit, by whose companionship sinners can receive their salvation."
19. Choe Pyonghon, "Sin 2," 444.

But the millennia-year-old root of original sin[20] is deeply enrooted in human hearts.

> But the root of sin that comes down for thousands of years has become nearly completely glued to human heart. It emerges from time to time. And like a heavy dose of sleeping pills, it makes the mind dizzy and the heart confused, and commands human beings like its own slaves. Thus they are unable to do what their hearts want to do and in fact do the evil that they do not want to do. Thus even if we desire to do the good, we will not obey the Lord's laws, though we know them, nor will be able to carry it out, if the Lord of heaven is not with us.[21]

God's Work of Salvation in Jesus

It is in this desperate human situation that Choe speaks of the prior actions God has taken to save humanity, which is destroying itself by sin.

> Rejoice! The patient love of Heavenly Lord did not abandon all humanity to sin, but desired to save them. Thus he early promised to send a Savior to our ancestors. He planted this way of salvation like sunlight hidden within darkness. He had all the believers wait in faith for the future coming of salvation. He also ordered the sacrificial system of atonement, to be a shadow of things to come, and made all the people recognize their sin. Thus all the infants are saved according to grace—despite their original sin—because they have not committed any actual sin. Also, foreigners who do not know the law were given their conscience to teach their spirits. They could know good from evil through their conscience. Even without the law, they established their own laws. On the Day of Judgment, they too will be made whole according to the gospel of grace.[22]

---

20. This image was prevalent in many of the earliest tracts that the missionaries penned or translated. See Kim Kunyong, "Interpretation of 'Sin' and 'Traditional Religion' in Early Evangelistic Tracts" (K), *CHK* 9 (1998): 221–54, esp. 222–34.
21. Choe Pyonghon, "Sin 2," 444.
22. Ibid., 445–46.

For Choe, God's great desire for human salvation is reflected in earlier gifts God has given to humanity to prepare them for his final act of salvation through Jesus. These gifts are to be found in the Old Testament: the sacrifice of atonement, human conscience, and the giving of laws.[23]

In the climactic paragraphs of the book, Choe describes the person and work of Christ in very poetic, and yet, theological language:

> All praise to the faithfulness of our Heavenly Lord! The ancient and mysterious revelation, being quiet, Christ now has appeared on earth for us sinners as promised. For Christ is the only Son of the true Lord of Heaven, one who is lifted up before all the people…Though the Lord of Heaven, he took on flesh and became a human being (*saram*); he walked on earth in the form of a humble servant (*ha-in*) and bore all kinds of suffering in patience. He only proclaimed the kingdom of heaven, healing all diseases and raising the dead. Therefore, through the one righteous man, Jesus Christ, will we all not attain life?
>
> This Savior offered his own body on the altar of the cross to atone for our sins, for once to be a perfect and holy sacrifice. At that time, the veil in the Holy Temple was torn from top to bottom, opening the way of reconciliation and communion with the Lord of Heaven. The wall of sin that stood between us was destroyed by the pounding sound of the nails. Glory be to God above and peace on earth, with whom he is pleased. The glory of the daylight has appeared on the world hidden in dark nothingness. It has washed away its entire dark destiny. So Jesus died once to sin, defeating the power of death. He rose once and lives again and is become the head of all those who were resurrected…
>
> Thus the blood of the Lord is abundant to wash away all original and actual sins of all peoples. One receives this salvation only by faith through the grace of the heavenly Lord and the blood shed by Jesus. The proofs of salvation are three inward signs; peacefulness, joy, and an absence of the fear of sin. Those who have these witnesses in their hearts have returned to the Garden of Eden. Those who do not have these witnesses are still outside the Garden of Eden. Believe with all your strength until the morning star appears in your hearts and you enter

---

23. Ibid.

therein. The Bible says, "Heaven will be entered by force, and those who are forceful will acquire it. Amen."[24]

In this flowery passage, Choe understands Jesus in two ways—as the only son of God (John 3:16), or the "beloved son of God" and the second person of the Trinity; God himself, who became incarnate to save humanity. "Though the Lord of Heaven,"[25] he became a *ha-in,* or a servant or slave, a member of the lowest class, and served as the mediator between humanity and God. It is amazing that he used the term, *ha-in,* to describe Jesus, particularly given their status in the Korean society of his day. It offered an alternative understanding of the traditional mediator (usually the king or emperor), who represented the human race in the sacrifice to the Lord of Heaven.

Choe's understanding of Jesus as mediator includes both the work of atonement and mediation; he sacrificed himself in place of human sin as the *taesokja* (substitutionary sacrifice).[26] In that sense, Jesus on the cross is the perfect sacrificial lamb given for the sacrifice of atonement. His sacrifice is placed within the framework of the Old Testament sacrificial system. But Choe does not pursue this image any further than the Biblical model, particularly in terms of the violent nature of the sacrificial system. Nor does he dwell on the suffering that Jesus went through.

Rather, Choe turns to another of his favorite Scriptural passages, Ephesians 2:13–15. It describes the work of repairing and renewing the broken-up communion and relationship between God and humanity effected by sin and Christ's dismantling of the barrier set up by human sin. After quoting from Ephesians 2:13–16, Choe writes, "From all these testimonies we can attest that a sinner can wash away

---

24. Choe Pyonghon, "Sin 2," 445–47.
25. In Choe Pyonghon, *Reflections on the Holy Mountain* (K: Songsan myongkyong) (Seoul: Tongyang sowon, 1911; reprint, Seoul: Chongdong sammun chulpansa, 1998), 75, we find the phrase, "by origin, he is God."
26. Choe Pyonghon, "Sin 1," 312; and idem, "Sin 2," 446.

the original sin and actual sin and receive his salvation by believing in the Savior and keeping the commandments."[27] Thus, in saving humanity, Jesus returns humanity to "the Garden of Eden" with its amazing potentiality; the relationship of love and communion with God restored; forgiveness of sin; freedom from fear; peacefulness; joy; and the restoration of the ability to rightfully use the human power of self-determination (*chajujang*) to follow the Savior in the great way of truth.

As this detailed look at the "Doctrine of Sin" has revealed, Choe adopts a robust doctrine of Christ's person and work. He is God himself, who is incarnated, come to deliver humanity from its self-killing. Humanity is caught up and tied up in the thousand-year-old tendency to fall enslaved to sin and its temptations. Sin breaks off the beautiful relationship of love with God, and banishes humanity from God's Garden of Eden. It also distorts the powerful faculty of choice and self-determination that God has endowed on humanity. But now, in Christ, there is the potential of a new humanity. It is restored to its original nature in the companionship of the Holy Spirit; it is reconciled to God; and it is made right in their souls to be able to do God's will with their God-restored power of self-determination. Now, humanity can become the true humanity, as God created Adam to live in fellowship with God and build a wholesome human society for each other's benefit.

6.4 The Evangelist's Work I: Preaching the Great Way of Jesus (*Chili Taedo*)

After his conversion, Choe threw himself into the work of the evangelist of the Gospel of Jesus, as outlined above, selling religious

---

27. Choe Pyonghon, "Sin 1," 313.

books and tracts; preaching in the marketplaces; visiting his hometown, which was caught up in the *Tonghak* Revolution, with the message of Jesus; debating with Confucian scholars about Christianity; and visiting the governors and officials of the provinces to persuade them with the Gospel message.

In every place and to everyone, Choe presented the saving message of Jesus: the Savior of the world can make us into true humanity. Eastern philosophies and religions are centrally concerned with the question of humanization, i.e., How can we become a true human being? All of them offer a goal and the means to achieve the goal: the human ideal of Confucianism is *kunja*, or noble person (Chinese *chuntzu*) or *songin* or holy man; for Taoism, *chinin* or authentic, true human; for Buddhism, Buddha or awakened being; and in Sondo, or shamanism, *sinson* or divine being.[28] So, Choe offered the new great way of becoming human through Jesus. Now that the Christian story of salvation had become his own story, Choe began to speak to the Confucian mindset of his society. He was also fully aware of the inability of the Confucian message to reform the people or renovate the society.

Choe makes several theological moves to help the people meet Jesus the Savior. First, he identified the God of Jesus with the Confucian *Sangje* (Sovereign Lord). By doing so, he was directly confronting the notion that Jesus was a foreign God. Once they overcame this initial prejudice, just as he had done, then the superior person and work of Jesus would naturally draw the people to him.

Second, Choe's stressed the role of human self-determination in attaining salvation in Jesus. This may have been a part of the Methodist emphasis on free will. But Choe went well beyond the traditional Wesleyan understanding of free will. For Choe, there is

---

28. Choe Chunsik, *Understanding Korean Religions*, 107–9.

almost no loss of the power of free will and its potentiality in sin. This move is best understood when seen in light of the Confucian emphasis on *sim* (heart) and *song* (nature) endowed by God or heaven. Korean neo-Confucianists followed Mencius' teaching on the innate goodness of human nature.[29] But Choe makes it clear that original sin distorts this goodness. He goes on to say that it is completely unable to win salvation on its own, apart from God's power, the Holy Spirit. Only when humanity is in full communion with God is their true nature and free will restored to their full capacity.

Third, Choe says that Jesus' salvation has the power to return the human race back to its original condition in the Garden of Eden. Jesus' work continues and finishes God's act of creation, which had the final goal of making humanity into his beloved sons and daughters. Believing in Jesus means the restoration of the human race and the cosmos back to its original blessing and destiny.

Through his own experience, Choe found the mercy and compassion of God as well as the comforting presence of the Spirit. He would receive the power to overcome the tragedy of his family's sudden and massive losses in the spring of 1901. He would also personally encounter God's presence in two separate spiritual experiences, which are recorded in the Choe biography. First, at the All Nations Prayer Meeting held on January 1, 1899, Appenzeller preached on Romans 11:1 and challenged all present to offer themselves as a living sacrifice by physically prostrating themselves on the ground. As Choe went down on his stomach, he was "slain in the Spirit" and "entered the seventh heaven" and experienced an ecstatic union with God, which filled him with an inexpressible joy:

---

29. See Heup Young Kim, *Wang Yang-Ming and Karl Barth: A Confucian-Christian Dialogue* (Lanham, MD: University Press of America, 1996), 15–60, for a discussion of the Confucian notion of self-cultivation compared to the Christian doctrine of sanctification.

> At that time, the Teacher was led by the Holy Spirit and he entered into the seventh heaven. He had no other thought and his holy body praised the Lord in inexpressible joy. From then on the Teacher received an internal testament of his rebirth from God and gave himself completely to the work of God's kingdom.[30]

After the harsh year of 1901 passed, Choe continued his work, but sought for a special experience of God, perhaps as a sign of God's comforting presence in light of the family tragedies.

> That time, the Teacher went into the sanctuary early in the morning and prayed, "Lord, let me see your special glory with my eyes, and let me hear your words with my ears." Then on 3 May, at 6 A.M., he suddenly heard a voice saying, "I am the light of the world. Look at my actions. The Scriptures are the teachings of the *Sangju* (Heavenly Lord). So listen to the words of the Scriptures. Why would you seek another?" After receiving such a witness, he never prayed that kind of prayer again.[31]

Through these experiences, Choe realized that the salvation wrought by Jesus had brought him face-to-face with God and his glory, and that God, through Jesus, is now in the process of enlightening the world through his word, actions, and presence.

Choe preached Jesus, the universal Savior, as the one who restores the people to their original goodness and stature by opening the channel of communion of love with God the Father and by sacrificing himself to atone for humanity's sins. This was Jesus' way, his *tohak*, his way of humanization. By the *tohak* of Jesus, the whole nation and world could be renewed and restored in each arena of their social life through a process of consciousness-raising and education.

---

30. Choe Chaewon, *Biography*, 119.
31. Ibid., 121.

6.5 The Evangelist's Work II: Renewing the Nation through the Jesus Way (*Tohak*)

In 1882, Choe had seen the confusion caused by the Imo Military Mutiny in reaction to the government's reform actions, and was forced to flee from Seoul with his family. Now, ten years later, he had become a Christian. In many people's eyes, becoming a Christian was identical to modernization, and modernization meant becoming a Westerner, and Westernization meant leaving behind all things Korean.[32] In addition to this domestic push for modernization was the nonstop pounding of foreign powers demanding to control Korea's economy and politics. Within a year of his conversion, Japan and China dueled for the control of Korean future. As Japan emerged victorious because of its modernized military, it redrew the map of East Asian countries and forced them to think in new ways.

The Call for Reform through Education in the Jesus Way

Before the turn of the century, Choe saw the signs on the wall of the social implosion on its way. In face of these realities, he looked around and saw the people still sleeping and the social systems unresponsive to the impending crisis. In particular, his trip to Japan from March 1 to May 15, 1898, opened up his eyes to the urgency of the situation. That trip left a deep impression on him about how Japan's modernization had brought prosperity and abundance to her people.[33] In comparison, the reality of Korea brought tears to his eyes.

> After I disembarked on land to look for the inspector's office, I saw the way our Korean people lived. It was so far below the Japanese situation

---

32. Han, "The Theology and Philosophy of Early Missionaries," 49–67.
33. See his ten-part report on his trip in the *Korean Christian Advocate*. Choe Pyonghon, "My Trip to Japan 1-10," *KCA*, May 25, 1898; June 1, 1898; June 8, 1898; June 15, 1898; June 22, 1898; June 29, 1898; July 6, 1898; July 13, 1898; July 20, 1898; and July 27, 1898.

that it naturally made me cry. The thatched-roof homes built on the ground faced the east or the west. Near the dirty road ditch, there were roadside bars where people were drinking rice wine, speaking loudly. In this civilized world, what poor souls![34]

Choe knew he must speak out in self-reflection and critique, calling for reforms, improvements, and a change of heart, but having tasted the power of Jesus' salvation, Choe was not a pessimist when he looked around his world.[35] Given his belief in the mutual relationship of religion and politics, Choe began preaching that the nation would be truly renewed when it experienced a spiritual rebirth. In other words, its citizens needed to be reborn, remade, and enlightened as new human beings, *first*. Then, they could engage in the building of a new society and civilization. Choe chose education as the path that would lead to a right process of self-cultivation and human development, but it was to be a particular kind of a humanizing education, based on the Christian way.

Choe's adoption of education as the path of national enlightenment was both missionary and Confucian, both of which highly valued the educational process. Appenzeller's name for the first foreign institution of education was Paichai Haktang (a school to "rear useful men"), reflecting his belief that education in Christ's way would help build a Christian nation in Korea. Out of his own background in Confucian education, Choe referred to this Christian-based (or religion-based) education as *tohak,* or humanistic education. In his article on "The Theory of Enlightenment," Choe writes, "The foundation of education is *tohak*. If people have no *tohak*, all the skills do not help, since they do not trust each other."[36]

---

34. Choe Pyonghon, "My Trip to Japan," *KCA,* July 20, 1898, 174.
35. In addition to his strong doctrine of salvation and theory of human self-determination, he had adopted a progressive and evolutionary worldview in which God was in control of world events and was leading it toward evolutionary progress. It depended on Koreans to respond to God's progressive march through history. Song, "Formation of Theological Thought," 182.

Likewise, in a speech at the opening of Younghwa Haktang, the first girl's school in Chemulp'o, Choe says that two main elements of education are virtue and skill, which must be integrated if true education is to take place.

> Virtue and skills are developed and nurtured only by the way (*tao*) and learning (*hakmun*). Thus without the true way (*tao*), virtue cannot be enhanced; without true learning, skills cannot be developed. The so-called "true way" is God's word found in John 1:1. True learning comes through good literature…In Korea there are thousands who have received education, but they worship only external culture and do not have the true way inside of them. Thus their education lacks effectiveness and cannot develop the students' wisdom.[37]

He goes on to say that in the West, the first task of a Christian student is to worship God, become renewed, and cultivate the spirit, so the Korean church must also educate in order to help nurture Christian men and women, humanized in the way of Christ. He ties the education of the young to the cultural progress of the nation, and calls on the church to get busy opening schools and teaching the youngsters the *tohak*.[38] By calling the church "father of learning," Choe asserts that learning worldly knowledge without the true principles of God's Kingdom can even be harmful. So, he calls on the church and the schools to be mutually supportive. Whenever a new church is started, a new school ought to be built alongside it.

6.6 "The Song of Independence"

Only when the people are humanized and properly educated in the

---

36. Choe Pyonghon, "The Theory of Enlightenment" (K), *The Independent*, August 21, 1897.
37. Choe Pyonghon, "Establishment of Younghwa Haktang at Chemulpo" (K), *SW* 1, no. 12 (1901): 492.
38. Choe Pyonghon, "The Present Generation's Duty to the Coming Generation" (K), *SW* 2, no. 7 (1902): 241.

Christian way can they look forward to protecting the independence that God has endowed on their nation. Choe has a very strong belief in God's act of creation, in which God established all the nations of the world, with the same promise of independence applying to all. In the "Song of Independence," published in *The Independent*, one can sense the deep love that Choe has for his native land, as well as the doctrine of creation that undergirded such love.[39]

To attain national independence, there was an order to be followed. Given his framework of the relation of religion and politics, internal religious work of spiritual rebirth and humanization through education was given primary and initial focus. At the same time, he took an active part in the sociopolitical movements during the last decade of the nineteenth century, such as the Independence Club and the YMCA. First, he concentrated his efforts into evangelistic outreach and the building of local faith communities. He crisscrossed the country on evangelistic tours while serving as a leader in the growing church in Seoul. At the same time, Choe established various educational programs and agencies geared to train the youth and the younger generations. As a teacher at Paichai Haktang, he mobilized the youth into debating clubs and political reform clubs under the name of *Hyopsonghoe,* or Mutual Assistance Society, and church youths under the Epworth League, and led the way for a new way of education that taught the people democratic process and participation.

On the contrary, unlike some of the radical reformist *sodo sokip'a* leaders, Choe saw the importance of renewing and reforming Korean indigenous cultural resources if true self-determination was to be won. Jesus did not come to make Koreans into Westerners, but more

---

39. Choe Pyonghon, "Song of Independence" (K), *The Independent*, October 31, 1896, printed here below. Yi Juik argues that Choe is also the author of the words of the Korean national anthem, which was originally a poem, "The Song of Eternity." Yi Juik, "Taksa Choe Pyonghon's Theology," 20–21.

authentic Koreans. His "Song of Independence," published in 1896, affirms the presence of God's Spirit in Korea's long history, directing it in the heavenly way of righteousness and unity with God.

"The Song of Independence"

Refrain:
The best foundation of an eternal independence:
Military, citizenry, and merchants[40]
O happy day, o happy day,
When Great Choson became independent.[41]

All things on heaven and earth created,
Heaven determined the five continents,
In the eastern region of the Asian continent,
Firmly stands the great nation of Choson.[42]

After giving us Tangun and Kija-ja,[43]
Silla's motto: Heaven's Way.
Country established, many people saved, people satisfied;
Koryo's heavenly way illumined the virtues.

Long live the beautiful plum tree flower of Wansan[44]
The new king, the outstanding head of heaven.
Even after 500 years of its happy beginning,
Its motto of heaven's way still shines.

---

40. This reflects the democratic vision espoused by the Independence Club, following the American model of a constitutional republic or parliamentary rule with a constitutional monarchy.
41. In 1897, King Kojong changed the name of the Choson Dynasty to *Taehan Cheguk* or the Empire of Taehan, in commemoration of Choson's "independence" from Chinese influence, following China's defeat at the hand of the Japanese. While its independence was hardly real, given the heavy hand of Russia on Korean internal affairs, this event was seen by many reformed-minded Koreans as the harbinger of new beginnings. For Choe, the content of independence was along the lines taken by the Independence Club.
42. Choe sees the existence of Korea as God's will. Thus, later on, Choe would argue that the greatest sin for a nation or a people is to lose the freedom that God has endowed them with.
43. The founder of the Korean race, Tangun, ruled in northeastern Asia with his capital in northern Manchuria. Kija-ja came from China into the Korean Peninsula to set up the first Korean kingdom and gave it its first legal code.
44. The founder of the Choson Dynasty was General Yi Songgye. His surname means "plum tree," and his family hails from Wansan.

> Lifting high like the sun and moon
> the Taeguk flag of yin-yang symbol.
> Our Choson truly is an ancient land:
> Now a time for enlightenment and reform.⁴⁵
>
> This great land of golden mountains and pearly fields
> Nine thousand five hundred li long
> Let the twenty million people together
> Sing the song of independence.

6.7 An Evangelist of God's Salvation in Korea

When Choe began to preach the Gospel of the New Great Way of Truth (*chili taedo*) in Jesus Christ, the Korean peninsula was going through a period of dramatic changes. His preaching on Jesus in this period focused on the person of Jesus as the Universal Savior, not a Western God. He presented Jesus as the mediator of the Great Way of God, who has always been present in the Korean people's history. Five hundred years of neo-Confucian rule of Choson had made them corrupted, through and through. The best answer to the Korean predicament was the message of the Universal Savior. Jesus is the Mediator, and is actually the *Sangje* (Heavenly Sovereign, the Confucian concept of God) himself who has become human. He came to restore humanity to its original goodness and destiny to be God's children.

In "The Doctrine of Sin," Choe pictured Jesus as the final Mediator who has come to restore humanity to its original union with the God of love. Choe's Jesus was thoroughly based on the Bible, taking the facts and narratives of the Bible as historically true. At the same time, he understood the Biblical truths in terms of his Confucian

---

45. *Kaemyong* (literally "open civilization"), *yushin* ("modernization").

framework. He taught that the universal God of the Bible is the *Sangje* of Korean history, who gave them the earlier Eastern sages in order to bring the Korean people to perfect salvation in Jesus.

Choe interprets the work of Jesus in terms of the *tohak*, the teaching of the Way. Its central aim is to form a new humanity, which has been the goal of the Confucian way of self-cultivation. The final goal of *tohak* is world peace that comes through a righteous polity, based on a harmonious family arising from right relationships between people, who are enlightened by the new great way of truth of salvation in Jesus. Thus, Choe believes that Jesus' *tohak* offers the best remedy for the social distress and disorder facing the Korean people. Whereas the weak Confucian *tohak* had failed to produce a virtuous people and society capable of modernizing itself and defending itself against foreigners, Choe promised that Jesus would make of the Korean people a righteous people, through whom a new civilization would emerge on the Korean peninsula. Only those who receive the salvation of their souls through Jesus would become sanctified or become authentic human beings. In turn, they would help build the foundation of a new civilization through the Christian *tohak*.

In the first decade of his life as a Christian, Choe worked tirelessly as the Lord's worker in God's new work in Korea. He preached the Good News with a clear voice. The Korean people can become true human beings by following Jesus' Great Way of Truth, and the corrupt and collapsing Choson can become a new nation by Jesus' *tohak,* through education, organization, and purposeful action.

PART IV

Part 4: Jesus the Savior of the Korean Nation

7

Jones, 1903–1910: Building God's Kingdom in Korea

"What did Jones's Christ promise to the Korean people, facing the loss of their identity and nation as Japan takes over Choson, and what would be required of them to rebuild a new one?" In this chapter, we see the ethical power of the new Way of Jesus at work, as Jones proclaims Jesus as the new Ethical Standard for a people and a nation seeking a new future.

7.1 Jones's Last Years of Service in Choson

In this chapter, we see Jones making important decisions about how he would preach Jesus as Japan gradually took away Korea's national sovereignty. It is in this context of a total sociopolitical collapse that two responses are forged during the last three years of Jones's missionary service in Korea: Jesus, the new "The Ethical Standard" (*Totokui pyojun*), and Jesus, the Purifying Lord of the Church. In addition, we look at Jones's analysis of two major events of this period—the 1905 Protectorate Treaty with Japan, which signaled the end of Korean sovereignty and independence, and the 1907 Revival, often called the "Korean Pentecost," that birthed the Korean church. These two events provided the ingredients for two of his most powerful images of Jesus the Savior.

After his work at Chemulpo ended in 1903, he took a long-deserved furlough in the United States and came back after three years. He returned with a deep sense of burden for the direction of the Methodist Mission in Korea. The sudden death of Henry G. Appenzeller in 1902,[1] the absence of Dr. Scranton in Korea during 1902–1904, his worsening physical illness, and the bureaucratic slowness of the Methodist Mission Board to the work in Korea made him realize the danger facing the Korean church. In particular, he worried about how the fast-growing church would sail through the rough waters of political instability and social chaos without clear leadership in place. These realities nearly led him to resign and give up his missionary appointment. But as he traveled throughout the United States, speaking about his missionary work in Korea and reflected on the developments in Korea, he regained his spiritual energy. He decided to focus his energies on the theological training of indigenous leaders, and returned to the mission field, appointed as President of the Biblical and Theological Institute of Korea.

Living back in the United States for three years, away from the frenzy of daily reactions to the ever-changing political scene, also allowed him to see Korea's place in the global context. It helped him form a clearer idea about the inevitable end of Old Korea. His return trip, via Hawaii, gave him an opportunity to see the good that his assistance had done in promoting Korean immigration to Hawaii. By sending along some of his most highly trusted assistants as leaders, he had built a strong presence of Christian churches among the immigrant workers, who now numbered 7,000.

---

1. See the following for a description of the tragedy that took Appenzeller's life. G. H. Jones to A. B. Leonard, June 28, 1902, Missionary Collection; William C. Swearer, "Memoir of Rev. Henry G. Appenzeller," *The Korea Review* 2 (June 1902): 254–61; No Pyongson, "Southern District Superintendent Appenzeller Dies" (K), *SW* 2, no. 8 (1902): 269–81.

The brutal famines of 1901–1903 had devastated certain parts of Korea, with the poor masses driven to survival by eating tree barks, or even soil. Jones saw immigration to Hawaii as a great opportunity for suffering Koreans and encouraged many in his churches to go. Of course, not that all people applauded his immigration "scheme." In his absence, Elmer M. Cable, presiding elder of the Chemulpo area, writes in the 1904 Missionary Report:

> The West Korea District has had to contend with the Hawaii emigration scheme in a way that other districts have not. Some of the most prominent men in the church, among them local preachers and exhorters, were secured at flattering salaries and placed at the head of the enterprise, and the result has been that these men have not only lost interest in the church work themselves but have used their influence to further the ends of the Hawaiian enterprise to the detriment of the church…On the Kyodong Circuit a whole church was entirely uprooted, and others have been decimated. The greatest harm to the church from this scheme was not due to the numbers we lost, but to the spirit of unrest, dissatisfaction, and jealousy which it fostered among our groups.[2]

7.2 Jesus as the "Ethical Standard" (*Totokui pyojun*)

In his new post as the head of theological education in Korea, Jones resumed publishing the *Sinhak Wolpo*—the Theological Monthly—in order that the magazine could be used as a theological curriculum for the training of Korean lay and clergy leaders. From 1907, *Sinhak Wolpo* began publishing articles with a clear emphasis on Christianity's social and ethical message.[3] It continued to focus on

---

2. For a description of his participation, see the letters written to his wife, Margaret B. Jones, between June 1902 and March 1903. George Heber Jones, Letters to Margaret Bengel Jones, June 8, 1902 to March 7, 1903, privately held by family, Tiburon, CA. BFM-MEC, *Annual Report*, 1904: 239.
3. Already in 1893, Richard T. Ely's economic writings were included in the theological

the vital, experiential nature of Christian faith, especially with an emphasis on spiritual gifts and practices.⁴

For example, Jones's closest friend and missionary in charge of the Pyongyang station, William Arthur Noble, gave a series of important lectures on Christology at a training event, which was then published in the Theological Monthly. His lecture begins with the thesis that a religion's power is measured by the ethical life of its believers, which ought to be identical with the standard set by its founder. Thus, Noble claims that Jesus is amply qualified to be the Ethical Model (*Totokui pyojun*) for all nations, since the Western nations that believe in Jesus are prosperous, powerful, and pious. Noble argues that Jesus' ethical purity is proven by his humility, as well as his opposition to sin and a lack of any consciousness of guilt before God. Jesus could approach God freely because he was in such a harmony with God. Jesus could judge others of hypocrisy because he knew everything about sin while remaining sinless himself. Jesus loved sinners, but truly abhorred sin. He himself models such an ethical standard indirectly through the power of his personality, i.e., true humility and true courage defeating all evils.⁵

If Koreans wanted to have a new nation strong as the Western nations, they must adopt Jesus as their national ethical model. In these introductory lectures on Christology, which Noble gave in many of the theological classes, one can see the aim that Noble, Jones, and many American missionaries were taking in a time of great

---

curriculum, and James S. Dennis' book *Christian Mission and Social Progress,* which argues that Christianity, above all other religions, is the only religion that is able to solve the social problems and evils facing the world, received a positive review in the *Korea Repository* in 1897. George Heber Jones, "Christian Missions and Social Progress," *KR* 5 (February 1898): 64–69. Also, in his 1900 MA thesis, Jones characterizes the influence of the Christian message ultimately in social terms, even if no concrete social policy or strategies are adopted. Jones, October 8, 1900, Diary.

4. Noble began his long series on "Psychology" with Cable on "Prayer," and Mrs. Noble translating excerpts from Western spiritual and devotional classics, such as the "Upper Room."
5. William Arthur Noble, "Christology," *SW* 7, no. 4–5 (1909): 511–25.

sociopolitical upheavals. The logic was simple—Jesus is more than qualified to be the new ethical standard. His powerful personality and his life example prove it. Most of all, Jesus' claim to be the new ethical standard has already been proven in history. The existence of powerful Western nations, which claim that Jesus is the foundation of their ethical system and nation, shows the truth and power of Jesus' moral example.

Jones and other missionaries began to preach Jesus as the Moral Model sent by God. It was "good news" to a people who were seeking an alternative to the failed religion of Confucianism that brought about the demise of the Choson Dynasty built on its famed ethical principles. Jones's article "Apologetics,"[6] published in 1909, but likely presented as a special lecture in the theological classes that had begun in the fall of 1906, reflects this new direction. In the article, Jones argued that the truth of Christianity was supported by three undeniable factors: its world-changing power, its revelation of the first duty of humanity toward God, and the foremost law of love. He proudly points to its practical powers and to the prosperity and power of all nations that have turned Christian. He adds that vast non-Christian nations have been colonized by Christian England, Germany, and Russia.

In line with Noble's naming of Jesus as the "Ethical Standard," Jones lays out its meaning in concrete and practical terms of a new

---

6. George Heber Jones, "Apologetics 4," *SW* 6, no. 5–6 (1909): 258–80. This is the concluding lecture of a four-part series. It is interesting that his final lecture ends with this contextual Christology. For Jones, there could have been no better time to present Jesus as the beacon in the darkness of Choson facing its demise. The earlier lectures are on apologetics as a method of examining the origins of a religion and the veracity of its scriptures, and the Christian Bible as the basis for Christian apologetics in "Apologetics 1," *SW* 5, no. 2 (1907): 504–11; God's existence and goodness proven by stars and planets, living plants, human body and soul in "Apologetics 2," *SW* 5, nos. 4–5 (1907): 599–631; all creation reveals the goodness of Creator God, all humanity has religions in "Apologetics 3," *SW* 6, no. 1 (1908): 8–20. Jones's definition of theology is found in "Systematic Theology: An Overview," *SW* 5, no. 1 (1907): 465–72; his doctrine of God is found in "The Doctrine of God," *SW* 7, no. 1 (1909): 341–48.

ethics. Jesus is the Revelator of the supreme principle (*suryun*), the Teacher of a new law of love, and the founder of a new civilization.

First, he portrays Jesus as the New Interpreter, or Revelator, from God, who revealed humanity's first principle (*ilryun*) of our duty to God. He chides Chinese Confucianism, which ignored the primary principle of duty to God, and only dwelt on the requirements of human duties to the earthly king and parents. Jesus had come to reveal the first (*ilryun*) and highest (*suryun*) principle that must be kept. Only then can the five principles of Confucianism governing human relations be rightly observed.[7] Earlier, he had criticized a lack of real spirituality in Confucianism. Here, Jones argues that Confucianism's "atheism" or lack of primary attention to God opened the door for the superstition of Buddha and Lao Tzu to run rampant. Confucianism had become confused about the core principles.

In other words, Jesus showed what was missing in Confucianism and in Korean communal life, despite its strict adherence to the five relations and its central principles of *chung-hyo*, loyalty to the king, and filial piety to parents. It had forgotten the number one principle about humanity's primary relationship to God. The neglect of this most high principle and rule of relationship had brought about chaos in every other human relationship. When the first principle is ignored, how can the rest of the system run smoothly?

Second, Jones argues that Jesus revealed the simple but central law of God's love (Matt. 5:44–49) that was universal, inclusive, non-prejudicial, and extensive in its reach. This love became actualized in Jesus' own life as the great high priest (Heb. 4:12). As the Son of Man, Jesus is both human and divine, and as such, fulfilled his dual "sonship" perfectly. He first showed his true *hyo,* or filial piety, to his Heavenly Father and true *chung,* or loyalty, to his Heavenly Lord, by

---

7. Jones, "Apologetics," 266.

obeying his commandments. He also showed the human duties of *hyo* and *chung* to his earthly parents and earthly king.[8] Since Jesus is from God and gave us a model, we ought to do as he did and lived by observing the first principle and the central law of love.

As a consequence of these two images, Jones's central apologetical point then leads to a third image of Jesus as the founder of a new civilization. Jones could be certain of his belief in Jesus because he could point to the historical proof of the power and truthfulness of Jesus' new revelation; all the Western nations that had Jesus as their Ethical Standard were prosperous and strong, and even controlled other heathen nations as colonies. Thus, the missionaries preached: "Believe in Jesus and accept the new Principle and the new Law of love. Then you will be able to live by the right standard and also make Korea into a Christian nation. Therefore, believe in Jesus and be saved. Join the *Yesukyo*, the *Kusekyo!*"

This is Jones's most developed statement about Jesus on the Korean soil, one that reinterpreted the traditional Western two-natures doctrine of Jesus in the Confucian cultural setting. Jesus is the true human being, the interpreter of the principles of God, and the incarnated mediator between heaven and earth. He himself taught and practiced true *hyo and chung*, both to his Heavenly Father and King and to his earthly parents and king. It was his divine nature that enabled Jesus to worship and honor God, his Father and Sovereign Lord and reveal the *suryun* to the human family. In his human nature, he was completely faithful in practicing *chung* and *hyo* to his earthly parents and king. It is his human nature that enables his brothers and sisters to imitate him in recognizing their true relationship to God, as God's sons and daughters. It is in light of this act that Jones brings up the Biblical images of the Son of Man and the Great High Priest

---

8. Jones does not elaborate on this point, but suggests that Jesus obeyed the laws of the land (his king) although he fought and struggled against evil laws and the evil practices of the Pharisees.

to emphasize the identity of Christ with the human family. He is compassionate in sharing their burdens, and yet, able to stand firm before temptations to lead his brothers and sisters forward into true faith.

What five hundred years of Confucianism had been unable to do, Jesus had done in his person. That made him the teacher surpassing Confucius, because he restored the cosmic order. He reordered the relationship of humanity toward God as being the primary and first relationship. He then formed the true human society, through which people were being changed to see humanity's primary relationship to God and to pay proper honor and love to their earthly parents and kings and neighbors.

In these ethical arguments, one can see that Jones has been an astute student of Choson society, its philosophies, and religions. One can almost imagine him growing in his grasp of the Confucian mindset as he listens and converses, debates, and argues with his teacher, Choe Pyonghon, from the very beginning, as he tries to persuade Choe to follow the new Way of Jesus. Then, as both become evangelists in Chemulpo and Chongdong, they face the challenge of making the message stick. How would they speak of ethics in a society whose "leading men" thought that Master Confucius had the last word on ethics? Choe's Confucian influence on Jones becomes dramatically clear in these images. These insights on Jesus resulted from Jones's perceptive political sense as well as the real need in the infant church for a clear message at a time of great social upheavals.

7.3 Jesus, the Purifying Lord of the Church

The image of Jesus, the New Ethical Model, was also strongly emphasized in the 1907 Revival. The Revival, which started in

Pyongyang in January, swept across the whole country and helped redefine what the Korean church would be at a time of national disaster. Jesus' own ethical standard had revealed the supreme law (*suryun*) of humanity's primary duty to God and the central law of love of Matt. 5:44–49. Now, it became clear in the 1907 Revival that the community of believers formed by Jesus—the New Interpreter, New Teacher, and New Founder—ought to practice his teachings as a way of life.

As their Lord, Jesus expected his followers to imitate his path of highest ethics. The path of the ethical life was not reserved for a select few, but for the whole community. The year-long experience of communal confessions, repentance, mutual forgiveness, and acts of restitution in 1907 has instituted the image of a rather stern and moralistic Jesus in the consciousness of the Korean church. While the Korean church has often used this image to fall into moralistic self-righteousness ("Christians don't smoke, drink, or dance"), conversion to Jesus always meant a new way of life and a new ethical standard. This standard, however, was different from others, for it was an ethic that emerged from a personal relationship with the living God. The experience of God resulted in ethical behavior. It is Jesus who alone saves our souls, not our culture or education, but once he does, it makes a difference in the person's life in this world.[9]

---

9. Thus one keeps the Sabbath because believers are those who have "cast out desires of the flesh and distinguish between the body and the soul." Thus, they need to spend one day for nurturing the soul. Jones emphasized the physical difference of paying attention to the things of the spirit on Sundays as the mark setting Christians apart from society, which, in turn, will make a difference in the world. George Heber Jones, "Sabbath Keeping," *SW* 1, no. 1 (1901): 10–13.

In his account of the 1907 revival,[10] Jones names the true knowledge of "the true and terrible character of sin," or "sinfulness of sin," and repentance as the most important impact of the revival.[11] What is the true and terrible character of sin, and what does it reveal about Jesus, who came to save humanity from their sins? In various accounts of the Revival, "sin" is defined as the lack of "great sorrow for sin," i.e., lack of contrition and true confession, or ignorance of the "true sinfulness of sin." Jones writes:

> Among a people like the Koreans, there is no definite and clear idea of the true and terrible character of sin, so that when first converted they are not prepared to manifest the deep and awful conviction that is found among those who have been taught what sin really is. This fact has led some into believing that the Koreans are incapable of deep feeling. This revival, however, has shown that having once come under the power of personal conviction, and having been placed in a position where the Holy Spirit can work on their hearts, they are capable of as overwhelming sense of sin as any people on earth. The one cry of the Korean Church was for heart cleansing.[12]

---

10. Jones and Noble, *The Korean Revival*. Yi Dokju traces the 1907 Revival back to 1901, when missionaries speak of "old-time Methodist revivalism" arising among people, which later became organized as a collective event in Wonsan in August 1903. At a meeting of the missionaries, R. A. Hardie confessed his lack of spiritual fervor and his pride and obstinacy. When he shared this with his members at Wonsan, it resulted in a time of "repentance, regeneration, and sanctification." Later, this was mirrored by "open confession" among Korean members, which continued for one year among the Methodist circles. Other denominations joined in September, 1904. Yi Dokju, *Formation of Indigenous Church*, 91–94.
11. Jones and Noble, *The Korean Revival*, 11, 35.
12. Ibid., 11–12.

For Jones, the sinfulness of sin is to have an actual sense or conviction of sin,[13] marked by deep remorse, emotional distress, and especially, physical expression, for

> If men ever discovered the terribleness of sin when revealed uncovered in the presence of God, they did in those days. First came the physical distress, penitents beating the floor with hands and with head, and their screams and outcries were as though the demons whose name is legion were tearing them, then followed sobbing confessions of sinful and unclean lives. One general characteristic of these seekers was their consciousness.[14]

In Jones's account, the deep awareness of sin meant recognizing any sin as an action directed against God and Jesus' first commandment of love, and becoming fully conscious of this reality, which leads to a comprehensive act of repentance, including physical, emotional, and mental distress or "deep feeling." For Jones, the Revival was about what the people felt and experienced as they repented of their sins.

In Blair's account, however, the consciousness of the "content" of sin was even more important than the emotional feelings that accompanied repentance. Blair clearly defined sin as "double-

---

13. See Yi Dokju, *Formation of Indigenous Church*, 89–133 for a comprehensive discussion of this issue. It is interesting to compare Jones's account with his contemporary Presbyterian missionary, William Blair, who came to Korea in 1901. He recalls that the occasion for the Pyongyang revival was an August 1906 missionary retreat where the missionaries were searching for a way forward for the Korean church, given the political instability and the emergence of an independent indigenous church and leadership. Again, led by Hardie, who used the I John text showing that "the way of victory for us would be a way of confession, of broken hearts and bitter tears." According to Blair, he called for three concrete confessions of sin; the Korean church's repentance of hating the Japanese, a deeper recognition of sin against God, given many Christians lack of "great sorrow for sin because of its familiarity," and "embittered souls needed to have their thoughts taken away from the national situation to their own personal relation with the Master." The spiritual direction of this retreat was repeated at the January 1907 Pyongyang Biblical Institute, which was the occasion of the start of the Korean Pentecost. I John was used as the text for the 1906 and 1907 Revival by Hardie and others. William N. Blair and Bruce F. Hunt, *The Korean Pentecost and the Suffering Which Followed* (Edinburgh: Banner of Truth Trust, 1977), 67.
14. Jones and Noble, *Korean Revival*, 14.

mindedness,"[15] or drawing one's loyalty and devotion from God to earthly concerns, especially becoming "embittered" and hostile because of the national crisis and the presence of the foreign occupying force. In addition to hating the Japanese, the Korean Christians were guilty of turning their eyes away from the things of God to worldly concerns. For Blair, this was a sign of the lack of love of God that Jesus revealed as the first principle and the first law. Jesus' first principle was greater than the love of one's native land.

While Jones preached that the truth of Jesus' saving message was proven by its power to change the world, the Revival of 1907 introduced into Korean church a church-focused Jesus who demanded the purity of his disciples, including a separation from worldly concerns. The more one became united with Jesus, the less care one entertained about the world. The more one became focused on church work, the less he or she had to do with the world, especially its political reality, which was passing away. It ended up painting Jesus into the corner of the church. The atonement, which he had made with his own life for the life of the world, was interpreted quite narrowly as the salvation of the sin-sick soul now becoming freed from its earthly connections and concerns. This dualism would be powerfully challenged in March 1919, but in popular accounts of the Revival of 1907, the Revival took the society out of the minds of the Korean Christians.

Thus, the purifying fires of the 1907 Revival formed a truly ethical faith community, filled with "the holiness of God" that was not of human origin, but from Christ alone. In particular, the works of restitution the now repentant purified Christians carried out on their own, as if driven by a most exacting spirit of rectitude and

---

15. Jones, December 9, 1899, Diary. The issue of double-mindedness was a theme that Jones often preached on. Preaching from James 1:8 on double-mindedness, he writes, "Our Koreans are in danger of becoming too engrossed in the occupations of this life."

righteousness, amazed the society at large. Grown men and women—from elderly grandparents to students in grade school—repented of their sins of commission and omission and sought out those whom they had wronged, hated, or misunderstood.

But in the accounts of the 1907 Revival by Jones and Blair, there is an element that contradicted the central premise of Jesus, the Ethical Standard. For twenty-five years, American missionaries had been preaching that Jesus is the saving and civilizing Savior. They had pointed to the Western nations, now Christianized and civilized, as the living, historical proof of the salvation wrought by Jesus and the truth of his message, but now it seemed as if the new ethical community of faith in Korea—established by the same Jesus and purified by his righteous Spirit, which judges the inner hearts of men and women—would not be held up to the same historical standard. There would be no need for this ethical community to seek to make its presence felt in the arena of world history. In fact, to do so would be a sign of turning away from the love of God, and thus, a sign of its sinfulness.

At the end of the article "Apologetics 4," Jones offers an interesting reason for shifting the attention away from local political realities to the heavenly Kingdom of God. He also gives another title to Jesus, the Lord of the Church: the universal Savior. Jones argues that while all religions are national and ethnic in nature, only Christianity is a universal religion. As such, the Old Testament goal of building a human society based on the true religion has been set aside.

> The New Testament carefully tells why the people are made new and did not discuss about ruling the government. The reason is (that) it is not a "national" religion, but the great way under heaven. Thus, it did not talk about national governance. In the Old Testament, the beginning of heaven and earth is recorded, and it is really a wonderful truth, but it does not give a careful explanation of all theories about astronomy. Because its basic concern is about the salvation of all people, it does not

deal with nature. The talk about heaven and earth in other religions all are alike in their uncertainty. Those who know the true principle know their falsehood and do not believe them. *It also spoke about national politics which has no relevance for us* (italics by the author). Now the Old Testament does not contain false words, thus it must be believed for generations. The New Testament does not speak about national governance, thus it is meaningful for all nations. The reason for the beauty of this teaching is because it comes from true God.[16]

He argues first that Jesus has opened the doors of a universal religion of the great way, compared to other "national" or "tribal" religions, which hold for only a specific time, place, or people. Thus, all doctrines and teachings related to the "local" have been done away with by Jesus, which includes the Old Testament language and doctrines about human society and politics. So, in the Christian church, any concern about local politics goes against the universal nature of the church. The understanding of *taedo* or The Great Way—of the universal nature of Christianity—both displaces it as a "Western" religion as well as shakes it from its "nationalistic" moorings. This phenomenon was very common in Korea and the East, where religions have served as the religious foundation for dynastic families, and then, were replaced by another when the dynasties changed. But the concern in this paragraph also has another audience. Christianity is apolitical, or non-political, and non-nationalistic; thus, by inference, Korean Christians must keep clear of the political process, political aspirations, and political participation.

However, emphasizing the universality of Christianity at this point introduces a paradox into Jones's preaching. It calls into question his earlier argument that all Christian nations are prosperous and have become powerful (enough to possess colonies). However, Jones does not address this apparent inconsistency nor deny the truthfulness of

---

16. Jones, "Apologetics 4," 280.

his first premise. Korean Christians faced a troubling predicament. They had been amazed by the dazzling signs of Christian power in building Christian nations and civilizations. They also had been amazed by this *taedo,* or great way, by which they had found God's truth. Now, they faced a dilemma. Would they be willing to dispense with the local expressions of Christian faith in Korea when, in the West, it had clear cultural influence, including political power?

7.4 1905 and Its Effect on Jones's Ethical Jesus

1905 was the beginning of the end of half a millennium of the Choson Dynasty, which was renamed the "Empire of Taehan" in 1897. Jones thought its end was already visible in 1884, when the radical reformers' revolution was overturned after three days, and Korea began to lurch between forces of reform and reaction for the next twenty-five years. In reality, after his 1892 study of the 1592 Invasion of Korea by Japan, Jones had concluded that the decline of Choson had begun several centuries back and that it was only waiting for another powerful nation to grab it.[17] The 1905 military victory of Japan over Russia, a Western Christian empire, signaled Japan's political predominance in Asia. The Emperor of Taehan could do nothing about the 1905 Treaty of Portsmouth signed between Japan and Russia, which gave Japan the right to control the destiny of Korea, putting Choson on the throes of its death.

It was a time when social disorder, collective despair, denial of reality, and occasional acts of self-determination against imperial domination were on the rise. Jones and the indigenous church seized this moment in Korean history to proclaim Jesus as the spiritual and

---

17. *Korean Repository* vol. 1 (1892) contains a seven-part series on "The Japanese Invasion," 10–16, 46–50, 116–21, 147–52, 182–88, 217–22, 308–11. For other comments on the Japanese invasion, see Jones, July 15, 1891, Diary.

temporal answer to the Korean crisis. Jones and the Korean church leaders blamed Korea's social problems on the failure of the traditional religions of Korea:

> Property is insecure, the standard of education is low, corruption prevails everywhere, the people are oppressed, and life is neither safe nor sacred. Such is the awful condition of the country. Christianity alone can save the individual and the state.[18]

In this context, Jones proclaimed Jesus as the One who comes to save both the individual and the state. He interpreted the three traditional religions as having become corrupted and degraded into crass idolatry, having lost any form of religious vitality they had before.[19] For example, he describes Buddhism as having lost its inner vitality so that even its priests and nuns had no idea of its subtle teachings. Thus, Jesus was held up as the religious and ethical Teacher, superior to other Founders, fully capable of correcting the limits of the Confucian system that had only known about the *samryun* and *oryun*, but not about the *ilryun* and *suryun*.

In light of the violence of the rule of law of Choson's rulers against their own people, which had already made the people's heart flee from the rulers, Jesus stood for the Law of love. His love was inclusive and sensitive to the rulers' victims and had restored dignity to everyone who entered his community. Above all, as the process of the collapse of Old Korea quickened at every level of society, everyone mourned the passing of their ancestral heritage and despaired of a new society. Jones points to Jesus and the mighty West as the new possibility that awaited Korea if it would only turn to *Yesukyo,* or the Teaching of Jesus, for his truth would help reconstruct Korea and enable her to find her true destiny in God and the world.

---

18. George H. Jones, Supplemental chapter to *Korea Mission of the Methodist Episcopal Church*, 2d ed., by Henry G. Appenzeller (New York: Open Door Emergency Commission, 1906), 35.
19. Jones, *Korea: The Land,* 1–2.

Likewise, the Purifying Lord of the Church that appeared in the 1907 Revival revealed the power of the Ethical Savior. Never had neo-Confucianism in its 500 years of rule in Choson reached such a level of ethical purity and discipline. It was not just Jesus, the Ethical Savior, who preached and practiced his *suryun* and law of love. It was not just the selected upper class who had the time to spend to cultivate virtue and practice ritual righteousness. In the church, all people, from the youngest to the oldest, from the poorest to the richest, both men and women, were expected to embody the first principle and practice the central law of love.

The people heard the message gladly. People by the thousands thronged to the Christian church. Jesus had become the Savior of the Korean people. Now, they waited for him to become the Savior of the Korean nation. So far, we have shown that Jones's newer thoughts about Jesus in this period were greatly informed and transformed by the sociopolitical developments surrounding the collapse of the Korean monarchy. The massive movement of the Korean *minjung* into the Christian churches where *Yesu*, the Ethical Lord, *the Ethical Example,* awaited them, testifies to his sensitivity to people's hearts, as well as meeting the aspirations of the people for the birth of a new society in their midst.

7.5 Jesus and the 1907 Korean Pentecost

1907 takes on a special place in Korean missionary lore, and in Jones's account as well,[20] as the "natal day of God's church in Korea."[21] The 1907 Revival was, in actuality, a long series of revivals that had its

---

20. Jones understands the event as "an exceptional time, one that rarely comes in the history of the church," a special work of the Holy Spirit on the church, Christians, to give them a "definite" and "clear" idea of the "true and terrible character of sin." Jones and Noble, *Korean Revival,* 10–11.
21. Jones, "Christian Missions in Korea," Papers, 9–10.

beginning and initiative among Methodist missionary circles, starting in 1904. But Jones also continues to compare "that day in January 1907" to the Day of Pentecost in the Christian Bible (Acts of the Apostles 2).

> The Korean Church now possesses its own spiritual history, which is the all-convincing evidence to itself that it is as much begotten of God as the Churches in more favored lands with their great historic past.[22]

However, no missionary would discount the first twenty years of Christian witness in Korea, which, before 1907, were frequently compared to the apostolic days.[23]

The centerpiece of the 1907 Revival, as it has been told, is the "confession," which sometimes lasted days and nights, after which the people were filled with a "deep and marvelous peace and souls were awed into silence in the presence of God."[24] Pyongyang, the hotbed of Christian growth, was remarkable for the scope and length of this spiritual "movement." Nearly all Christians there and over two-thirds of all Christians in Korea shared in this common experience, almost like a rite of passage.[25] Wonderful descriptions of this amazing event are available. The crowds were impressed with the people's repentance and their effort at restitution to correct the sins and wrongs of the past.[26]

---

22. George Heber Jones, *The Korea Mission of the Methodist Episcopal Church* (New York: BFM-MEC, 1910), 47–48.
23. Already in 1901 and in 1904, Jones recognized the characteristic marks of the Korean church and asked about the source of their power. "One answer alone there is: It is the Spirit of God" that has enabled them to withstand the persecution as well as to become self-sufficient in financial support and be a church of prayer. Jones, *Successes and Opportunities*, 10. Jones likened the Korean church, its growth, and its catechetical system to the apostolic times. Jones, "The Growth of the Church in Korea," 13–14.
24. Jones and Noble, *Korean Revival*, 29.
25. Ibid., 14. "No half work would satisfy them. If any of them allowed himself to be betrayed into being satisfied with less than complete cleaning, he would soon discover how futile were his attempts, and would be brought low at the foot of the cross, there to remain on his face until God had completed his work."
26. Ibid., 26.

It brought the Korean church in touch with the living God and his Mediator, Jesus. Moreover, by its experiential power and force, it made Christian faith and experience a palpable reality. "It made him (Christ) a fact and a reality to each one personally, and to each church."[27] This led to a deepened spiritual life of prayer, fervent evangelism that resulted in over 80,000 new converts, and the formation of an ethical community with "moral possibilities of the highest order."[28] These facts are acknowledged in most accounts of the Revival.

However, another aspect of the 1907 Revival needs to be examined further, in particular, two revealing points in Jones's account. He writes,

The political disturbances had greatly agitated the people throughout that section, and there is little doubt that many of the church members had for a time lost sight of the blessedness of the gospel and were seeking for political aid and personal advantage.[29]

As a result of the revival, "The revival had an indirect bearing on the maintenance of law and order during a time of great national disturbance."[30] The revivals had prepared the soil so the Christians "were more ready to stand for law and order."[31] In other words, they were more ready to accept Japanese colonial rule (for, in Jones's eyes, Japan stood for the rule of "law and order").

How did this happen? One can read the first step in Jones's words: the separation of whatever happened to the nation from "the blessedness of the gospel." But this separation was bound to confuse the members, especially socially minded members. In another part of his account, Jones had remarked how the missionaries had seen in the

---

27. Jones, "Christian Missions in Korea," 10.
28. Jones and Noble, *Korean Revival*, 40.
29. Ibid., 32.
30. Ibid., 41.
31. Ibid., 42.

native Christians the potential for "moral possibilities of the highest order," and that the crowds had been impressed by their voluntary acts of repentance and restitution. After all, this was taking place in a Confucian society, which had promised to make the people virtuous according to the mandate of Heaven, but now had been reduced to a land of robbers and corrupt rulers, from top to bottom; even the people themselves had become evil. But now, they recognized their sins and the sin of the land.

Thus, they repented. Jones's account contains a very revealing paragraph about what was happening in the confessions and prayers of repentance. While many accounts dwell on the public confession of private sins, Jones reports that in these prayers he heard what today is called the *han*[32] of the people, revealing something of the inexpressible depression surrounding the Korean people's lives.

> It is the sorrows and griefs (*sic*) of life that have molded Korean ideas and susceptibilities…the scenes of violence and crime, the ruin of individuals and homes, the innumerable cases of oppression and violence which were told would fill many volumes and can be explained only on the ground of imperfect laws and an astonishing disregard of human life. It was into hearts shadowed by tragedies untold that God sent the power of the Holy Spirit to redeem and save.[33]

For Jones, it wasn't so much that people were making a list of their individual sins, although there was that. It was more a collective cry to God, much like the prayers of lament in the Psalms, "How long, O God, must we live in this sinful land, filled with poverty, suffering,

---

32. *Han* maybe loosely translated as lament or sadness, covering many different kinds of sadness. There is no literal English translation. "It's a state of mind. Of soul, really. A sadness. A sadness so deep no tears will come. And yet, still, there's hope," says President Josiah Barlet after he attempts to find out the meaning of the word in the West Wing. The West Wing. Season 5 Episode 4. "Han." See Andrew Sung Park, *The Wounded Heart of God: The Asian Concept of Han and the Christian Doctrine of Sin* (Nashville, TN: Abingdon Press, 1993), 15–86 for a Christian appropriation of the idea of *han*.
33. Jones and Noble, *Korean Revival*, 22.

corrupt and vile leaders, violence, war, killing?" Like Jones, they also saw the writing on the wall, warning of the coming disaster. They could easily imagine the future suffering under the cruel oppression of Japanese colonialism. They had already witnessed Japanese merchants buying up the best rice for export back to Japan when there was not enough rice to go around in Korea during the famine of 1901–2.

There is no doubt that Korean Christians repented for their personal sins. But they also repented of their collective sin in allowing their society to become so twisted from their original goodness, so full of idolatry and so filled with violence and corruption. They repented of their sin in allowing evil rulers to oppress the poor; they also repented of their sin in allowing the nation to become so weak as to allow foreign armies to trample their native land underfoot. In these prayers and laments of the revival, Jones recognized a revolutionary power—and trembled. Christians were repenting not only for their own sins, but were going beyond the church walls to embrace the entire society into the magnetic field of their prayer and concern. If the Confucian society was to be blamed for the sorrows and tribulations of life, Korean Christians were declaring that they would pray *and work* to make their homeland truly Christian, truly ethical, beneficial, and civilization-building, and edify and save the people from sin, slavery, and despair.

It is in this sense that the 1907 Revival can be understood as the indigenization of the Korean church—not in their *tongsong kido* (collective audible prayer), nor in their open confessions (well-known in Finneyan revivals), nor in their physical displays of distress (a revival staple). Rather, in the darkening years following 1905, as the force of Japanese imperial rule began to be felt, Korean Christians made the entire society their arena of intercessory concern and prayerful action. They began with a personal, prophetic identification with the sins of the land, which always began with confession of wrongs committed against their closest neighbors.

Interestingly, Blair called for repentance of "Christian hatred of Japanese," which Jones does not mention. For Blair, the Revival came just in the right time as an answer to the intractable and revolutionary situation, especially for the Korean church, in which "hotheads" were urging a more active role for the church.[34] But neither account mentions the fact that in many churches, special prayer services and patriotic actions were held for the dying nation.

For example, Kil Sonju, who would become the most celebrated revivalist of the 1907 Revival in Pyongyang, began holding early morning prayer meetings from the fall of 1906, focusing on prayers for the salvation of the nation. Some of actions taken by the Korean churches in the post-1905 era were public prayer meetings for the nation, a signature movement to regain national sovereignty, protest suicides, armed struggle, mobilization to pay back national debt, participation in the Righteous Army, and Christian leaders appointed as peace commissars to work out ceasefire terms with the Righteous Army.[35]

For the Korean Christians, it was a time of Christianizing *and* civilizing the land for Jesus, the Ethical Standard and the Purifying Lord of the Church. It was a time to claim their rightful place in society because they were willing to bear the suffering of the people. Their ethic would be an ethic of love and self-sacrifice, one less of judgment and one of mercy, one of inner transformation and less of external rites, and one of action and not so much words.

Unfortunately, the missionaries believed in "law and order," not

---

34. Blair and Hunt, *Korean Pentecost*, 61–70; see also William N. Blair, *Gold in Korea*, 3d ed. (New York: Board of Foreign Missions of the Presbyterian Church, 1957), 60–68, for the connection he makes between the political situation and the revival.
35. See Yi Dokju, *Formation of Indigenous Church*, 163–94, for a detailed discussion of these activities by the Korean Christians.

the freedom-filled wind of the Spirit. For Jones, the loss of the nation was not meaningful or helpful to dwell on, for "history has shown that a people may lose their national influence without losing their influence on the life of the world."[36] Instead, the missionaries called for peaceful nonintervention. Carl Rufus, commenting on the sacrificial spirit and intercessory prayer life of Korean Christians, observes in 1909, "The Christian principle of nonresistance seems to fit serenely into the life of the Korean Christian. In a word, the Korean seems to be made for the Gospel and the Gospel for the Korean."[37] To be a Korean Christian now meant to close one's eyes to the social changes around him or her.

Thus, it is important to ask why Jones and most of the missionaries took such a strong stance of non-intervention in Korean affairs. What accounts for the discrepancy between their proclamation from the beginning about Christ, the renovator of souls and nations, and their actions? In particular, what did they mean by their earlier proclamation of Jesus as the universal "Ethical Standard" who would create a different kind of community for a different kind of a world?

7.6 What Would Jesus and Jones Do about Japan and Korea?

No one disputes the fact that Jones and most missionaries welcomed the Japanese involvement in Korean affairs after Japan defeated the Chinese in 1894, and especially, after the 1905 Treaty of Portsmouth, following the Russo-Japanese War, which de facto placed Korea under Japanese power.[38] It has also been acknowledged that the

36. Jones and Noble, *Korean Revival*, 42.
37. BFM-MEC, *Annual Report*, 1909, 348.
38. The historical record is clear that "most of the missionaries stationed in Korea, both Catholic and Protestant, in 1910 openly supported, tacitly consented to, or ignored the Annexation of Korea to Japan." They believed that the church would further develop under the Japanese rule; thus, their main concern was not about the Korean people and their aspirations, but about maintaining their freedom to evangelize, trusting the Japanese "guarantee of missionary

American missionary community acquiesced to Japanese pressure and prohibited the Korean church from political activism for two main reasons—their principled stance on the separation of church and state,[39] and their belief that the Japanese would not hinder the missions, but that the Korean church would blossom under Japanese rule. The 1910 Annual Missionary Report for Korea states: "The changed political situation in Korea will, it is believed by many, hasten rather than hinder the evangelization of the people, given the religious liberty guaranteed by the Japanese authorities."[40] In addition, Bishop Harris, who oversaw the Methodist work in both Japan and Korea, was an ardent supporter of Japanese policies in Korea.

The missionary community preached Christ and civilization, supported the Independence Club from the beginning, and championed the ideal of American constitutional democracy among progressive Koreans. So, the two reasons given do not add up to a persuasive case for suppressing the aspirations of the Korean people for independence and supporting a colonial rule for Korean Christians. In addition, while the missionary community adopted a policy of separation of church and state in Korea, neither the American church nor the missionaries, in general, abided by such a principle.[41] In fact, the opposite was the practice. Most missionaries

activity." Cho Kwang, *200 Years of Korean Catholicism* (K) (Seoul: Haitbit Ch'ulp'ansa, 1989), 63–64.
39. "Ultimately a great gap in understanding the role of Christianity appeared between the Koreans who in their long history of national suffering expected Christianity to play a political role of overcoming national crisis, and the missionaries who were used to the affirmation of ruling system of those in power due to their separation of religion from politics." Wells, *New God, New Nation*, 46.
40. BFM-MEC, *Annual Report*, 1910: 358.
41. After Queen Min was murdered on Oct. 18, 1895, American missionaries, Jones included, stood guard at the royal bedroom for seven weeks. They also tried to rescue Kojong on Nov. 27, 1895, which failed, but finally helped him to escape to the Russian legation on Feb. 11, 1896. No doubt these actions influenced Kojong's decision to give official permission for open religious activity in June, 1898.

did not abide by this principle, since most of them were highly critical of the Korean government and hoped for its demise. Thus, we are forced to look for other reasons to explain this important missionary policy change at a critical juncture in Korean church history.

It is clear from Jones's public and private writings that he was probably the most astute political analyst among the missionaries in Korea, and enjoyed the friendship of many of the movers and shakers in Korean diplomatic circles, especially American ambassador Dr. Allen.[42] With these ties, it was easy to adopt the American policy line regarding the "Korean problem." By 1905, the United States and Japan had signed a gentlemen's agreement regarding each other's colonial interests, called the Taft-Katsura Pact, through which the US agreed to let Japan have its way in Korea, and Japan allowed the US uncontested rule in the Philippines.

Jones believed that Old Korea lacked internal moral and human resources to become independent and that "union with Japan" would help the Korean people in the long run. From the very first, Jones detested the old feudalistic ways of Old Korea, especially in comparison to its relatively modernized neighboring Japan, to which he often took refuge for his illness as well as mental health. His first research on Korean history was on the 1592–98 Japanese invasion of Korea, by which he concluded that Korea had been on the decline since the sixteenth century and that Japan had a more vital and "masculine" culture.[43]

---

42. The Jones and Allen families were very close. Jones was privy to many government secrets and served as Allen's private interpreter several times when Allen spoke to Emperor Kojong about very critical affairs regarding Korean politics. Once, Allen offered Jones a position in the American embassy, which Jones refused for its low salary. See George Heber Jones to Margaret B. Jones, 1902–3, Letters. For Allen's role in Korea, see Fred Harvey Harrington, *God, Mammon, and the Japanese: Dr. Horace N. Allen and Korean-American Relations, 1884-1905* (Madison, WI: University of Wisconsin Press, 1944).
43. For a relatively positive analysis of US–Japanese and Japanese–Korean relations, see George Heber Jones, "American Japanese Relations—A Review," *The Journal of Race Development* 3

In addition, Jones had little respect for the leadership of the Independence Club and considered them inept and pompous, except for Yun Chiho. Yun told him, in 1899, after the Club was banned,

> If Korea could be protected from interference by Japan & Russia, the Koreans themselves would soon settle matters here. But it is to the interest of Japan and Russia to maintain the present farce of a Gov't, for it is so venal they can buy from it anything they want. The Japanese have proven most mean and contemptible and have sold out both sides in Korea repeatedly... He thought that there is material in Korea out of which to erect a stable upright and honest Gov't, provided a public opinion can be created to which they must be amenable. This is the only hope of the country.[44]

While he sympathized with Yun's patriotic concerns, he did not believe nor agree with him.

After 1894, Jones was astute enough to recognize Japan's talk of Korean "independence" as a cover for colonial rule, although he believed Japanese "reformers" such as Marquis Ito would bring Korea under a civilizing, not an imperialistic, policy. Thus, Jones's obituary in the *Seoul Press* (a Japanese newspaper) reads in part,

> When the Residency-General regime was inaugurated in this peninsula, he was among the few far-sighted foreign missionaries, who were thoroughly sympathetic with the Japanese Government. He helped in every way to establish and promote good relations between the Japanese authorities and the resident foreign missionaries and rendered great service in this line to all concerned.[45]

Since this notice was placed after the March First Movement of 1919, and the Japanese were hard pressed to find Western supporters of its violent repression, the words "thoroughly sympathetic" may need

---

(July 1912): 55–64; and George Heber Jones, "Some Aspects of Reform in Korea," *The Journal of Race Development* 1 (July, 1910): 18–35.
44. Jones, August 12, 1899, Diary.
45. "Death of Rev. G.H. Jones," *Seoul Press*, June 13, 1919.

to be questioned. However, there was no doubt in the minds of the Japanese that Jones was a friend.

But it was no crime to be a friend of Japan in early twentieth century, for most Western intellectuals, including Jones, always viewed Korea through the lens of Japan.[46] One need not rehearse the story of Japan's modernization[47] to realize that the West adored Japan, and especially, its complete makeover as a Western society. Radical Japanese reformers such as Fukuzawa Yukichi and his book *Break With Asia* (1885) echoed the sentiments of the foreign minister of Japan who said in 1887, "Let us change our empire into a European-style empire. Let us change our people into a European-style people."[48] Given the popular social Darwinist worldview that supported American manifest destiny in Asia and placed Japan on the top of ladder in terms of national development, it was natural that Jones would welcome Japan as a reforming and modernizing power in Korea. His personal knowledge of the failure of reform in Korea due to the government's corrupt ineptitude and a lack of alternate viable leadership outside the government made it easy to look to Japan for change.

In many ways, Jones's relationship with George T. Ladd, who was hired by the Japanese government as a propagandist and supporter of Japanese imperial purpose in Korea, is reflective of his overall attitude. Ladd's book, written after his tour of Korea in 1908, *In Korea with Marquis Ito*, has three simple messages that repeated the Japanese propaganda: Korea is corrupt through Chinese influence; Japan and Korea are one people; and Korea is incapable of self-

---

46. Of course, there were intellectuals and labor leaders who opposed American and Japanese imperialism. See Howard Zinn, *A People's History of the United States 1492-Present* (New York: HarperCollins Publishers, 1999), 297–320.
47. See, for example, John Hunter Boyle, *Modern Japan: The American Nexus* (Fort Worth, TX: Harcourt Brace College Publishers, 1993), 78–117.
48. Quoted in Boyle, *Modern Japan*, 112.

government, and thus, must be dependent on Japan. Ladd argues that Koreans need to be saved from their insurgents, customs, and themselves, from their "misguided patriotism, with a large mixture of hypocritical sentimentality…unwilling to admit the incapacity of their country to manage its own affairs," and argues at length on why Korea is "unfit for self-rule." He concludes, "The case of the nation is hopeless…they are an effete race, destined to give way before the invasion of members from any more vigorous race."[49] Jones agreed with Ladd, who called on the American missionary community to assist the "imperial task" of Japan "to accomplish the task of industrial development and political redemption in the land which was now so dependent upon Japan for its future,"[50] since Christianity is "the most important help toward the success of his (Ito's) policy in uplifting the Korean people."[51]

Jones and the American missionary community did write a letter of protest to Ladd regarding his prejudicial view of Korean Christianity. Ladd writes,

> Among the so-called civilized nations of the world, there is probably not another where the prevalent native religion is of a more depressing and degrading character than in Korea… In fact, not only do missionaries inflate the number of converts, the underlying motives for a first adherence to Christianity are, in a large percentage of so-called converts, economic and political rather than moral and spiritual.[52]

He thought the Revival of 1907 had nothing to do with spirituality or morality, but infantile Korean emotionalism, for it is reflective of the "infantile condition of the Korean mind, united, alas!, with a morality

---

49. George T. Ladd, *In Korea with Marquis Ito* (New York: Charles Scribner's Sons, 1908), 69–73, 162.
50. Ibid., 143.
51. Ibid., 67.
52. Ibid., 390–91, 408–11.

that is far removed from the innocence customarily attributed to the human infant."⁵³

However, Jones did not differ much from Ladd's perspective because he largely shared his worldview.⁵⁴ First, like Ladd, Jones did not think all imperialism was bad. In his later writings, Jones would praise the American occupation of Philippines and its military incursions around the world. Second, both assumed that when the ruling government is stable, the church must maintain the separation of state and religion, support the government's policy, and limit its work to the spiritual realm. Third, both assumed that in the evolution of nation states, Japan was superior to Korea and had the God-given right to rule over Korea. There is an explicit social Darwinism at work in the later Jones. Fourth, both worked out of an orientalist framework that the underdeveloped countries deserved to be controlled, reconstructed, and rebuilt by the advanced ones.⁵⁵ Fifth, both reflected a liberal belief that social progress is God-ordained, and that anything that stands in the way of progress stands in God's way as well.

How then shall we understand Jones's decision to disregard Korean independence and to support Japanese colonial rule? Dae Young Ryu argues that Jones acted from his deep-seated sense of American patriotism and support for its increasing imperialistic role in world politics. In addition, Jones's middle-class aspirations and his support for the American political agenda prevailed over his own Jesus-

---

53. Ibid., 411.
54. Ibid., 395. Ladd argues that Korea needs something more than what even the missionaries can provide. "The purification of Korea required, and still requires, the firm, strong hand of the civil power." Ladd was a theologian of some repute from Yale Divinity School. After Jones returned to the US, he served on the Board of Directors of the *Journal of Race Development* with George Ladd and wrote several articles on US–Japan relations and on developments in Korea.
55. For a discussion of orientalism, see Edward Said, *Orientalism* (New York: Pantheon Books, 1978).

inspired imagination. Not only was Japan destined to rule Korea, the American policy of manifest destiny in Asia also benefited from it.

But this interpretation is too simplistic and overlooks several important facts. First, while it is true that Jones was an American patriot, he also taught Korean Christians to love their country. Many of the elite Korean leaders such as Yun Chiho regularly sought out his opinions and advice in regards to the fate of the Korean state. In his heart, he considered himself a Korean. Thus, he did not see himself making a choice between two loyalties, i.e., supporting the American agenda and neglecting the Korean agenda.

Second, as one of the most astute readers of East Asian politics, Jones saw the writing on the wall. His journals after the end of the Sino–Japanese War in 1895 are filled with premonitions of the Korean collapse. He read the signs of the times and realized that Korea was "destined" to fall to Japan. He wanted to believe that self-initiated reforms would be enough. But what saddened him greatly was the lack of indigenous leadership that was organized, strong-willed, and astute enough to overcome great odds. Old Choson had completely depleted the people's will, as well as its military and technological resources. From early on, Jones despaired of a self-determining independent Korea.

Third, Jones honestly believed that Japan had the best of intentions in mind for Korea. In this sense, he believed in the imperialistic propaganda and refused to believe information available to him about the violence of Japanese rule and policies. Here, it was his modern, positivist belief in progress, social Darwinism, and imperialism that betrayed him, blinding him to Japan's imperialistic aims.

Fourth, Jones did not believe the Christian church in Korea was ready to play the kind of sociopolitical role it did in other countries. It was a fledgling community of faith. If it were thrust into the limelight, such action would only lead to disaster. Just as there was a lack of leadership in the larger society, he believed that the same leadership vacuum existed in the Christian church. In 1908, when the Korean mission was finally organized in a regular Annual Conference of the Methodist Episcopal Church, it had only 6 native ordained preachers, 29 local preachers and workers, 14,967 Sunday School scholars, and 24,244 communicants.[56] In his eyes, to encourage an unprepared, fledgling church to take on a leadership position in the society, especially political, would be suicidal. Jones thought he had the best interests of the Korean church in heart when he and the missionary community prohibited Korean Christian participation in anti-Japanese activities.

Fifth, the most important reason for rejecting Dae Young Ryu's analysis is Jones's later theological teaching, centered on the image of Jesus as the Ethical Model. It is amazing that it was in the aftermath of 1905 that Jones would begin teaching that Jesus is the Ethical Model in the theological classes (*sinhakhoe*) for the clergy and in the Bible institutes (*sakyonghoe*) for the laity. He recognized that Ethical Jesus was the only relevant message for a people about to lose their motherland. Jones really believed that the community of faith under Christ needs to be an ethical community. And in the Biblical and Confucian ethics, a person was not alone, but always connected in a network of relationships. Transforming one person held the promise of the transformation of an entire society. It was based on this principle that Jones taught a new vision for the people and the society in the three metaphors of Jesus.

But if this is what Jones believed about the efficacy of the Gospel, why did he stand in the way of the Spirit and the Gospel in Korea? Even while preaching Jesus as the Ethical Model, Jones failed to see the power of the Living Lord in preparing his ethical community

---

56. AR, Missionary Reports by the Corresponding Secretaries, 1908, 23 (308).

for the task of transforming Korea into a new nation. Whereas the Korean Christians heard and believed the proclamation of the Ethical Model and accepted the vocation of saving and renewing their society in the power of the Spirit, Jones trusted his own judgment about the flow of history that said Korea could not be independent, Japan is more powerful, and thus, more modern, and the institutional church is nonpolitical.

Some scholars argue that Jones's sociopolitical self-identification with the policies of his native country helped to direct his Christian missionary work. But if Jones and the missionaries were simply vanguards of American imperialism, as Dae Young Ryu and others suggest, it would have been foolish to preach Christ as the Ethical Model, which helped rally a despairing people. Rather, it would have been better to preach a transcendental Christ isolated in heaven, as far away from the realities of the day as possible.

But Jones was too good of a teacher and missionary to miss an opening to proclaim the salvation of Christ. The Spirit had rightly led the Korean church to proclaim Jesus as God's Ethical Standard of the Old Korea that was passing. It had even birthed an ethical community of love and right relations under its Purifying Lord, but Jones's policy outlook favored Japanese policies along the lines of American agenda in Asia, and his social Darwinian worldview made it impossible for him to imagine that Koreans could determine their own national fate. These perspectives conflicted with his own teaching about Jesus, the Ethical Model.

Instead of critically examining and changing his own views in light of his insights about Jesus, Jones ended up going against these important truths with a hollow argument about the "universality" of the Gospel. With that move, he ended up opposing all attempts to incarnate or recreate the new life in Christ in human society. All the effects of Christ's atonement and salvation were now shipped out to the spiritual realm. Had he paid closer attention to the work of Jesus among the people, perhaps Jones would have seen the social reality in a different light. Because he did not consider the Japanese to be an oppressive presence in Korea, he could not identify fully with the Korean people, who felt the chains of oppression becoming heavier every day. He was unable to fully fathom how liberating the Gospel of Jesus was to the people of Korea. He did not feel the deep hope Jesus gave them in the Gospel promise to renew and remake the people's hearts and the structures of the society.

Fortunately, Korean Christian leaders under Jones and the missionaries learned their Jesus well in the Bible institutes and theological classes. While it seemed the church was abiding by the missionary injunction against political participation, the church took leadership in the nonviolent resistance against oppressive Japanese colonial rule in the March First Movement of 1919, merely nine years after Korea was annexed to Japan in 1910. During those intervening nine years, the Korean church had not turned inward or heavenward, as the missionaries wanted. Neither did they become benign spectators on the sidelines of Korean history. Rather, they followed Jesus, their Ethical Model, imitating him in his self-sacrifice and nonviolent resistance against evil. We will see how this took place in the next chapter, as we follow Choe's ministry after 1905.

7.7 A Recap of Jones's Life and Work in Choson

The American Christ Who Came to Korea with Jones

In this story, which spans the first twenty-five years of Protestant Christianity in Korea, 1885–1910, as well as the last twenty-five years of the Choson Dynasty, a young American goes to Korea after hearing a voice from heaven, telling him to go. In the process, he becomes an "apostle" to the Korean people. The longer Jones stayed in Korea, his American Christ not only spoke Korean, but became a Korean—the Jesus of Korea.

When Jones came to Korea, he brought to its shores an American Christ whose image had been forged in the lives of various people who had immigrated to the New World and formed themselves into a new people. They had battled a world power in a revolutionary war for independence, started the world's first political experiment in people's democracy, conquered a continent, fought a bloody civil war, and were waiting for its chance to make history on the world's stage. Jones's Christ was a uniquely American creation. It grew out a particular, confident vision that God was building his kingdom in America. His Christ focused on the human side of God, who was loving, compassionate, and creative. The salvation he wrought was a holistic one, covering the entire gamut of human experience. As his love knew no national boundaries, it sought out people everywhere needing salvation and liberty. As his follower, Jones saw a new sign in the sky: Christianize and civilize.

However, Jones did not start his work in Korea to impose his American Christ on the Korean people. He first learned to appreciate its culture, history, and aspirations. He felt their pains and hurts. He had found his "inestimable" teacher, Choe, who opened his eyes to the realities facing the Korean people and the rich cultural resources at their service. He quickly saw that people everywhere wanted to live fulfilled lives, in harmony with God, themselves, and the world. They wanted to be free from guilt and to do the good. They wanted to leave a better society for their children and their children's children. Jones knew that his basic message of Christianize and civilize was pointed in the right direction. What it needed was some tweaking. In the twenty-year process of intercultural interactions, Jones looked for new ways to speak about his American Christ and what he had to offer to the Korean people facing a tough reality—corrupt and inept leaders at home and powerful imperialistic neighbors at the doors. Jones used the rich social, religious, and cultural resources of Korea to shape his image of Jesus in Korean realities. Just as Jesus had taken on humanity in his incarnation, Jones made Jesus become "Korean" in his incarnation on the Korean peninsula. At the same time, he did not feel he had to slavishly copy the Christian traditional language about Jesus. He had to speak so that his American Christ could touch and save their sin-sick souls and renovate their dying nation.

Jesus the Mediator and Builder of Civilization

In the first period of his missionary life (1881–92), Jones brought to Korea two images of Christ out of his own conversion experience and church life—the Experimental Christ who expresses the union of God with humanity, and the Missionary Jesus as world-renovator and builder of civilization. In speaking of Jesus, Jones focused on Christ's person, with his divinity seen as the sign of divine life in world history, becoming actualized in the American Christian experience. While he used the traditional theological language of atonement to describe Jesus' work of salvation, Jones leaned toward a commonsense understanding of Christ's divinity as a divine presence in human life; the church, in that sense, continued Christ's incarnation on earth through its exemplary communal life with God and others.

Jesus, the Revealer of *Hananim* and Savior of the Common People

In the second period (1892–1903) of his ministry at Chemulpo, two images of Jesus became central—Jesus the Revealer of the Living

Hananim (God) of Korea, and Jesus the Incarnated Mediator, who saves the common people. Jones saw the real meaning of ancestral worship in the Confucian world and its impact on the people. It robbed the people of true spirituality, and it oppressed the common people, especially the women, through its control. As a metaphor of the Korean society, ancestral worship pointed to the dead religion of Confucianism and the oppressive social conditions which it masked.

At the same time, Jones recognized the religious genius of Korean traditions and the people's spiritual longings. He seized two indigenous concepts—*Hananim* (God) and *hwamok* (reconciliation)—to preach Jesus, the Savior of the Korean people. He also made an important theological decision to discard Western theological categories as meaningless for the Korean Christians. With these two moves Jones helped the Korean Christians adopt the Christ of the Bible, which portrayed Jesus in his various images and names as presented in the Bible. Recognizing that all people seek God, Jones defined the Korean people's spiritual longings in terms of the Confucian vision of humanization and social harmony. By his insightful analysis of ancestral worship, Jones reached out to the spiritual as well as the sociopolitical yearnings of the people. His Jesus would save the people's souls and renovate their society. His Jesus would lift their souls to their rightful place as God's sons and daughters. By modeling the life of Jesus, they would also build a new society on the Korean peninsula.

Jesus, the New Ethical Model and Purifier of the Church Community

In the last period of his missionary service (1905–10) in Korea, Jones faced the time of greatest crisis—the death of a nation—and proclaimed a very hopeful message of resurrection through two images of Christ—Jesus, the Ethical Standard, and Jesus, the Purifying

Lord of the Church. Old Choson had been weighed and found wanting. Jones preached that Jesus was the new Ethical Standard. His Great Way of Truth now overshadowed the waning way of the ancestral masters.

The 1907 Revival demonstrated the power of the Christian message to form a new society in which ethical behavior was not something reserved for only the educated or the upper classes. All Christians, from the youngest to the oldest, were being renewed. It seemed Jones had his fingers on the pulse of the Korean people and nation who were desperate for a message from heaven in their darkest hour. People poured into the church. Many expected the Christian church, as the largest and most organized of remaining social institutions of Choson, to become the leading instrument of salvation and national renewal. This led to a wide range of Christian participation and action for independence and salvation, which made the missionaries fear for the survival of the church.

Jesus, Whose Power Is Hidden by the Missionaries

Unfortunately, Jones and most missionaries turned their backs on the aspirations of the Korean Christians and people for independence and freedom. It was a decision made for a variety of political and religious reasons. For Jones, it had already become apparent, as early as 1895, that Korean independence was an impossibility. The failed coup of 1884 by radical reformers, and the failure of the reform policies of 1895, signaled to Jones that the entrenched political leadership, including the Korean Court, would not be able to win Korean independence. Nor did he see any other viable force emerging on the horizon, not even the Christian-influenced, Western-educated, Korean progressives.

For Jones, it was clear that Japan, with its earlier successes in self-reformation and modernization, was destined to rule in East Asia. Given his belief in the practical impossibility of Korean independence, Jones saw it fitting that Korea would be tutored under Japan. With most of the missionaries, Jones believed Japan would be a good neighbor, itself having been nurtured under Western influence, but that turned out to be wishful thinking that disregarded the history of Japan's many attempts to conquer Korea. Accordingly, Jones's decision to accept Japanese colonial rule cannot be seen solely as a sign of his growing identity with the policies of his native land, the United States. While he did share a belief in the American imperialist role in the world, it does not offer the most complete explanation for his actions.

Despite his highly creative response to the national crisis, Jones failed to carry out the implications of his teachings about Jesus. His talk of "universal Christ" undercut any nationalist aspirations by Korean Christians. Compared to this stance, five years later, he returned to America and became an out-and-out advocate of social gospel in the United States.[57] He would preach that Jesus is the true "democrat" whose message is ultimately geared for the transformation of the political arena! He threw himself enthusiastically into a religious battle against Germany's autocracy. But in Korea, Jones was a child of the nineteenth-century American ethos. He held cultural imperialist notions and a social Darwinist outlook that led to unexamined assumptions, both political and religious. These ideological "shades" over his mind blinded him to the real movement of the Spirit that was changing Korea for the emergence of a new people and a new nation. Thus, in spite of his creative images of Christ emerging out of the Korean soil, Jones was not able to disengage himself completely from his cultural worldview

---

57. For an overview of American social gospel, see Robert T. Handy, ed. *The Social Gospel in America 1870-1920: Gladden, Ely, Rauschenbusch* (New York: Oxford University Press, 1966).

long enough to see the work of the living Christ among the Korean *minjung*. Behind Jones's cultural blinders, Jesus was changing a despairing people into a people of the way of the cross, willing to sacrifice themselves in nonviolent resistance against evil.

Jones's Legacy: Jesus in the Twenty-First-Century World

Jones's vast theological insights, as well as his failure to overcome his own cultural biases, are historical legacies for the American and Korea churches. For the American Christian church, Jones's contextual method of theology and missionary work is instructive in its effectiveness and its ideological temptation. Jones's highly creative and contextualized Christology in Korea was built on the traditions of the postmillennial and evangelical visions of nineteenth-century American Christianity. Yet, he became a lifelong student of the Korean way of being and believing. His last lectures in Korea on the Ethical Christ show a level of creativity that needs to be emulated. He not only knew Korean culture, he lived it in his theology.

For the Korean church, it would be important to remember that when Jones and the missionaries preached Jesus as Savior, the Korean people received the "Good News" in its fullness, without any dichotomy between soul and body, spirit and secular, earth and heaven, religion and politics. Jesus Christ is the Savior of the Korean soul, people, and nation. Jones's motto of "Christianize and civilize" may seem too simplistic for our times, but it still casts a vast vision that can inspire a spirituality that seeks wholeness in human hearts and human societies. God's Spirit continues to groan among the people as it did in the 1907 Revival, awaiting the arrival of the true sons and daughters of God on earth, who would fulfill their destiny to reclaim their original humanity and become a channel of blessing to all people. It may be important to ask if the Korean church is fulfilling the promise of the 1907 Revival for the emergence of a faith community of people with "moral possibilities of the highest order."

As a theologian of great power and ability, Jones recognized the provisionality and provinciality of all theological concepts and construction. Despite his own failings, he would warn us today to recognize the narrowness and particularity of our ethnic and national identities, which may keep us from recognizing the presence and action of Jesus, the universal Savior, at work among the peoples of the world. In our increasingly pluralistic world, where competing world religions reside side by side, with all virtues highlighted and faults well-rehearsed, Jones's insight is instructive. His example of speaking to the Korean people's dreams and aspirations, using the common people's language and cultural resources, remains an important historical legacy for the American and Korean churches. Who is Jesus for twenty-first-century America? What image of Jesus inspires Christians today to do the good? What is the content of Jesus' salvation to Koreans living on the cutting edge of cyberworld? What would Jesus have us do today to help build a better world? Or has Jesus been relegated to a room in the attic or cellar of human existence? What would Jones say about our theological thinking and activities on behalf of Jesus today?

Sent to a land that was completely foreign to him, young Jones brought his American Christ of his conversion and life experiences to Korea. In Old Choson, he witnessed to the power of Jesus to change people and transform their world. This change was most dramatically seen in his language teacher and colleague, Choe Pyonghon. It was Choe who proved in his life that the Christ of the West brought by Jones was his Savior, the One who would remake the Korean people and reform the Korean nation. The American Christ *becomes* Jesus of Korea in Choe Pyonghon's pastorate at Chongdong Church.

8

Choe, 1903–1910: Birthing a New Korea

"How does Choe's Jesus help the Korean Christians confront the national crisis, and what does Jesus demand of his followers in Korea?" In this chapter, we see Choe living out his belief that religion and politics are united; a right religion would give birth to a righteous political system. He hears Jesus on the cross calling him to help build a new nation, albeit through suffering and heroic self-sacrifice.

8.1 Choe's Pastoral Goals at Chongdong Church

As Choe began his fruitful ministry at the Chongdong Church in 1903, he saw old Choson collapsing right before his eyes. He could feel the hands of Japanese imperialism squeezing tightly around Choson's throat. In light of the inevitable loss of his native land, Choe began preaching salvation in Jesus with his creative image of Jesus as the founder of a new nation.

About the same time, Choe writes an interesting article, "The Present Generation's Duty to the Coming Generation," in which he outlines three tasks that he owes to the coming generations: morality (*todok*), industry (*kongop*), and word (*malssum*). In other words, he defines his task in three areas: evangelism, education,[1] and literature. For example, in the area of literature, he saw it as his duty to publish books and articles that will reinforce *susin cheka* (self-cultivation, including family life and the education of children), *chungkun hyochin* (loyalty to the king and filial piety to parents) "with words that teach right opinions about *aekuk aemin*" (love of nation and love of people). After listing famous figures from Chinese and Korean history, Choe shows how they left useful literature that is beneficial for the people, especially for the education of children. "By respecting God and believing in the Savior, we will be able to establish the foundation of *tohak* among the coming generations by the help of the Holy Spirit."[2]

True ethics or faith[3] is to "proclaim God's *tohak* (teaching of the way), the most important thing."[4] He emphasizes the "principles of true way," which would undergird both education and his literary output. By establishing schools everywhere, Choe believes that by educating the coming generation, he would both "proclaim far and wide the faith in the Savior and make of the *Taehan* nation a civilized society."[5] In a nutshell, this would be his vision statement for over a decade of ministry at Chongdong Methodist Church, which grew numerically[6] and spiritually. At Chongdong, he established many educational channels in and out of the church, participated in the

---

1. *Kongop* can mean industry or collective work; here, it refers to modern public education from elementary to college, covering all areas of academic subjects that will educate people to be useful. It also includes establishing orphanages, nursing homes, and schools for the deaf and the blind.
2. Choe Pyonghon, "Present Generation's Duty," 241.
3. Only by knowing the Christian faith can one save "one's soul." For Choe, salvation includes the notions of forgiveness of sins, reconciliation with God, sanctification of life, and eternal life. Love can come only from those who believe in the *tohak*, while virtues are the by-products of love.
4. Ibid., 239.
5. Ibid., 242.
6. See Ryu Tongsik, *History of Chongdong First Methodist Church*, 179–80 for membership statistics of Korean Methodist Church and the Chongdong Church from 1903 to 1913.

political process, and wrote his most important work, *Reflections on the Holy Mountain*.

Similarly, he outlines two tasks facing the pastors of his day in another article: 1) to "obey the commandment, with Jesus as our model" by sharing the food of eternal life with a starving people, and 2) to share the truth, not depending on one's own natural talents or knowledge, but by the power of the Spirit.[7]

Ever since Ryu Tongsik's early studies on Choe Pyonghon, it has been common to view Choe as a cultural theologian, a comparative religions scholar, and a poetical minister. He was viewed as being much more comfortable in the retreat in the mountain, writing of ethical truths and idealistic ideals of loyalty to the king and love of the nation in Chinese characters, rather than getting involved in the nitty-gritty work of reforming a nation through the political process. Even those who note the importance of national salvation in Choe's theology end up pigeonholing Choe into the religious and educational arena, separated from the political arena.

However, recent discoveries of Choe's unpublished materials have begun to challenge this traditional view.[8] These articles show that Choe was indeed very much involved in the political process of building a new nation while old Choson was collapsing all around him. He did this not only through evangelism and education, but also through direct and indirect political actions. We will examine how these acts of "national salvation" were based on his deepening understanding of Jesus. He began preaching Jesus who atoned for universal human sin, reconciled humanity to God, and brought the human race back to its original nature. Now, this same Jesus was

---

7. Choe Pyonghon, "Theological Study at Chongdong" (K), *SW* 2, no. 3 (1902): 31.
8. Currently, there is not even an elementary biography of Choe Pyonghon available. In the 1990s, Korean scholars began to recover more materials written by Choe and about Choe from family and historical archives. This book makes use of several recently discovered materials.

calling and leading his Korean followers to carry their cross through a most difficult time of social and political crises toward a new society.

8.2 Jesus, the Foundation of a New Nation

During his ministry at Chongdong, Choe took the Jesus of his conversion and first phase of nonstop evangelistic outreach into the political arena. If Jesus was the foundation of Western civilization and nations, surely he was now leading his Korean believers into a new nation and new culture, even as the old society was disappearing right before their eyes. It became important for Choe to show how this would come about and how Jesus would help create a new nation.

At the same time, his writings show a deepening reflection on Jesus and his self-giving sacrifice on the cross. In this decade, one finds Choe speaking often and unashamedly of laying down one's life, like the Savior, for the sake of others and for the nation. He reasons that one can lay down one's life since the world and its glory is not the goal of our earthly lives, and our eternal life with God is already guaranteed in Jesus' resurrection. In addition, he begins to look critically at the social processes that make up the life of a nation and how Jesus' salvation becomes actualized in these processes. Thus, the true principles of Christianity are understood as the new *tohak,* or the curriculum of the Way, that should undergird all activities of the church, especially its educational ministry. Choe is clearly aware that the eyes of the nation were turning to Jesus and his message of salvation. The Korean people were starting to believe the good news of Jesus, that he would indeed bring about a new Korea.

The Three Great Laws of God

As he did in the previous period (1893–1902), Choe thinks about Jesus from within the framework of his doctrine of creation. In "The Doctrine of Sin," Choe argued that God created the world and filled it with his glory, giving humanity free autonomy and establishing God's law on the earth. In *Reflections on the Holy Mountain*,[9] there is a more detailed discussion of the three principles or rules (*sam taeryun*) established by God to maintain his sovereign rule in the universe. Three great principles govern the relationship between God, humanity, and nature. The natural world is ruled by the law of matter, the human world by the law of humanity, and the spiritual world by the law of spirit, or heaven.

The law of matter refers to the "grass, tree, metal, and animals," which live according to their instincts in the way God created them to propagate themselves in the service of humanity.[10] The law of humanity refers to the human race, which God created with spirit, soul, and intelligence that enables it to make progress, develop cultures, and advance intellectually.[11]

> Becoming a true human being is valuable, for only then is it able to obey the principle of spiritual law by honoring *Hananim* and worshiping the Savior above, and to examine the law of matter in order to rule over grass, tree, metal, animals, and the insects and fish below. Humanity's proper task is to honor and respect their parents on earth, be loyal to the king, treat others as themselves, carefully observe the way of three bonds

---

9. *Reflections on the Holy Mountain* (K: Songsan Myongkyong) was published in 1911. It was an expansion of a four-part series published in 1907 in the *Sinhak Wolpo*: Choe Pyonghon, "Pilgrimage to the Holy Mountain (K: Songsan Yuramki), *SW* 5, no.1 (1907): 486–91; no. 2 (1907): 541–46; 5, no. 2 (1907): 584–90; no. 4–5 (1907): 689–97. There are sections of this amazing book which are copied word for word from articles in the *Sinhak Wolpo* written by Jones and Noble on the "Theory of the Soul" and "Human Psychology." The book is a dialogue between disciples of four religions of Korea—Confucianism, Buddhism, Taoism and Christianity.
10. Choe Pyonghon, *Reflections*, 36–37.
11. Ibid., 37–38.

and five principles (*samkang oryun*)[12] and carry out the affairs of *sushin cheka* and *chiguk pyongchonha*,[13] so that they can be saved eternally and receive the endless glory of heavenly blessings.[14]

When Confucian understanding of the human is merged with the Christian belief in creation and salvation, its borders are widened. Humanity's true place within God's order is restored. The seamless merging of core Confucians concepts with a Christian framework is a sign of Choe's growing ingenuity in theological thinking. Choe's strong doctrine of anthropology says that *all* human potentialities are restored by Jesus' work of salvation. While sin has distorted human abilities and its free will so that humanity cannot save itself, God's grace is seen as actively involved in human affairs and human history, despite human sinfulness. Human laws that govern its relationships, society, and communal life are all seen as gifts of God to humanity. These are hardwired into human society and human nature. Jesus comes to restore everything "human" to humanity so that it may claim to its rightful place in God's creation and its rightful relationship with its Heavenly Parent.

What Choe refers to as the law of heaven is the doctrine of God and God's nature, including the doctrines of Trinity and the nature of God and the church. These teach us that:

> The holy Father is the Creator of all things in heaven, earth, and the seas. The holy Son is the Messiah who became incarnate on earth, endured countless suffering, died nailed to the cross and by his outpoured blood

---

12. *Samgang,* or the three bonds, refers to the three central human ties: the relationship between king and subject, father and son, husband and wife. *Oryun,* or five moral rules, refers to five basic human relations and its natural virtues. Affection (*chin*) between parents and children; righteousness/loyalty (*ui*) between ruler and subjects; distinction (*pyol*) between men and women; hierarchy (*so*) between elder and younger; and trust (*sin*) between friends and confidants.
13. The goal of cultivation of the self (*susin*) is to bring order to the family (*cheka*) that contributes to the righteous rule of the nation (*chikuk*) which ultimately leads to cosmic peace and harmony (*pyong chonha*).
14. Choe Pyonghon, *Reflections*, 37–38.

atoned for the sins of all people of all nations. The holy Spirit comes to this earth to touch the hearts of evil humanity to make it good, to illuminate the hearts of the dull ones, to make wise those who are ignorant. He is the Comforter.[15]

Choe understands God as the origin of human souls, compared to earthly parents who give the physical body. So, God is "elder father" (*kun apoji*),[16] who is the source of "real" humanity, its soul. Thus humanity is also born of the law of heaven. He who does not worship God is ignorant of this law. So, in a typically Confucian way, Choe says that since we honor our earthly parents, we ought to first honor God, our spiritual father.[17] In his discussion of the law of humanity, we can see the development of Choe's doctrine of humanity. He understands the human being as being made up of body and soul (a spiritual being), which controls the body and is eternal. "Thus in reality, humanity refers to the soul (*yonghon*) that controls the body, and the body is the *ha-in*, or slave, of the soul's work."[18]

In this discussion of the three great principles, we see Choe firmly planting the Christian doctrine of creation in the Confucian notions of three bonds and five principles. This bold move elevates the law of heaven as the basis for the other two laws. It forces Confucianism back to its primitive form; the primary duty of humanity is to be in relationship with the Heavenly Lord or *Sangje*. Jesus comes to save and restore humanity so that it may truly live by the three great laws which God gave to humanity at its creation.

---

15. Ibid., 39–40.
16. Ibid., 41.
17. Ibid., 70–71.
18. Ibid., 71.

8. 3 Jesus in *Reflections on the Holy Mountain*

To the question why one must believe only in Jesus when everyone desires to enter heaven, Choe writes,

> God is truly holy Spirit; how can earthly sinners approach the throne of the Almighty? When the sins of human race increased mightily, God, in his love of humanity and mercifulness, did not destroy humanity but rather had pity on them. He sent the second person of the Trinity, his only begotten son, Jesus and sent him to earth to become a human being by borrowing the womb of the Virgin Mary. He lived together with earthly sinners, eating and clothing himself like others. He taught the sinners, healed the sick, received our deadly sins on himself, and was crucified on the cross and died. With his blood, he washed away the sins of all people and cleansed them. He himself became the atoning sacrifice, giving himself away as the atoning sacrifice. Everyone who believes in Jesus will have their sins redeemed and receive their salvation. Human beings can approach God only if they have no sin. Jesus was originally *Hananim*. Also, he is a human being; thus he can become the mediator between God and humanity…When people want to go up to a higher level, they must use a ladder between them. To enter heaven, there is a mediator, Jesus, our Savior.[19]

This Bible-based understanding of Jesus does not seek to explain the Trinity or the two-natures theory of Christ. These are accepted on faith.[20] The focus is on the person of Christ as the mediator and the restorer of true humanity through his self-sacrifice on the cross. When Choe joins the work of Christ, as atonement for sin and as mediator between God and humanity, with the restoration of the human law in humanity, he ends up connecting the work of Christ with what humanity must do here on earth: *sushin cheka chiguk*

---

19. Ibid., 74–76.
20. In earlier generations, Confucian scholars rejected Buddhism and Christianity for the logical "absurdity" of their many doctrines, such as Buddha's repeated reincarnations and Jesus' crucifixion and incarnation. However, the richness of spiritual experiences in shamanism, as well as Buddhism, made Incarnation and Trinitarian notions not so strange to Korean ears. See Pak Kyonghwan, "Buddhist-Confucian Controversy," 71–110, for Confucian rejection of Buddhist spirituality.

pyongchonha. This is the nine-character (in Chinese) summary of Confucian philosophy of self-cultivation that is the basis of all human existence, "Self-cultivation leads to an orderly household which is the foundation of a just government which aims at world peace." The classic Confucian text, *The Great Learning* (Taehak (Korean) or Ta-hsüeh (Chinese)) is an extended meditation on these foundational phrases. Choe says that Jesus' salvation aims to complete the Confucian goal once and for all.

Jesus' salvation brings about the complete restoration of humanity's capacity to do what God has created it to do: fulfilling its destiny to live as God's sons and daughters. Humanity is majestic and superior because God has placed the soul in its body and dwells with humanity through his Holy Spirit in humanity's *yongdae* (literally "soul house"), or heart. The human problem, then, has two dimensions—its separation from God by its sins, and the distortion of human existence and personality as a result of its separation and its sins. Therefore, Jesus came to defeat the power of sin and save humanity from its deadly hold and to reconcile humanity to God, its true Father.

Near the end of *Reflections on the Holy Mountain,* in which the Christian has argued for the superiority of the spirituality of Christianity over Confucianism, Buddhism, and Taoism, the Confucian scholar Jindo concludes that Confucian social ethics and polity are still better than Christianity despite its complex spiritual principles.

> Jindo (Literally, True Way: the Confucian scholar) continued to disagree and said, "After hearing about the religious knowledge and purpose of Christianity, I am certain that the principles of higher ethics evolved from the ancient peoples. Christianity has many ideas that Eastern sages cannot believe. Neither do I think it can best the principles of governing nations and political philosophy found in Confucianism.
> Sinch'onong[21] (the Christian) again said, "Teacher Jin has still closed the door of his heart and cannot open it. How can Confucianism be

better than Christianity in terms of its political theory and its patriotic spirit? Although he roamed over the world, Confucius was not able to implement his political ideas. When he was the justice minister in the state of Lo (Lu in Chinese), he was unable to repel the eighty dancing girls sent by the state of Che (Qi in Chinese) and so was forced to resign.[22] Confucius could not make the state of Lo prosper. Mencius and Chasa (Zisi in Chinese), during the Warring States Period, sought out the rulers to advise them, but they, too, could not help build prosperous states.

The English Queen Victoria, as a Christian ruler, rules her people by the words of the New Testament Bible. During her 60 years of rule, England has become one of the most advanced nations in the world and the leading nation of the world. During eight years of a stormy war with countless difficulties and suffering, (George) Washington never retreated and went on to defeat the British Army. He made America an independent nation, freed from British control. Garibaldi and Mazzini reformed Italian politics and made it an independent and advanced nation. They, too, were all devout believers in Jesus… Bismarck…and Nelson… were all Christian believers, loved their nation, and were loyal to their kings. They were willing to sacrifice their own lives for them. And with brave and unwavering minds, they reformed their national politics, fought in fierce wars, making their native lands into advanced civilized countries among the world's nations. They are no less than Confucianists. In Confucian scriptures, it says, "If there is *tao* in the land, then serve; if there is no *tao*, hide." And "when the king doesn't listen to you, resign your appointment, withdraw to the mountains and fish in the lakes saying, 'I did not meet my opportunity.'" History creates heroes, and heroes create history. How can we call these people patriotic when they do not attempt to make the politics of their day civilized,

---

21. This is the name of the Christian in the story. Literally, it means "the old man who looks up to heaven." In the story, it is said that the pelican is called by this name because it floats on the water with its wide beak open and waits for fish to jump in. Likewise, the young Christian adopts this name since a Christian lives by God's grace and is made righteous by faith through grace.
22. According to the *Records of the Grand Historian*, the neighboring state of Che (Qi) was worried that Lo (Lu) was becoming too powerful. Che decided to sabotage Lo's reforms by sending one hundred good horses and eighty beautiful dancing girls to the Duke of Lo. The Duke indulged himself in pleasure and did not attend to official duties for three days, which disappointed Confucius greatly. Sinchonong takes liberty with history and lays the blame on Confucius for the Duke's indulgence. Confucius looked for a way to leave the services of the Duke of Lo, and did so later.

but withdraw from it for their own comfort? As Christian patriots who fought for their kings and nation…

And so Jindo replied, "(Now I can see that) Western civilization is in fact based on the influence of the virtues of Christianity." (At last convinced), he became a Christian.[23]

In these final paragraphs of the book, Choe makes the strong case that these Western patriots were Christians who loved their native homes. They were willing to lay their life on the line for the protection of their nation, as well as to win and protect their independence. For Choe, independence and freedom has been God's will for all peoples since the beginning of the world. It should be noted that all the named heroes were nationalist revolutionaries who fought for the independence and freedom of their respective countries. In Choe's eyes, they were able to achieve their goals because they were Christians. As Christians, they were people who had now recovered their original human nature and were able to fulfill their destiny, directed by the law of humanity to live freely on earth, worshiping God. It is their God-given and God-endowed gift to enjoy these human rights and to fight to keep them, since Jesus has paid for such human salvation by his blood.

These final paragraphs make it clear that Jesus' salvation of human souls is not a matter of taking the human soul out of this sinful world for the heavenly realm. Nor does it mean that there is a dualism of soul and body. Rather, Jesus' work of salvation—reconciling humanity to God and restoring their true humanity by forgiving them of their sins through his own sacrifice on the cross—enables the Christians to become fully human on earth. By following Jesus, they grow in their spirits (*yongdae*), where the Holy Spirit has made his home. It is imperative, therefore, for this human body to be free to worship God and live in freedom. This earthy and practical reading

23. Choe Pyonghon, *Reflections*, 77–79.

of Christian salvation of the soul reflects Choe's Confucian outlook that pays great attention to human motivations and actions and their role in society. It shows Choe's creativity and originality in clarifying the doctrine of creation in light of Jesus' work of atonement and reconciliation.

8.4 Jesus Builds a New Nation: Spiritually

In *Reflections on the Holy Mountain*, Choe uses an interesting term to describe the Christian's life of discipleship which will lead them to heaven. Christians are

> …those who believed in the Savior on the earth; love humanity and peace; suffer patiently through tribulation and troubles; overcome worldly traditions and desires of the flesh and temptations of the devil; seek to be meek and humble, honest and loyal people; and always follow Jesus bearing their own cross.[24]

Increasingly, we find references in Choe's writing to the suffering of Jesus and its ethical implications for Christian living, especially in troubled times such as the one Choe and the Korean church were facing. As part of his task, Choe became the chief advisor and advocate of the Christian youths, especially the Methodist Epworth League and the YMCA. In his speeches to them, one can see his own self-understanding as a teacher, a mentor, and an elder statesman, whose task is to instill in them the right vision for the future. There is a clear note in his biography that from 1903, he preached regularly on "The Cross."

In this connection, it is very instructive to examine the emerging theology of the cross among the Korean Christian youths taught by Choe in the Epworth League. The writings of Yi Sung-man, or

---

24. Choe Pyonghon, *Reflections*, 73–74.

Syngman Rhee,[25] reflect this deepening understanding of the cross. After his release from prison in 1903, Rhee writes four articles for the *Sinhak Wolpo*,[26] in which there is a progression of understanding about Christ's suffering on the cross. In them, he draws out its saving significance for the individual and the nation, as well as its demand on Christian disciples to carry the cross with Jesus. One can clearly hear Choe's voice in these words by Rhee.

In "The Growth of the Christian Church in Korea," Rhee writes that only Jesus can transform "life-takers" into "life givers" such as Jesus, who enables the believers to "love others as yourself," and "by grace to sacrifice one's life for other's sins." Only by becoming "life-givers" will Koreans "save the body, protect the house, and restore the nation." He repeats the claim that "nations which accept the religion of Jesus are civilized, wealthy and peaceful," and that it is through "our own faults that we are recipients of a broken society," full of "life-takers." He believes Koreans are not ready and prepared for independence because they have not been internally transformed.[27]

In "Two Contradictions," Rhee scolds both the political radicals and the politically disinterested. He especially directs his criticism against those who profess disinterest in politics because of the Protestant principle of the separation of religion from politics. He criticizes them for not recognizing the inner message of the Gospel, in which there is a call for self-denial and love of the neighbor, which includes the nation.

---

25. The first president of the Republic of Korea in 1948 (South Korea); a leader among the Paichai students taught by Jones and Choe, Rhee later became a Christian while in prison for his involvement in the Independence Club. See Choe Chaewon, *Biography*, for relationship between Choe Pyonghon and Syngman Rhee.
26. Syngman Rhee, "Christianity: The Foundation of Korean Future," *SW* 3, no. 8 (1903): 240–45; idem, "Two Contradictions," *SW* 3, no. 9 (1903): 299–305; idem, "The Growth of the Christian Church in Korea, *SW* 3, no. 11 (1903): 383–89; "The Task of Korean Christians," *SW* 4, no. 8 (1904): 231–38.
27. Rhee, "Growth," 242, 244, 245.

> Jesus died on our behalf, thus saving the world. If we will not care for other's tribulation, suffering, and desolation, where is our faith and where is our work? We must certainly think about the world, think about the nation, and think about our neighbors. We know a person's faith only by seeing his actions for others, no matter how small or big. If a tree has no fruit, what is its usefulness?[28]

Rhee does not hide the fact that he does not have the answer for the Korean crisis. He believes Korean Christians will find a way by imitating Jesus' way of the cross. He goes on to stress the point that Koreans must not become dependent on foreign missionaries and their resources, but stand on their own. They need to recover their God-given inalienable right and pursue the independence of the Korean people on their own. He repeats this point in "The Task" article, where he objects to the "rescue mentality" of waiting for missionaries or the US to save them. Perhaps, in these words, we are being introduced to Choe's honest thoughts, transferred to his best students at Paichai Haktang.

But given that the Korean people were not yet prepared for independence, Rhee does not counsel outright political actions. For now, he says that their task is to dwell and walk with Jesus, who came for the weak and the victims of world's woes. It is the task of the Christian church to stand with these ones, waiting until there is a unity of will and a willingness to take the right course of action.

Finally, in "The Task of Korean Christians," Rhee calls on Korean Christians to nurture their self-determining, self-sacrificing spirit shown by Jesus' salvation.

> (Jesus) freed all people from all sins. All people think, "Only I exist," and do not recognize that others exist. They think "Only today exists," and do not recognize that there is a tomorrow. They think, "Only this world exists," and do not recognize that there is an eternal world afterwards. Each person seeks for his own survival and tries to live only for today.

---

28. Rhee, "Contradictions," 304–5.

> So they kill each other, and all are destroyed. Jesus came and unknotted all these thoughts in order that each will lay down his life for others. He enables them to refuse the happiness before their eyes for eternal blessedness, since he helps us to think about the bigger and deeper things. There is none high or low, strong or weak; all are together the children of God. The hope of true Christians is for all people to enjoy God's blessings.[29]

Rhee recognizes in Jesus a person who suffered on behalf of others. He foresees that one day, the Korean Christian church may be called to share in the suffering of the nation. Until that day, he counsels caution to the political radicals. To the majority of Christians, who turn their eyes away from the social problems around them, he pointed to the cross of Jesus and his Gospel. Not thinking, not praying, and not being socially concerned is to betray the message of Christ, who came to save the weak and stand with those rejected by society (or family of nations, as Korea would be). Jesus' atonement, for Rhee, is related to his sacrificial self-giving, which should be imitated by Christians, regardless of their political stance. This was the criticism of young Korean Christians directed against the American missionaries who counseled turning their eyes away from the reality of national crisis for the heavenly realm. To do so is to turn our backs on Jesus' atoning work. We will hear many similar themes when we examine Choe's political writings below.

A similar perspective is developed in a "Declaration of War of the Soldier of the Cross" by Pak Yongman, a member of the Epworth League, in 1904, before the crisis of the 1905 Protectorate Treaty.

> I urge our soldiers of the Cross to awake and think again. Why did our Lord Jesus give his life for us, and why did God send Jesus? It

---

29. Rhee interestingly emphasizes the point that Koreans must not become dependent on foreign missionaries and their resources, but stand on their own and recover their God-given inalienable right and pursue independence of the Korean people. He repeats this in "The Task" article against the "rescue mentality" of waiting for missionaries or the US to save them.

is only because God desired to save us and atone for our sins? If we do not hate our present world and are not hostile to it, then we are saying that God has lied, that Jesus has died in vain…Think about it. We are indeed citizens and descendants of Korea. Our souls have been entrusted to this land, our bodies have been nurtured on this land. Alive, we are its citizens; dead, we are its citizens. This is because God has made us the owners of this peninsula. Its riches and its ruin, its gain and its loss; they are our responsibility. Thus, we must take responsibility for its prosperity or ruin, its ascent or decline. Its survival is in our hands. For when we look around our country, who is there to handle this responsibility or embrace this cause? Are there such people among the Confucianists or the Buddhists? After much thought, I can only conclude that it is the soldiers of the Cross of our Lord Jesus Christ who can confront this world and save human lives. Indeed, we are loyal citizens of this land, the chosen soldiers of our Lord.[30]

Pak understood Jesus' work of atonement for human sin as an act that Christians must imitate, despite the harm or death that may or may not follow. By emphasizing the cross—as a sign of victory and a mark of ongoing struggle against the evils of the world—this youth leader lifts up the "direction" that the cross points to. Based on his firm belief that it is God who has placed the Korean people in a particular place called Korea, Pak calls on the Christian youths to embrace the task of taking responsibility for Korea's prosperity or ruin, its rise or fall.

Jesus' cross is seen as a sign standing against this present world filled with evil, injustice, oppression, and sin. To carry the cross in a time of national crisis is to carry the burdens of a land that is lost and leaderless. The Korean Christians were beginning to discover that the Korean people were looking to them for leadership. These youthful leaders worried whether the church was already becoming like the Confucianists of old Choson—those who only spoke lovely words, but did not care to live out their beautiful talk in everyday life. For Pak, to follow Jesus in his time meant to pray and work patiently

---

30. Pak Yongman, "Declaration of War of the Soldiers of the Cross," *SW* 4, no. 6 (1904): 154–58.

to recover the independence as a sovereign nation and to regain the freedoms that God had given them as God's children and Christ's vanguards.

This examination of Choe's Christology in the *Reflections on the Holy Mountain* and through the Epworth League shows that there is a deepening understanding of Jesus' work of salvation and the task given to the Korean Christians by their cross-carrying Savior. For Choe, Jesus' saving work continues to have power in his day as atonement and reconciliation. In practical terms, it meant that Korean Christians needed to rediscover and renew the law of humanity in their society. They were to see themselves as human beings who were becoming the dwelling place of the Holy Spirit and the agents of their original destiny as residents of the Garden of Eden. The result of Jesus' saving work is understood in its various dimensions; Jesus is spawning a new breed of humanity, back to its original nature and destiny. In this section, we have also noted how Choe creatively merged the Christian teaching on creation with the Confucian notions of three great laws and the principle of three duties and five relationships (*samgang oryun* and *sam taeryun*). Last, we note that in his teaching and preaching, Choe begins to emphasize the cross of Jesus. Jesus on the cross speaks with a clear ethical mandate, inviting the Korean Christians to carry their own cross in a time of great sociopolitical crises. Now, we turn to Choe's educational and political work and writings to see how his developing doctrine of Jesus and the cross becomes reflected in his political perspectives and actions.

8.5 Jesus Builds a New Nation: Politically

Even before the 1905 Protectorate Treaty[31] was imposed on Korea,

Choe saw the writing on the wall warning of the death of the nation. The article, "The Time for Diligent Study" reflects something of the crisis and urgency that Choe felt as the Russians and the Japanese were waging war on the Korean peninsula to determine who would control its fate.

> How sad it is my brethren! What time is it? It is the season of mutual competition and daily struggle between the peoples of the nations for their interest and power. It is the time for diligent education in order to become an advanced enlightened civilization (*munmyong kaehwa*) in this global world... At the present, England is one of the superior nations of the world and wants to be the leader of Europe. But if you look back one hundred years in history, their people were illiterate and little educated, commerce was unorganized and the nation was weak... Little by little the people became educated, and the system slowly grew... The nation naturally became wealthy through the productive industries of the people. In conclusion, the people of our *Taehan* (Korea) must awaken at once from their sleep. They must dive into any area related to commerce, agriculture, manufacture, and trade. They need to learn their systems and start new enterprises. Only then will we not fall behind the people of other nations.[32]

Choe knew the Korean people had to change their mentality and become educated if they were to survive in the new world that had been thrust upon them. Thus, he thought long and preached much on the ideals of enlightened civilization and self-determined independence that was pervasive in the society. However, in the following year, 1905, the Empire of Great Han fell to the Japanese, unable to enter the modern world on its own terms.

---

31. On the night of November 17, 1905, Marquis Ito forced Korean cabinet ministers to sign the "Ulsa Poho Choyak" or the 1905 Protectorate Treaty, which included the following: a) Japan will represent Korea in its foreign affairs; b) Korean cannot enter any treaties without Japan's approval; and c) Japan will establish a Resident General under the Korean emperor to carry out these duties. It signaled the loss of national sovereignty. See Lee Ki-baik, *A New History*, 309–11.
32. Choe Pyonghon, "The Time for Diligent Study," *SW* 4, no. 10 (1904): 326.

Chongdong and Sangdong: Two Models of Political Participation?

Ryu Tongsik has argued that the Sangdong Church adopted the path of political activism while the Chongdong Church took the path of religious educational consciousness-raising.[33] However, historical records do not show that Choe's actions can be so defined or categorized.[34] Choe's and his eldest son, Chaehak's, relationship with Chon Tokki, the pastor of the Chongdong Church, Choe's organizing of other youth organizations when the missionaries disbanded the Epworth League, and his close relationship with the YMCA, which became the hotbed of the Korean independence movement, all demonstrate that Choe's theology of national salvation cannot be so easily defined only in terms of "nonpolitical" consciousness-raising campaigns or "apolitical" educational programs. In light of Choe's clearly political actions, it is no longer possible to accept Ryu's judgment or his typology of Choe's theology.[35]

Ryu and others use Choe's 1906 YMCA speech on the relationship

---

33. In the history of Chongdong Church written in 1992, Ryu describes the politically-oriented strategy of Chon Tokki's Sangdong youth movement, "But the faith approach of Chongdong Church was different. While both were involved in national salvation movement based on Christian faith, Chongdong Church under Rev. Choe Pyonghon carried out the national salvation movement following its religious approach (contrary to political approach) to national salvation." Ryu Tongsik, *History of Chongdong*, 162–64.
34. In support of his assertions, Ryu interprets the 1906 YMCA speech as Choe's theory of national salvation through religious renewal. Thus, "he aggressively carried out faith movements and founded new churches as the form of national salvation." He also says that unlike the Sangdong Youth School, the Chongdong Night School carried on "Christian education," not "nationalist education" like Sangdong. Ibid., 166. In addition, he sees the difference in numerical growth between 1906 and 1908 as a sign that more people were attracted to the "faith approach and mission policy" of Chongdong than Sangdong. Ibid., 168–69.
35. See Choe Pyonghon, *Mongyangwon*, 100–103 for a description of Choe's political involvement. His overt activities included writing newspaper editorials severely critical of the government (e.g., Dec. 22, 1903 letter to the *Hwangsong Sinmun*); organizing forums on Korea's political future, which threatened the government so much that the Emperor threatened to imprison them (1904 printing of *Taechiso*); participating in anti-1905 Treaty movement; sponsoring a memorial service for those who carried out ritual suicide in protest of the 1905 Treaty; serving as a peace commissioner to appease the Righteous Army; and being imprisoned in 1910 for five months in connection with the organizing effort of the *Sinkanhoe*.

between religion and politics³⁶ to support their argument that Choe chose religious activism over political activism. The thesis of the speech is simple. Religion and politics have a mutually dependent relationship, of an inner with an outer. When the root of the nation (its religious infrastructure) becomes weak, the national life (its political superstructure) suffers. To restore national sovereignty and strength, the religious life must be revived. They understand this speech as Choe's strategy of distancing himself from overt political reforms for a more religious-oriented movement of consciousness raising, education, and religious activity. But when the speech is placed in its wider historical context, this interpretation cannot be held.

Choe argues in his speech that Korea needs a new spiritual basis for the creation of a new nation. Nowhere does he call on the Christians to abandon their political vision. Just as Confucianism has been the foundation of Choson's collective life through its motto of "loyalty to king and love of nation," Choe argues that Christianity must now play the same social role. He sought to give hope by pointing to a new *tohak* in Christianity that would show a new way forward for a new national identity. It is not a call to give up political responsibility. Choe, like Rhee and Pak, is very critical of those who are naive enough to believe that religion and politics can be kept apart, or that they have no responsibility for it at all, as many missionaries seemed to argue.

Choe's biographers remain silent about his actions during the 1907 Revival.³⁷ Fortunately, Jones has an interesting anecdote about

---

36. Originally titled, "Non kyochong kwankye," (literally, "Theme: the relationship of religion and politics"), it was published full-text in the *Hwangsong Sinmun*, Oct. 5–6, 1906. The translated version is reprinted in Choe Pyonghon, *Mongyangwon*, 74–82.
37. Chongdong Church history shows, however, that the church grew tremendously during this period, as did other churches. It seems natural that Choe's clear message of national salvation would have drawn a hopeless people to the church, especially from the upper classes.

Choe's activities during this period. In his report of the 1907 Revival, Jones reports that in the beginning, Choe participated reluctantly in the revival occurring at Chongdong.[38]

> When the elder from Pyongyang came and the pastor saw the terrific (emotionally-charged) character of the revival, he shrank back and hardened his heart against it, determined that he would have no part in opening the way for such a visitation of God among his people.[39]

Later on Jones says that Choe surrendered to the Holy Spirit and "from that instant he was a changed man." Choe also confessed to Jones about how "formality and indifference had reduced his service for the Master to a mere perfunctory performance of his duties"[40] and about him spending few pennies from the office cash box when he was Jones's language teacher fifteen years earlier! It is not clear in what ways Choe became a changed man. But it is clear that he did not become changed by the Revival as the missionaries wished. Given his Confucian understanding of the strong relationship between religion and politics, he could not accept the missionary attempt to redirect the frustration and disappointment of the people away from their social reality to a Christian spiritual life that was divorced from everyday realities. Chongdong and Sangdong churches were two sides of the one coin of salvation wrought by Jesus.

---

38. According to Jones, Chongdong church never displayed the kind of spiritual vitality, or at least, its physical expressions, that Chemulpo churches did. Thus, he complained several times in his journals about the lack of response to his preaching among the members at Chongdong! Perhaps it was more reflective of the upper-class origins of many of Chongdong members as well as Choe's own style, that of a quiet Confucian teacher who would not have encouraged extravagant emotional outbursts!
39. Jones and Noble, *Korean Revival*, 30.
40. Ibid.

8.6 Jesus Builds a New Nation: Heroically

In 1999, a collection of speeches given by Choe in 1908 was published.[41] It consists of four speeches given to women at the Changhaksa (literally "Hall of Scholarship") on June 28, 1908 and a set of speeches at the YMCA for its students. What is significant about these speeches is their timing, coming after the year-long 1907 Revival, which, in large measure, had channeled the Korean church's attention away from the national disaster to a more heavenly and spiritual realm, as the missionaries had planned. In these speeches, Choe offers a Christian social vision with a clear political agenda. Rather than withdrawing to the inner walls of the church or the inner world of the soul, Choe spoke of the social responsibility of the Christians and the church in a time of national crisis. He never lost hope that the Gospel of Jesus would bring about a new nation in Korea, one day. He never gave up his calling to train a generation of Korean Christians who would be willing to lay down their lives for their love of their neighbor and their nation. He also kept his eyes on the prize: the reform of Korean society and the winning of Korean independence and equality before the international community.

In these speeches, Choe envisions a future world of love for neighbors and enemies alike, where God is worshiped, people are respected, and a global culture is created. Despite the competitive nature of the modern world, he sees the potential of a common culture of the East and the West. Choe believed that Christ's law of love can guide the world forward, but it is education that will teach the people not to "sit dumbly while receiving oppression and indignity."[42] By their collective action, they will overcome the shame and indignity placed on the whole nation.

---

41. It was first given as a part of a series of student lectures, and then, published in the Kiho Scholarship Fund Newsletter. Choe Pyonghon, *Mongyangwon*, 30.
42. Choe Pyonghon, "Be Diligent," in *Mongyangwon*, 31.

With the life and death of Jesus in the background, the speech, "Life Through Death" recalls the death of late Honorable Min Yonghwan,[43] and calls him a national hero for his act of ritual suicide protesting against the 1905 Protectorate Treaty. To die in loyalty to the nation is to "live in the blue sky." Their name will also be remembered for a thousand years. "Though his glory dies, in reality it is alive today and is born and reborn in heaven."[44] Choe goes on to argue that only those "who are ready to die can really live." Then, he tells the story of Wilhelm Tell, the father of Swiss independence whose long journey toward independence included banishment, imprisonment, and hunger.

> He lived in hiding in Swiss for ten years like a prisoner, but did not dampen his lively spirit. He organized "Young European League" and became involved in often bloody murderous battle, never retreating and never giving up, always standing up like a lion. He kept on moving toward his mark, saying, "Those who seek to fulfill great deeds must ignore victory or defeat, wise or foolish actions. If it cannot be achieved today, then they must look to the following year. If it cannot be achieved in ten years, then a hundred years are necessary. If my body cannot achieve it, then my sons or grandchildren will achieve it." Finally, he won his revolution and got rid of corrupt authorities and rulers. He led his three million compatriots into freedom. Why cannot we believe with Wilhelm Tell that there is life *through* death? Let us take him as our model and gain life through death.[45]

This certainly is no easy ethics or civics lesson. Still, Choe seizes the historical moment as the time of the battle for the soul of the Korean nation that may require the Christians to lay down their lives. He sees in the Resurrection of Christ, a promise of life eternal for those who

---

43. Min Young-hwan (1861–1905), was a member of the powerful Min clan and a nephew of Empress Myongsong. He was a minister of the Empire of Taehan. He committed ritual suicide in protest against the 1905 Treaty placing Korea under Japanese "protectorship."
44. Choe Pyonghon, "Life Through Death" in *Mongyangwon*, 40.
45. Ibid., 42.

would lay down their lives for their brothers and sisters, including their native land. This act would be to imitate Jesus, who came down to earth and brought life and forgiveness to all people through his death. Calling on the Korean Christians to die to the world, and thus, earn eternal life, Choe goes on to urge them to a different conclusion:

> I beg you to hear me out. Believe in the Lord with your heart of virtue. When they want to kill you by crucifying you, throw your life away! March courageously into the civilized world with unbended hearts. Perhaps in death we may be like Apostle Paul and the revolutionary hero Mazzini.[46]

This "nationalistic" speech is firmly Jesus-centered in its approach. Just as Jesus took on death gladly in order to deliver humanity from its sins and to give it life, Korean Christians must be willing to give up their lives and face death. In so doing, they will have eternal life. More important, their sacrifice will also become the seed that will cause life to sprout among the people by giving them "civilized culture" as they fight against forces of oppression, just like other Christian heroes of the West. There is no discussion about the right or wrong of dying for a nation. He takes it as a natural good and a Christian virtue, since guarding one's freedom is a divine mandate.

In an earlier speech, "The Need for Women's Groups" given on June 1, 1908, at the opening of the City Center for the Association of Women's Education, which had been organized during the 1905 Anti-Treaty Movement,[47] Choe once again sounds the trumpet for education as the guardian of human freedom.

> The weak always lose their freedom and easily turn into slaves. If you are friendly, then you will love; if you love, then you will come together; if you come together, you will get organized; if you organize, then you

---

46. Ibid., 43.
47. *A History of Korean Church* (K), vol. 1, sixteenth century to 1918, ed. Hankuk kidokkyo yoksa yonguso (Seoul: The Christian Literature Press, 1989), 350.

are wise; if wise, then strong; if strong, then you can defend yourself against other's attacks and protect your right of freedom.[48]

Choe understands Korea's loss of freedom as originating from its lack of love and unity. Thus, he regards unity[49] as the key to winning "independent national sovereignty," which was not an impossible goal to seek. His vision is always very clearly stated: a free, independent, self-determining Korea, with its people living in harmony, not only among themselves, but also with the world's peoples. His strategy, then, is to find the heroes who can serve as models for his students.

In "Types of Heroes,"[50] Choe again turns to heroes of both the East and the West who, interestingly, are mostly military generals who led wars of independence. In this roll call of heroes, Choe includes George Washington, Martin Luther, and Christopher Columbus. While it is not clear what makes them such "heroes," one characteristic that sets them apart is their ability to withstand the difficulties and the suffering of the moment for the greater good and future hope of eternal life in Christ. He calls on the students to be like them, pushing themselves in study, which will result in a modern and prosperous nation.

Such heroes are only born of God. Since the soul is the engine of one's personality, it is important who—the Lord or the devil—dwells in the house of the soul (*yongdae*). Believers are people who have received the Lord's love, righteousness, truth, and holiness in their bodies. So, they are able to "love others as they love themselves, and thus love their compatriots. When they pray to the Lord…the Holy

---

48. Choe Pyonghon, "The Need for Women's Groups" in *Mongyangwon*, 48.
49. Ibid., 49. He thought the organization of many social groups in which men and women could easily mix and communicate was a key to maintaining Korean independence and developing a new civilization in Korea.
50. Choe Pyonghon, "Types of Heroes," in *Mongyangwon*, 53–55.

Spirit himself enters my soul's house and renews my being."[51] This is the way a human being becomes united with the transcendent God.

Finally, Choe speaks unambiguously about Christianity and nationalism.

> Some say that we believers (Christians) all belong to the Westerners and so do not have any independent spirit of patriotism. Surely, this is a great fallacy (literally, "deserves to be punished by beating on one's stomach"). America is America for the American people while Korea (Taehan) is Korea for the Korean people. How can people lose their identity (*kunpon*) just because they belong to the same religion? It is my sincere desire that we can unite the spirit of our people through our religious faith. Then we will be able to engage in competition (with the rest of the world, for this will lead to a right kind of competition).[52]

In this speech, one can clearly read Choe's "nationalistic" spirit based on his doctrine of creation. God has created all the nations of the world as his own, including Korea. So, God desires to dwell in the hearts or *yongdae* (house of soul) of Koreans to change them back into his children. For Choe, then, becoming a Christian means becoming a Christianized Korean, who is responsible for the stewardship of the land in which one is born.

In these speeches, it is the same victorious and militant Christ who leads the people toward a new nation. His act of self-sacrificial giving is lifted up as a model for the Korean Christians. One is able to sacrifice oneself and carry the cross because the human soul has already been saved and has eternal life through Christ's salvation. The Holy Spirit who dwells within human souls will grant them the strength and the wisdom to obey the three great laws. This includes the safeguarding of the freedom and liberty given by God at creation and won back by Christ's work on the cross. By the power of the

---

51. Choe Pyonghon, "Elements of Human Nature," in *Mongyangwon*, 61.
52. Choe Pyonghon, "The Relation of Competition and Power of Many," in *Mongyangwon*, 62.

Spirit, people are able to bear the cross of Jesus and lay down their life for the love of one's neighbor, which, by extension, includes the neighbor's land and one's own native land. What is most interesting are the heroes that Choe lifts up as models for his students. All of them are Christian independence fighters who did not fear for their own lives, but regarded suffering as part of the process of winning and protecting their God-given freedom and liberty.

The 1908 speeches show that it would be a mistake to categorize Choe simply as a religious activist who believed that increasing the number of Christian churches would somehow make Korea into a civilized and independent Christian nation. His study of the Christian church in the West and the list of "Christian" heroes that appear in his writings show that he understood that a new nation could not be born without a struggle that would often involve self-sacrifice and even bloody battles.

Some have seen a lack of "direct" political activism as a sign of Choe's quietism. That is to misread the role that he had in the Korean society as a *sonbi,* or a scholar, an elder statesman, and a leader of the church. It would have been enough for him to provide advice and direction. Yi Juik has pointed out that six assistant pastors who served under him all went overseas to serve as secretaries or assistants to nationalist leaders, such as Syngman Rhee and Kim Ku.[53] As a Confucian scholar, it was enough for a master of his stature to cast the vision and enable his disciples and the coming generations to actualize the vision, for by their fruits, you shall know them.

8.7 Pastor Choe, a Nation-Builder in the Jesus Way

In a time when the sovereignty of his homeland was being trampled underfoot and the freedoms of the people taken away, Choe

---

53. Yi Juik, "T'aksa Choe Pyonghon's Theology," 103.

proclaimed Jesus as the universal Savior who has come to save the Korean people from their troubles by saving their souls. To save the soul did not mean to take them out of the world into heaven. For Koreans, Jesus' atonement and reconciliation meant that the Korean people are being restored to their rightful place under God's created order. They were meant to live fully as the people of God and to become true human beings destined to live as a free people. In that sense, Christ's salvation required Christians to stand up against the evils that would keep humanity from its God-given gifts of freedom, dignity, and human rights.

Choe preached that Jesus' salvation would enable them to dream of a new world, and move them closer to its reality day by day as they educated themselves and others through the *tohak* of God's great truth, and lived according to the three great laws. Then, just as God is one and there is one heaven and one Savior, the world will one day become one family and live in righteousness, engage in fair competition, and grow intellectually.

Until that day when Korean Christians can breathe liberty and fully become liberated humanity, there will be a struggle and a call to self-sacrifice, just as Jesus suffered on the cross. It is interesting that in these 1908 speeches and in the *Reflections on the Holy Mountain*, Choe lists the same names of the heroes of the West who won their nation's independence through bloody battles and personal sacrifices. Choe dared to call them heroes worthy of Christian imitation. His roll call of global Christian heroes is not a subtle hint, but a clear clarion call. There will be no life without sacrifice, suffering, and perhaps, even death. There will be no self-determining independent Korea without Christians fighting against the evils that keep Korea from such God-given inheritance. Jesus' death and resurrection has relativized the power of physical death for Choe. Therefore, it behooves Christians to follow after Jesus in the name of the love of God's mandate of freedom (*inryun*) and in the name of the love of the neighbor, which includes the love of one's homeland (*chungkun aekuk*).

Is it still possible to say that Choe was not politically active, given his program of "national salvation through religion?" To say so is to misunderstand his 1906 YMCA lecture on the relation between religion and politics, as noted above. Nor did Choe adopt a dualistic outlook that favored consciousness-raising education over political activism. Rather, he saw the necessity of both for the creation of a new beloved national community. Thus, statements like the one below cannot be said about Choe.

> The basic perspective and strategy of his national self-determined independence thought was focused not on participation through political actions, but focused more on a more fundamental dimension of people's consciousness-raising and development of capabilities through religious activities.[54]

It is no wonder that Choe spent the first five months of 1910 locked up in prison, accused of being a secret organizer for the independence movement. While his activities after 1910 became limited because of increasing police surveillance, his action in sending six of his assistant pastors overseas to serve as secretaries of leading independence thinkers and fighters cannot be discounted in understanding his doctrine of national salvation.

Wilhelm Tell, the father of Swiss independence, becomes an attractive model for Choe because he exemplified the persistence, perseverance, and suffering necessary to win the independence of his native land from foreign aggressors. Choe's selection of Tell, in many ways, was prescient, for Tell would spend nearly thirty years moving from country to country, hiding and in exile, but always planning new activities for his native land before Switzerland won

---

54. Song, "Formation of Theological Thought," 198.

her independence. Many of Choe's best students and assistants would live a life that would match Tell's until Korea won her independence in 1945. Choe himself was the Lord's prophet and poet at home, having tasted death through his disciples and students, but living because they were willing to die for him and others in exile by the sacrifice of their lives, just as Jesus did for all of humanity. If there is true religion, then there will be true expressions of political life as God mandated.

8.8 A Recap of Choe Pyonghon's Thought and Work

Jesus, the Teacher of the New, Great Way of Truth

As a typical Confucian scholar of his day, Choe sought to cultivate himself to serve the king and the people. Yet, the push and pull of change in his life and Choson itself brought him ever closer to Western civilization and the American Jesus. From his conversion in 1893 to the Japanese annexation of Korea in 1910, Choe grows in his understanding of the way in which the Great Way of Truth of Jesus would become actualized in society—first as an ideal of a new faith, then as the way of forming a new humanity as all Korean religious traditions have done before, and finally, as the social expression of the ideals of a newly transformed people in the construction of a new society and a new nation.

At the time of his conversion, Choe understood Jesus as the Teacher of a new Way, the great way of truth (*chili taedo*), a new faith, which would save both the people and the nation. For him, it was the unique self-sacrificing death of Jesus on behalf of human sin that sets him apart from other religious founders. In response to the people's initial prejudice against the foreign origins of Christianity,

Choe stressed the universal nature of the God of Jesus as the God of love and mercy. This reframing of the Western Christ was done in light of his own personal experience of the powerlessness of Confucian religiosity and the inability of a corrupted Confucian polity to care for its people, or to modernize itself, or to withstand foreign aggression on its own soil. The advanced civilizations of the West, symbolized by American missionaries, stood as a guarantee of this new Way. For Choe, Jesus and his Great Way of Truth were powerful and spiritual enough to deliver the Korean people out of their spiritual chaos and national troubles.

Jesus, the Restorer of True Humanity

The first ten years as a new convert, now turned an evangelist, became an experiment in faith; to try put in practice the ethics of this new faith as it formed a new people. As Choe grew in faith, he located Jesus in the salvation history that not only included the Biblical narrative, but also the history of the Korean people who lived under one heaven under the One God. By inserting the Korean people into the salvation story, he was able to reframe the Confucian understanding of human autonomy in light of the Christian doctrine of creation. Jesus came to save humanity from its separation from God and its own self-inflicted brokenness. As God incarnate, Jesus restored humanity to its rightful place. Now, it could exercise its free will in all areas of life, according to God's great way of truth.

By believing in Jesus, the Korean people received the Holy Spirit in their souls and began the process of being reborn as a new people. In addition to the churches, schools and other educational institutions of all kinds were necessary to enable them to reach their destiny as the sons and daughters of God. While there was much talk of reform and counter-reform in the land, Choe recognized that the fulcrum of the matter was whether a new people could be reborn who would become owners of a new Korea. In a society where education was seen as the key to social success and national development, Choe offered Jesus' way as the new *tohak* (process of humanization) that would enable them to become true human beings, living in connection with God and in harmony with others.

Jesus, the Savior of Peoples and Nations

In his pastorate at Chongdong Church, Choe saw his native country undergo a slow death as a nation as it was forced into a colonial relationship with Japan. The anger and sadness of the people at the loss of their homeland filled the air. In this context, Choe preached Jesus as the Savior who would bring a new civilization and a new political culture to Korea. To make the message of Jesus take root in Korea's religious soil, Choe turned to the Confucian notions of the three great principles to explain the Christian doctrine of the salvation of the soul.

To be saved by Jesus did not mean a flight from the world. Rather, Jesus enabled them to live as God's people in all spheres of their life. Here, he came to favor increasingly the image of the cross of Jesus and his suffering. Jesus is the model for Christians living in troubled times. They, too, should not be afraid to die in the service of the love of their neighbors and nation. Their souls would live forever with God. Jesus enabled heroes to arise in times of crises because to die for Christ is to gain life. In the dire crisis facing old Korea, Choe dared to preach that Jesus was, indeed, the Savior of the Korean nation. One day, Jesus would make it into a free nation in which people will live according to the great laws with which God has endowed all people.

Jesus of the Bible, Savior of the Korean People

Choe's understanding of Jesus was thoroughly based on the Bible. Western theological debates did not interest him. The controversies of church history meant little in the Korean context. Rather, Choe's understanding of Christ was made fertile in Korea's religious and sociopolitical soil. Choe understood Jesus as the Savior of the *taedo*, the great way, similar to other religious sages and founders of Asia, but Jesus was superior to them all. Choe succeeded in weaving Jesus seamlessly into the Korean tapestry of religious spirituality and history. By so doing, the person and work of Jesus were never seen from a dualistic framework that separated body and soul, politics and religion, Earth and Heaven. His teaching was interpreted as *tohak*, the philosophy of the way that would save the people and enable them to fulfill their calling as God's sons and daughters in the world.

From the beginning, Choe understood Jesus out of his own religious and political background. Choe regarded religion as the root and the origin of the political realm. Many people have misunderstood the 1906 YMCA speech because they did not give full attention to the context out of which Choe lectured. While there is priority and order in the religion–politics relationship, Choe never entertained the thought that one could exist without the other. The 1908 speeches, which followed the 1907 Revival, reaffirmed his vision of the connection between a society's religion and its political health. While the 1907 Revival was seen by many missionaries as a way to channel the people's anger and disappointment at the loss of their nation, Choe strongly objected to the accusation that Korean Christians were controlled by Western political interests and lacked a sense of patriotism.

Jesus, the Revolutionary Hero and Suffering Servant

Choe's roll call of Western Christian heroes, which appears in the *Reflections on the Holy Mountain* and the 1908 speeches, was revolutionary in the worsening political situation after 1905. He paid dearly for such sentiments and activities in his 1910 imprisonment. It is true that his call was not a call to arms (armed resistance), but a call to the cross. He called on Korean Christians to suffer with the nation in its time of tribulation, and not abandon it or ignore it. But it was also a hopeful call, for he believed that beyond the crucified Jesus stood the resurrected Jesus. Choe's theology of the cross makes sense only in the context of national suffering. He did not seek an easy way out, for he recognized that the Western Christian heroes also dared to follow Christ's path by bearing the cross of their neighbors and their nation. To do less would be to deny that Christ had come to save the people of the world by his self-giving death on the cross.

Choe did not live to see an independent and free Korea, as he hoped. He lived through the early decades of Japanese colonial rule, suffering with the Korean people and the Korean church, which stood by the people's side. The Korean church followed his path of social and political engagement even as it suffered greatly under Japan's harsh colonial rule. Its heroic leadership and suffering in its nonviolent, yet powerful resistance against Japanese imperialism in the March First Movement (1919), and subsequent years, showed that it had indeed become a heroic church of the Korean people, just as Choe had taught a decade earlier. Today, the heroic witness of the Christian believers in 1919 continues to inspire new generations of Christians as well as non-Christians in Korea.

Choe's Legacy: how Jesus Still Saves the People and the World

Choe leaves behind many legacies which the church universal—and especially, the Korean church—must grapple with: his subtle insights about Jesus, and the new message of the Great Way of Truth; his creative use of core Confucian terms and concepts to shed light on traditional Christian doctrines; his ability to bend both Christian and Confucian ideas to serve the people; his call for the church to bear the cross of the people and the nation it serves; his unapologetic recognition of God's presence in every culture and people's history; his belief in the power of the *tohak* of Jesus to rescue not only human souls, but the cosmos itself; his challenge to become heroes of Christ wherever we live as an expression of our faith in the gift of eternal life; and his core belief in the love of God, which transcends all boundaries and melts all human barriers.

For example, Choe's insights about the person and work of Jesus from the perspective of a Confucian *sonbi* raise interesting questions for a church in a world that is becoming increasingly global, pluralistic, and diverse. As a good Christian *sonbi,* he may ask us how we account for God's presence and action in our cultures, histories, and lives. He may ask us how we are becoming more authentic human beings because we follow Jesus, the True One. He may ask how we effect change in our own lives so that it is reflected in the harmony of the universe.

It is said that in his later years, when he had retired from all pastoral and teaching responsibilities, he went back to the old "books" of his ancestors. Jesus had opened his eyes to see the hand of the One God in the actions, stories, and lives of his ancestors. It no longer mattered what name was given—the American Christ or the Jesus of Korea. What mattered was that this American Christ/Korean Jesus opened his heart, his mind, and his life, and changed him forever. When he became changed, the world he knew was no longer the same. It and everything in it were becoming new and reborn. The only thing that remained was the central law of the universe: Love.

It was this same Love that had brought his erstwhile student and lifelong colleague, George Jones, from an upstate New York town to Old Choson. And it was this same Love that had brought them together as brothers in faith—to open the hearts, the minds, and the lives of the Korean people to feel, experience, and follow the mandates of this Love. Whither American Christ? Whither Jesus of Korea? He is found wherever Love is for God *is* Love.

Conclusion

When George Heber Jones and his family suddenly left Korea in 1909, to return to the United States, he had no idea that it would be the last time any member of his family would ever step on Korean soil in the twentieth century. It was to have been an extended furlough to see George's dying parents, continue their two daughters' higher education in America, and coordinate the fundraising campaign of the 25th anniversary (1885–1910) of Korean missions. The girls promised their friends in Seoul that they would return as missionaries right after their education. However, after Jones's death from illness due to an accident ten years later, at the age of 52, Jones's connection to Korea became faded as time passed. Unlike other missionary families such as the Appenzellers and the Underwoods and Moffatts of the Presbyterian mission, the Jones's daughters and their children did not return to Korea to continue the work George Jones had started.

At various farewell events before they left Seoul by rail on July 13, to cross Eurasia to Berlin, and on to London, from which they took a steamer to arrive in New York on August 15, the Jones family received many gifts of appreciation. One of these was a hand-embroidered work of art measuring fourteen by thirty inches. On the top half of the black silk canvas was embroidered an American flag and Korean flag standing crisscrossed, with the red cross of Christ between them. Below it is a golden bell ringing a new world into birth. In the bottom half of the panel are the gold-embroidered words that Jesus spoke while teaching in the synagogue at Capernaum, "Whoever eats my flesh and drinks my blood remains in me, and I in him" (John 6:56).

It was the perfect gift to show and honor Jones's work in Choson. He had come to Choson as a young twenty-two-year-old missionary, bringing with him the American Christ of his conversion and experience. Through Christ, who had come to reveal divine life in human history, Jones had become united with God through the cross of Christ. He had been sent by this same God of Jesus Christ to be an apostle, carrying this universal message of God's salvation to a land unknown to him, and through his preaching of this Savior in Korea, he had succeeded in bringing the same divine life (flesh and blood) to a people and a nation in dire need of salvation, on a personal and communal dimension.

The words of Jesus embroidered on the silk fabric captured what had happened to him, to Choe, and to the people of Korea, individually and corporately. If the Choson Jones first entered had been the "Hermit Kingdom," as people have often called it, in a short twenty-five years, its hearts, its minds, and its doors had been opened—from the inside and the outside. In the process, Jones and the missionaries were given a special privilege of entering the life of a seeking people with a message that made a difference in their life and for their future. It was as if Jones found the fulfillment of his union with God completed when he shared bread and wine with his new brothers and sisters in Korea.

Although he had spent the most productive years of life away in a part of the world most Americans couldn't locate on the globe, it had been a purposeful life, put to great usefulness in God's hands. He had become an apostle, a messenger with the perfect message that fulfilled the tremendous need of the Korean people who progressively lost their identity and their country to a superior foreign power. He had introduced them to a Savior—of their souls and nation—through his tireless work of praying, preaching, publishing, teaching, and organizing.

Through his American Christ, they had received the power to re-create themselves into a new people. Through his diligent work, the Korean people were able to rekindle a burning hope in their hearts that enabled them to re-imagine a new future for themselves and their dying nation. He had invested his own life (flesh and blood) to the "largest possible usefulness." And these words of Jesus would have reassured him that the returns from his life investment would never end, but only continue to grow. While the memory of Jones and his missionary endeavors may have become faint, his American Christ continues to live on in his followers in Korea, urging them to live up to their destiny as sons and daughters of God on Earth.

The golden bell on the embroidered art piece was probably Choe Pyonghon's idea.[1] Henry G. Appenzeller died unexpectedly in 1902 in the aftermath of a shipwreck off the southeastern coast of Korea as he was on his way to a Bible translation meeting. Appenzeller apparently dove under the sinking ship to rescue a girl who was drowning, but ended up sacrificing himself in the rescue effort. Appenzeller had shared the message of his self-sacrificing Savior even in his own death. It was Choe Pyonghon who suggested that the Korean church cast a monument and a bell in Appenzeller's memory. The bell was to be named "The Bell That Awoke the People."

For Choe, the missionaries from America were sent by the *Hananim* of the East and the West to awaken the Korean people from their spiritual, moral, and political slumber. At first, the people

---

1. Yi Juik. "The Thought and Theology of Taksa Choe Pyonghon," The First Appenzeller Memorial Lectures. (Seoul: Chongdong First Methodist Church, 1995).

resented the cacophony introduced by the ringing bell of the missionaries in a society ruled by Confucian orthodoxy. In the past, it had only meant danger and death, as so many Catholic martyrs had shown. But as time went on, the sound of the bell had begun to speak to him; it resonated with something in his spirit. And one day, the bell had awakened him to the Great Way of Truth (*chili taedo*) in Jesus.

Jones's message of the American Christ had awakened and enlightened him to become the noble human being that Master Confucius had taught centuries earlier. Choe had been able to reclaim their rightful place as sons and daughter of God. Choe was always grateful to them for their willingness and courage to speak the Great Way of Truth (*chili taedo*) that Jesus had shown them in their lives and countries. The golden bell had also awakened Choe to his God-endowed right of freedom to live as a free people under heaven. Having recovered true humanity in Jesus, he set about to carry out heaven's mandate on Earth, "Thy kingdom come on Earth as it is in heaven." Choe knew it from his childhood days as the motto of the *Great Learning*: *sushin cheka chiguk pyongchonha* (controlling the self leads to order in the family that enables a just society leading to peace and harmony of the cosmos). Only in Jesus could this universal purpose be carried out completely.

It was now up to the Korean Christian leaders such as Choe to continue the work of awakening the Korean people and nation—and the rest of the world—to their God-given destiny; to become solid and authentic human beings using all the capacities and cultural resources God had given them; to build the beloved community where the least, lost, and the last of the society were welcomed; and to live by the simple but central law of love towards all.

In his later writings, Choe returned often to the books of his ancestors—books he had set aside as he learned, practiced, and preached the *chili taedo* of Jesus. Now, through Jesus, he was able to see how far the love of God had reached. Unknown to them, the God of Jesus Christ had been at work in the Korean people's lives and history. So, it was his joy and pride to see the Korean flag with its mysterious yin-yang symbols standing crisscross with the Stars and Stripes of a country such as the powerful United States, from where Jones had come. Despite the insurmountable problems facing his native land, Choe thanked God for his ancestors and the future he had in store for them. God's grace and love had been secretly present in Korean history all along. God had taken the enormous efforts of his bell-ringers, such as Jones and Appenzeller, to spread its melodious sounds into every corner of Choson. Now, it would be up to him to continue ringing the golden bell of warning and blessing.

Choe would go onto write his major opus on comparative religions, *Manjong illyon* (variously translated as *The World of Religions* or *Many Religions, One Love*). Based on his own lived experience, Choe recognized the limits and errors of all religions, including even Christianity, in that they can only point to a partial vision of the *Great Way of Truth,* or *chili taedo*. But for him, Jesus the self-sacrificing Savior, with his simple, but central law of love, is the living model for all religions and all peoples. It is only when all religions dare to learn from each other in humility like this One on the cross that they can practice this love, which Jesus taught and practiced in his person.

So, we come to the end of the story of these two men—two brothers who met in the Great Way of Truth. But the story of Jesus of Nazareth, whom both Jones and Choe followed, continues to make a difference in the lives of the people in Inchon (Chemulpo) and Chongdong, Rochester in upstate New York, and every corner of the world where it has been told. May the echoes of the golden bell rung by Jones, Choe, and countless other messengers of *Hananim*—The

One Above—continue to awaken the peoples of the world to live in love. Ubi caritas, Deus ibi est.

Primary Sources

Manuscript Materials

George Heber Jones and Margaret Bengel Jones. Mission Geographical Reference Files 1880s–1960, Folders 1467-1-3:23, General Commission on Archives and History of the United Methodist Church, Drew University, Madison, New Jersey.

George Heber Jones Journals. Privately held by family, Tiburon, California.

George Heber Jones Miscellany. Privately held by family, Tiburon, California.

George Heber Jones Papers. Missionary Research Library Archives, The Burke Library, Union Theological Seminary, New York, NY.

George Heber Jones Writings and Photographs. Mission Geographical Reference Files 1880s–1960, Folders 1466-4-7:22. General Commission on Archives and History of the United Methodist Church, Drew University, Madison, New Jersey.

Minutes of Committee on Japan and Korea (1886–1913). Mission Geographical Reference Files 1880s–1960, Folders 1307-4-7:01 to 1307-4-7:04. General Commission on Archives and History of the United Methodist Church, Drew University, Madison, New Jersey.

Missionary Collection. Letter Books 209–213. General Commission on Archives and History of the United Methodist Church, Drew University, Madison, New Jersey.

Newspapers, Journals, and Published Official Records

Independent, 1896–1899. Seoul.
Korea Review: A Monthly Magazine, 1901–1906. Seoul: Methodist Publishing House.
Korean Repository, 1892, 1895–1899. Seoul: Trilingual Press.
Methodist Episcopal Church. Board of Foreign Missions. *Annual Report, Korea Mission 1884–1943*, collected and bound as *Annual Report of the Board of Foreign Missions of the Methodist Episcopal Church Korea Mission 1884–1943*, ed. Institute of Korean Church History. Seoul: IKCH, 1993.

George Heber Jones: Published Works

Christian Medical Work in Korea. New York: Board of Foreign Missions of the Methodist Episcopal Church, Korea Quarter-Centennial Commission, 1910(?).
Korea: The Land, People and Customs. Cincinnati: Jennings and Graham, 1907.
Supplemental Chapter to Henry Gerhard Appenzeller. *The Korea Mission of the Methodist Episcopal Church*. New York: Open Door Emergency Commission, 1905(?).
The Korea Mission of the Methodist Episcopal Church. New York: New York: Board of Foreign Missions of the Methodist Episcopal Church, 1910.
The Korean Revival: An Account of the Revival in the Korean Churches in 1907. with W. Arthur Noble. New York: Board of Foreign Missions of the Methodist Episcopal Church, 1910.

www.ingramcontent.com/pod-product-compliance
Lightning Source LLC
Chambersburg PA
CBHW071153070526
44584CB00019B/2769